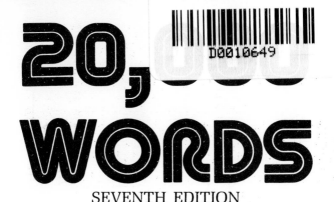

# 20,000 WORDS

## SEVENTH EDITION

Spelled and Divided
for Quick Reference

Compiled by
Louis A. Leslie

**McGRAW-HILL BOOK COMPANY**

*New York   St. Louis   San Francisco*
*Düsseldorf   London   Mexico   Sydney*
*Toronto*

**20,000 WORDS, Seventh Edition**

6789 DODO   832

ISBN 0-07-037392-2

aba·cus
abaft
ab·a·lo·ne
aban·don
aban·don·ment
abase
abash
abate
abate·ment
ab·at·toir
ab·bé
ab·bess
ab·bey
ab·bot
ab·bre·vi·ate
ab·bre·vi·at·ing
ab·bre·vi·a·tion
ab·di·cate
ab·di·ca·tion
ab·do·men
ab·dom·i·nal
ab·duct
ab·duc·tion
ab·duc·tor
ab·er·rance
ab·er·rant
ab·er·ra·tion
abet
abet·ting
abet·tor

abey·ance
ab·hor
ab·horred
ab·hor·rence
ab·hor·rent
ab·hor·ring
abide
abil·i·ties
abil·i·ty
ab·ject
ab·ject·ly
ab·jure
ab·la·tive
ablaze
able
able—bod·ied
ab·lu·tion
ably
ab·ne·ga·tion
ab·nor·mal
ab·nor·mal·i·ty
aboard
abode
abol·ish
ab·o·li·tion
ab·o·li·tion·ism
ab·o·li·tion·ist
A—bomb
abom·i·na·ble
abom·i·nate
abom·i·na·tion
ab·orig·i·nal
ab·orig·i·ne
abort
abor·tion·ist
abor·tive

abound
about
about—face
above
above·board
above·ground
abrade
abra·sion
abra·sive
ab·re·act
abreast
abridge
abridg·ing
abridg·ment
abroad
ab·ro·gate
ab·ro·ga·tion
abrupt
ab·scess
ab·scis·sa
ab·scond
ab·scond·er
ab·sence
ab·sent
ab·sen·tee
ab·sen·tee·ism
ab·sent·mind·ed
ab·sinthe
ab·so·lute
ab·so·lute·ly
ab·so·lu·tion
ab·so·lut·ism
ab·solve
ab·sorb
ab·sor·ben·cy
ab·sor·bent

1

ab·sorb·ing
ab·sorp·tion
ab·stain
ab·stain·er
ab·ste·mi·ous
ab·sten·tion
ab·sti·nence
ab·sti·nent
ab·stract
ab·strac·tion
ab·stract·ly
ab·stract·ness
ab·struse
ab·surd
ab·sur·di·ty
abun·dance
abun·dant
abuse
abus·ing
abu·sive
abu·sive·ly
abu·sive·ness
abut
abut·ment
abut·ted
abut·ter
abut·ting
abys·mal
abyss
ac·a·dem·ic
ac·a·de·mi·cian
acad·e·my
ac·cede (to agree;
   cf. *exceed*)
ac·ce·le·ran·do
ac·cel·er·ate

ac·cel·er·a·tion
ac·cel·er·a·tor
ac·cent
ac·cen·tu·ate
ac·cept (to take;
   cf. *except*)
ac·cept·abil·i·ty
ac·cept·able
ac·cep·tance
ac·cep·ta·tion
ac·cept·ed
ac·cess (admittance;
   cf. *excess*)
ac·ces·si·bil·i·ty
ac·ces·si·ble
ac·ces·sion
ac·ces·so·ry
ac·ci·dence
ac·ci·dent
ac·ci·den·tal
ac·ci·den·tal·ly
ac·claim
ac·cla·ma·tion
ac·cli·mate
ac·cli·ma·tize
ac·cliv·i·ty
ac·co·lade
ac·com·mo·date
ac·com·mo·dat·ing
ac·com·mo·da·tion
ac·com·pa·ni·ment
ac·com·pa·nist
ac·com·pa·ny
ac·com·plice
ac·com·plish
ac·com·plished

ac·com·plish·ment
ac·cord
ac·cor·dance
ac·cord·ing·ly
ac·cor·di·on
ac·cost
ac·count
ac·count·abil·i·ty
ac·count·able
ac·coun·tan·cy
ac·coun·tant
ac·count·ing
ac·cou·ter·ment
ac·cred·it
ac·cred·i·ta·tion
ac·cre·tion
ac·cru·al
ac·crue
ac·cru·ing
ac·cu·mu·late
ac·cu·mu·lat·ing
ac·cu·mu·la·tion
ac·cu·mu·la·tive
ac·cu·mu·la·tor
ac·cu·ra·cy
ac·cu·rate·ly
ac·cursed
ac·cu·sa·tion
ac·cu·sa·tive
ac·cu·sa·to·ry
ac·cuse
ac·cus·ing
ac·cus·tom
ac·cus·tomed
acer·bi·ty
ac·e·tate

ace·tic
ac·e·tone
acet·y·lene
ache
achieve
achieve·ment
achiev·ing
ach·ro·mat·ic
ac·id
ac·id—fast
ac·id·head
acid·i·fi·ca·tion
acid·i·fied
acid·i·fy
acid·i·ty
ac·i·do·sis
acid·u·late
acid·u·lous
ac·knowl·edge
ac·knowl·edg·ing
ac·knowl·edg·ment
ac·me (highest point)
ac·ne (a disease)
ac·o·lyte
ac·o·nite
acorn
acous·tic
acous·ti·cal
ac·ous·ti·cian
acous·tics
ac·quaint
ac·quain·tance
ac·qui·esce
ac·qui·es·cence
ac·qui·es·cent
ac·quire

ac·quire·ment
ac·quir·ing
ac·qui·si·tion
ac·quis·i·tive
ac·quit
ac·quit·tal
ac·quit·ted
ac·quit·ting
acre
acre·age
acre—foot
ac·rid
acrid·i·ty
ac·ri·mo·ni·ous
ac·ri·mo·ny
ac·ro·bat
ac·ro·bat·ic
ac·ro·nym
acrop·o·lis
across
acros·tic
acryl·ic
act·ing
ac·tin·ic
ac·tion
ac·tion·able
ac·ti·vate
ac·tive
ac·tive·ly
ac·tiv·ism
ac·tiv·ist
ac·tiv·i·ties
ac·tiv·i·ty
ac·tor
ac·tu·al
ac·tu·al·i·ty

ac·tu·al·ly
ac·tu·ar·i·al
ac·tu·ar·ies
ac·tu·ary
ac·tu·ate
ac·tu·at·ing
acu·ity
acu·men
acu·punc·ture
acute
acute·ness
ad (advertisement;
    cf. *add*)
ad·age
ada·gio
ad·a·mant
adapt (adjust;
    cf. *adept, adopt*)
adapt·abil·i·ty
adapt·able
ad·ap·ta·tion
adapt·er
add (plus; cf. *ad*)
ad·den·da pl.
ad·den·dum sing.
ad·der
ad·dict
ad·dict·ed
ad·dic·tion
ad·dic·tive
ad·di·tion (increase;
    cf. *edition*)
ad·di·tion·al
ad·di·tive
ad·dle
ad·dress

ad·dress·ee
ad·dress·ing
Ad·dres·so·graph
ad·duce
ad·duc·ing
ad·e·noid
ad·e·noi·dal
ad·ept (skillful;
   cf. *adapt, adopt*)
ad·e·qua·cy
ad·e·quate
ad·e·quate·ly
ad·here
ad·her·ence
ad·her·ent
ad·her·ing
ad·he·sion
ad·he·sive
ad·he·sive·ly
ad hoc
adieu
ad·i·pose
ad·i·pos·i·ty
ad·ja·cent
ad·jec·tive
ad·join (to be next to)
ad·journ (suspend)
ad·journ·ment
ad·judge
ad·judg·ing
ad·ju·di·cate
ad·ju·di·cat·ing
ad·ju·di·ca·tion
ad·ju·di·ca·tor
ad·junct
ad·ju·ra·tion

ad·jure
ad·just
ad·just·able
ad·just·ment
ad·ju·tant
ad lib adv.
ad—lib adj., v.
ad·min·is·ter
ad·min·is·tra·tion
ad·min·is·tra·tive
ad·min·is·tra·tor
ad·mi·ra·ble
ad·mi·ral
ad·mi·ral·ty
ad·mi·ra·tion
ad·mire
ad·mir·ing
ad·mis·si·bil·i·ty
ad·mis·si·ble
ad·mis·sion
ad·mit
ad·mit·tance
ad·mit·ted
ad·mit·ting
ad·mix·ture
ad·mon·ish
ad·mo·ni·tion
ad·mon·i·to·ry
ad nau·se·am
ado·be
ad·o·les·cence
ad·o·les·cent
adopt (accept;
   cf. *adapt, adept*)
adop·tion
adop·tive

ador·able
ad·o·ra·tion
ador·ing
adorn
adorn·ment
ad·re·nal
adren·a·line
adrift
adroit
ad·sorp·tion
ad·u·late
ad·u·la·tion
adult
adul·ter·ant
adul·ter·ate
adul·ter·a·tion
adul·ter·er
adul·ter·ous
adul·tery
ad·um·bra·tion
ad va·lo·rem
ad·vance
ad·vanced
ad·vance·ment
ad·vanc·ing
ad·van·tage
ad·van·ta·geous
ad·vent
ad·ven·ti·tious
ad·ven·ture
ad·ven·tur·er
ad·ven·ture·some
ad·ven·tur·ous
ad·verb
ad·ver·bi·al
ad·ver·sar·ies

ad·ver·sary
ad·verse (unfavor-
    able; cf. *averse*)
ad·ver·si·ty
ad·vert
ad·ver·tise
ad·ver·tise·ment
ad·ver·tis·er
ad·vice n. (counsel;
    cf. *advise*)
ad·vis·abil·i·ty
ad·vis·able
ad·vise v. (give
    counsel; cf. *advice*)
ad·vised
ad·vise·ment
ad·vis·er *or*
    ad·vi·sor
ad·vis·ing
ad·vi·so·ry
ad·vo·ca·cy
ad·vo·cate
ae·gis
ae·on
aer·ate
aer·a·tion
ae·ri·al adj.
aer·i·al n.
aero·dy·nam·ics
aero·med·i·cine
aero·nau·tic
aero·nau·ti·cal
aero·sol
aero·space
aes·thet·ic
aes·thet·i·cal·ly

aes·thet·i·cism
aes·thet·ics
af·fa·bil·i·ty
af·fa·ble
af·fair
af·fect (influence;
    cf. *effect*)
af·fec·ta·tion
af·fect·ed
af·fec·tion
af·fec·tion·ate
af·fi·ance
af·fi·ant
af·fi·da·vit
af·fil·i·ate
af·fin·i·ties
af·fin·i·ty
af·firm
af·fir·ma·tion
af·fir·ma·tive
af·firm·a·to·ry
af·fix
af·flict
af·flic·tion
af·flu·ence
af·flu·ent
af·ford
af·fray
af·fright
af·front
af·ghan
afield
afire
afloat
afoot
afore·said

afore·thought
afore·time
afraid
afresh
Af·ri·can
Af·ro—Amer·i·can
af·ter
af·ter·burn·er
af·ter·care
af·ter·ef·fect
af·ter·glow
af·ter·life
af·ter·math
af·ter·noon
af·ter·taste
af·ter·thought
af·ter·ward
again
against
ag·ate
ag·ate·ware
aga·ve
agen·cies
agen·cy
agen·da
ag·glom·er·ate
ag·glom·er·a·tion
ag·glu·ti·nate
ag·glu·ti·na·tive
ag·gran·dize
ag·gran·dize·ment
ag·gra·vate
ag·gra·vat·ing
ag·gra·va·tion
ag·gre·gate
ag·gre·gat·ing

ag·gre·ga·tion
ag·gres·sion
ag·gres·sive
ag·gres·sor
ag·grieve
ag·grieved
aghast
ag·ile
ag·ile·ly
agil·i·ty
ag·i·tate
ag·i·tat·ing
ag·i·ta·tion
ag·i·ta·tor
aglow
ag·nos·tic
ag·o·nize
ag·o·niz·ing
ag·o·ny
ag·o·ra·pho·bia
agrar·i·an
agree
agree·abil·i·ty
agree·able
agreed
agree·ing
agree·ment
ag·ri·cul·tur·al
ag·ri·cul·ture
agron·o·my
aground
ague
ahead
ahoy
aid (help; cf. *aide*)
aide (assistant; cf. *aid*)

ail (be ill; cf. *ale*)
ai·le·ron
ail·ment
air (atmosphere;
    cf. *heir*)
air  bag
air  base
air·borne
air  brake
air·brush
air  coach
air  com·mand
air—con·di·tion v.
air—con·di·tioned
    adj., v.
air  con·di-
    tion·er n.
air—cool v.
air—cooled adj.
air  cool·ing n.
air  cor·ri·dor
air  cov·er
air·craft
air·drome
air·drop n.
air—drop v.
air—dry adj.
Aire·dale
Air  Ex·press
air·field
air·flow
air·foil
air  force
air·frame
air·freight
air·glow

air  gun
air  hole
air·i·ly
air·i·ness
air  lane
air·lift
air·line
air·lin·er
air  lock
air·mail
air·man
air  mass
air  mile
air·plane
air  pock·et
air·port
air·proof
air  pump
air  raid
air·screw
air·ship
air·sick
air·space
air·speed
air·stream
air·strip
air·tight
air—to—air
air·wave
air·way
air·wor·thi·ness
air·wor·thy
airy
aisle (passageway;
    cf. *isle*)
akim·bo

Al·a·bama
al·a·bas·ter
a la carte
alac·ri·ty
a la mode
alarm
alarm·ist
Alas·ka
al·ba·tross
al·be·it
al·bi·no
al·bi·nos
al·bum
al·bu·men
Al·bu·quer·que
al·che·mist
al·che·my
al·co·hol
al·co·hol·ic
al·co·hol·ism
al·cove
al·der·man
ale (beer; cf. *ail*)
ale·wife
al·fal·fa
al·fres·co
al·gae
al·ge·bra
al·ge·bra·ic
al·ge·bra·ical
alias
al·i·bi
al·i·bied
al·i·bi·ing
alien
alien·ate

alien·at·ing
alien·ation
alien·ist
align
align·ment
alike
al·i·men·ta·ry
al·i·men·ta·tion
al·i·mo·ny
al·i·quot
al·ka·li
al·ka·line
al·ka·loid
al·kyl
all (wholly; cf. *awl*)
al·lay (soothe;
    cf. *alley, ally*)
al·le·ga·tion
al·lege
al·leg·ed·ly
Al·le·ghe·nies
Al·le·ghe·ny
al·le·giance
al·leg·ing
al·le·gor·i·cal
al·le·go·ry
al·le·gret·to
al·le·gro
al·ler·gy
al·le·vi·ate
al·le·vi·a·tion
al·ley (passage;
    cf. *allay, ally*)
al·leys
al·li·ance
al·lied

al·lies
al·li·ga·tor
al·lit·er·a·tion
al·lit·er·a·tive
al·lo·ca·ble
al·lo·cate
al·lo·cat·ing
al·lo·ca·tion
al·lo·cu·tion
al·lo·path·ic
al·lop·a·thy
al·lot
al·lot·ment
al·lot·ted
al·lot·ting
al·low
al·low·able
al·low·ance
al·lowed (permitted;
    cf. *aloud*)
al·low·ed·ly
all right
al·lude (refer to;
    cf. *elude*)
al·lure
al·lu·sion
al·lu·vi·al
al·ly (associate;
    cf. *allay, alley*)
al·mighty
al·mond
al·most
alms (charity; cf. *arms*)
al·ni·co
aloft
alone

along
aloud (audibly;
  cf. *allowed*)
al·paca
al·pha·bet
al·pha·bet·ic
al·pha·bet·ize
al·ready
al·tar (for worship;
  cf. *alter*)
al·tar·piece
al·tar   rail
al·tar   stone
al·ter (change;
  cf. *altar*)
al·ter ego
al·ter·ation
al·ter·ca·tion
al·ter·nate
al·ter·nat·ing
al·ter·na·tion
al·ter·na·tive
al·ter·na·tor
al·though
al·tim·e·ter
al·ti·pla·no
al·ti·tude
al·to
al·to·geth·er
al·tru·ism
al·tru·ist
al·tru·is·tic
al·um
alu·mi·num
alum·na sing. fem.
alum·nae pl. fem.

alum·ni pl. mas.
alum·nus sing. mas.
Alun·dum
al·ways
amal·gam
amal·gam·ate
amal·gam·ation
aman·u·en·sis
am·a·teur
amaze
amaze·ment
amaz·ing·ly
am·bas·sa·dor
am·ber·gris
am·bi·dex·trous
am·bi·gu·ity
am·big·u·ous
am·bi·tion
am·bi·tious
am·biv·a·lence
am·bro·sia
am·bu·lance
am·bu·la·to·ry
am·bus·cade
am·bush
ame·lio·rate
ame·lio·ra·tion
ame·lio·ra·tive
ame·na·ble
amend (to change;
  cf. *emend*)
amend·ment
ame·ni·ties
ame·ni·ty
Amer·i·can
Amer·i·can·ism

Amer·i·can·iza-
  tion
Am·er·ind
am·e·thyst
ami·a·bil·i·ty
ami·a·ble
am·i·ca·bil·i·ty
am·i·ca·ble
amid·ships
amidst
am·i·ty
am·me·ter
am·mo·nia
am·mu·ni·tion
am·ne·sia
am·nes·ty
amoe·ba
among
amor·al
am·o·rous
amor·phous
am·or·ti·za·tion
am·or·tize
am·or·tiz·ing
amount
am·per·age
am·pere
am·per·sand
am·phib·i·an
am·phib·i·ous
am·phi·the·ater
am·ple
am·pli·fi·ca·tion
am·pli·fied
am·pli·fi·er
am·pli·fy

am·pli·fy·ing
am·pli·tude
am·ply
am·pu·tate
am·pu·ta·tion
am·pu·tee
am·u·let
amuse
amuse·ment
amus·ing
anach·ro·nism
anach·ro·nis·tic
an·a·con·da
an·aer·o·bic
ana·gram
an·al·ge·sia
an·a·log·i·cal
anal·o·gies
anal·o·gous
anal·o·gy
anal·y·sand
anal·y·ses pl.
anal·y·sis sing.
an·a·lyst (one who
   analyzes; cf. *annalist*)
an·a·lyt·i·cal
an·a·lyze
an·a·lyz·ing
an·ar·chic
an·ar·chism
an·ar·chist
an·ar·chis·tic
an·ar·chy
an·astig·mat·ic
anath·e·ma
an·a·tom·i·cal

anat·o·mist
anat·o·mize
anat·o·my
an·ces·tor
an·ces·tral
an·ces·try
an·chor
an·chor·age
an·cho·vies
an·cho·vy
an·cient
an·cil·lary
and·iron
and/or
an·ec·dote
ane·mia
ane·mic
an·e·mom·e·ter
anem·o·ne
an·er·oid
an·es·the·sia
an·es·the·si·ol·o·gist
an·es·thet·ic
anes·the·tist
anes·the·tize
an·gel (a spiritual
   being; cf. *angle*)
an·gel·fish
an·gel food cake
an·gel·ic
An·ge·lus
an·ger
an·gi·na
an·gle (in geometry;
   cf. *angel*)
an·gle iron

an·gler
an·gle·worm
An·gli·can
an·gli·cism
an·gli·cize
an·gling
an·glo·phile
an·glo·phobe
An·glo—Sax·on
an·go·ra
an·gri·ly
an·gry
an·guish
an·gu·lar
an·gu·lar·i·ty
an·i·line
an·i·mad·ver·sion
an·i·mal
an·i·mate
an·i·mat·ed·ly
an·i·ma·tion
an·i·mos·i·ty
an·i·mus
an·ise
ani·seed
an·is·ette
an·kle
an·kle·bone
an·klet
an·nal·ist (writer of
   annals; cf. *analyst*)
an·nals
an·neal
an·nex
an·nex·a·tion
an·ni·hi·late

9

an·ni·hi·la·tion
an·ni·hi·la·tor
an·ni·ver·sa·ries
an·ni·ver·sa·ry
an·no·tate
an·no·ta·tion
an·nounce
an·nounce·ment
an·nounc·ing
an·noy
an·noy·ance
an·noyed
an·noy·ing
an·nu·al
an·nu·al·ly
an·nu·itant
an·nu·ity
an·nul
an·nu·lar
an·nulled
an·nul·ling
an·nul·ment
an·nun·ci·a·tion
an·nun·ci·a·tor
an·ode
an·od·ize
an·o·dyne
anoint
anom·a·lous
anom·a·ly
an·o·nym·i·ty
anon·y·mous
anoph·e·les
an·oth·er
an·swer
an·swer·able

ant (insect; cf. *aunt*)
ant·ac·id
an·tag·o·nism
an·tag·o·nist
an·tag·o·nis·tic
an·tag·o·nize
ant·arc·tic
ant·eat·er
an·te·bel·lum
an·te·ced·ent
an·te·cham·ber
an·te·date
an·te·di·lu·vi·an
an·te·lope
an·te me·ri·di·em
an·ten·na
an·te·pe·nult
an·te·ri·or
an·te·room
an·them
an·ther
ant·hill
an·thol·o·gy
an·thra·cite
an·thrax
an·thro·poid
an·thro·pol·o·gy
an·thro·po·mor·phic
an·ti·air·craft
an·ti·bi·ot·ic
an·ti·body
an·tic
an·tic·i·pate
an·tic·i·pat·ing
an·tic·i·pa·tion
an·tic·i·pa·tive

an·tic·i·pa·to·ry
an·ti·cli·mac·tic
an·ti·cli·max
an·ti·dote
an·ti·freeze
an·ti·gen
an·ti·ma·cas·sar
an·ti·ma·lar·i·al
an·ti·mo·ny
an·ti·pa·thet·ic
an·tip·a·thy
an·ti·per·son·nel
an·tiph·o·nal
an·tip·o·des
an·ti·pov·er·ty
an·ti·quar·i·an
an·ti·quary
an·ti·quat·ed
an·tique
an·tiq·ui·ty
an·ti—Se·mit·ic
an·ti·sep·sis
an·ti·sep·tic
an·ti·so·cial
an·tith·e·sis
an·ti·tox·in
an·ti·trust
ant·ler
ant·onym
an·trum
an·vil
anx·i·ety
anx·ious
any
any·body
any·how

any·one
any·thing
any·way
any·ways
any·where
ao·rist
aor·ta
apace
apart
apart·heid
apart·ment
ap·a·thet·ic
ap·a·thy
ap·er·ture
apex
apha·sia
aph·o·rism
Aph·ro·di·te
api·ary (for bees; cf. *aviary*)
api·cal
api·cul·ture
apiece
apoc·a·lypse
apoc·a·lyp·tic
apoc·ry·pha
apoc·ry·phal
apo·gee
apolit·i·cal
Apol·lo
apol·o·get·ic
apol·o·get·i·cal·ly
apol·o·get·ics
apol·o·gies
apol·o·gize
apol·o·giz·ing

ap·o·logue
apol·o·gy
ap·o·plec·tic
ap·o·plexy
apos·ta·sy
apos·tate
a pos·te·ri·o·ri
apos·tle
apos·to·late
ap·os·tol·ic
apos·tro·phe
apos·tro·phize
apoth·e·car·ies
apoth·e·cary
apo·the·o·sis
Ap·pa·la·chian
ap·pall
ap·palled
ap·pall·ing
ap·pa·ra·tus
ap·par·el
ap·par·eled
ap·par·ent
ap·pa·ri·tion
ap·peal
ap·peal·ing·ly
ap·pear
ap·pear·ance
ap·pease
ap·pease·ment
ap·pel·lant
ap·pel·late
ap·pel·la·tion
ap·pel·lee
ap·pend
ap·pend·age

ap·pen·dec·to·my
ap·pen·di·ci·tis
ap·pen·dix
ap·per·ceive
ap·per·cep·tion
ap·per·tain
ap·pe·tite
ap·pe·tiz·er
ap·pe·tiz·ing
ap·plaud
ap·plause
ap·ple
ap·ple·jack
ap·pli·ance
ap·pli·ca·bil·i·ty
ap·pli·ca·ble
ap·pli·cant
ap·pli·ca·tion
ap·plied
ap·pli·qué
ap·ply
ap·ply·ing
ap·point
ap·poin·tee
ap·point·ive
ap·point·ment
ap·por·tion
ap·por·tion·ment
ap·po·site
ap·po·si·tion
ap·prais·al
ap·praise (value; cf. *apprise*)
ap·prais·ing
ap·pre·cia·ble
ap·pre·ci·ate

ap·pre·ci·a·tion
ap·pre·cia·tive
ap·pre·hend
ap·pre·hen·si·ble
ap·pre·hen·sion
ap·pre·hen·sive
ap·pren·tice
ap·pren·ticed
ap·pren·tice·ship
ap·prise (inform;
   cf. *appraise*)
ap·proach
ap·pro·ba·tion
ap·pro·ba·to·ry
ap·pro·pri·ate
ap·pro·pri·ate·ness
ap·pro·pri·a·tion
ap·prov·al
ap·prove
ap·prov·ing
ap·prox·i·mate
ap·prox·i·ma·tion
ap·pur·te·nance
ap·pur·te·nant
apri·cot
April
a pri·o·ri
apron
ap·ro·pos
ap·ti·tude
apt·ly
apt·ness
aqua·cade
aqua·lung
aqua·ma·rine
aqua·plane

aqua·relle
aquar·i·um
aquat·ic
aqua·tint
aq·ue·duct
aque·ous
aq·ui·line
ar·a·besque
Ara·bi·an
Ar·a·bic
ar·a·ble
arach·noid
ar·bi·ter
ar·bi·tra·ble
ar·bi·trage
ar·bit·ra·ment
ar·bi·trari·ly
ar·bi·trary
ar·bi·trate
ar·bi·tra·tion
ar·bi·tra·tive
ar·bi·tra·tor
ar·bor
ar·bo·re·al
ar·bo·re·tum
ar·bor·vi·tae
ar·bu·tus
arc (curved line;
   cf. *ark*)
ar·cade
ar·chae·o·log·i·cal
ar·chae·ol·o·gist
ar·chae·ol·o·gy
ar·cha·ic
arch·an·gel
arch·bish·op

arch·dea·con
arch·di·o·cese
arch·du·cal
arch·duch·ess
arch·duchy
arch·duke
arch·en·e·my
ar·cher
ar·chery
ar·che·type
arch·fiend
ar·chi·epis·co·pal
ar·chi·pel·a·go
ar·chi·tect
ar·chi·tec·tur·al
ar·chi·tec·ture
ar·chi·trave
ar·chives
arch·ness
arch·way
arc·ing
arc·tic
ar·dent
ar·dor
ar·du·ous
ar·ea (space; cf. *aria*)
area·way
are·na
ar·gon
ar·go·naut
ar·go·sy
ar·got
ar·gue
ar·gued
ar·gu·ing
ar·gu·ment

ar·gu·men·ta·tion
ar·gu·men·ta·tive
ar·gyle
Ar·gy·rol
aria (melody; cf. *area*)
ar·id
arid·i·ty
ari·o·so
ar·is·toc·ra·cy
aris·to·crat
aris·to·crat·ic
Ar·is·to·te·lian
arith·me·tic
ar·ith·met·i·cal
arith·me·ti·cian
Ar·i·zo·na
ark (refuge; cf. *arc*)
Ar·kan·sas
ar·ma·da
ar·ma·dil·lo
ar·ma·ment
ar·ma·ture
arm·chair
arm·ful
arm·hole
ar·mies
ar·mi·stice
arm·let
ar·mor
ar·mor·er
ar·mo·ri·al
ar·mory
arm·pit
arm·rest
arms (of body;
    cf. *alms*)

ar·my
ar·my    ant
ar·my·worm
ar·ni·ca
aro·ma
ar·o·mat·ic
around
ar·peg·gio
ar·raign
ar·raign·ment
ar·range
ar·range·ment
ar·rang·ing
ar·rant
ar·ras
ar·ray
ar·rayed
ar·ray·ing
ar·rear
ar·rear·age
ar·rest
ar·riv·al
ar·rive·
ar·riv·ing
ar·ro·gance
ar·ro·gant
ar·ro·gate
ar·row
ar·row·head
ar·row·root
ar·royo
ar·se·nal
ar·se·nate
ar·se·nic
ar·son
ar·te·ri·al

ar·ter·ies
ar·te·rio·scle·ro·sis
ar·tery
ar·te·sian
art·ful
art·ful·ly
ar·thri·tis
ar·ti·choke
ar·ti·cle
ar·ti·cled
ar·tic·u·late
ar·tic·u·la·tion
ar·ti·fact
ar·ti·fice
ar·ti·fi·cer
ar·ti·fi·cial
ar·ti·fi·ci·al·i·ty
ar·til·lery
ar·ti·san
art·ist
ar·tiste
ar·tis·tic
art·ist·ry
art·less
Ary·an
as·bes·tos
as·cend
as·cen·dan·cy
as·cen·dant
as·cend·ing
as·cen·sion
as·cent (motion
    upward; cf. *assent*)
as·cer·tain
as·cer·tain·able
as·cer·tain·ment

as·cet·ic
as·cet·i·cism
as·cribe
as·crib·ing
as·crip·tion
asep·sis
asep·tic
asep·ti·cal·ly
ashamed
ash  can n.
ash·can adj.
ash·en
ash·tray
ashy
Asian
Asi·at·ic
aside
as·i·nine
as·i·nin·i·ty
askance
askew
asleep
as·par·a·gus
as·pect
as·pen
as·per·i·ty
as·perse
as·per·sion
as·phalt
as·phyx·ia
as·phyx·i·ate
as·phyx·i·at·ing
as·phyx·i·a·tion
as·pic
as·pi·rant
as·pi·rate

as·pi·ra·tion
as·pi·ra·tor
as·pire
as·pi·rin
as·pir·ing
as·sail
as·sail·ant
as·sas·sin
as·sas·si·nate
as·sas·si·na·tion
as·sault
as·say (analyze;
    cf. *essay*)
as·sayed
as·say·ing
as·sem·blage
as·sem·ble
as·sem·bling
as·sem·bly
as·sem·bly·man
as·sent (consent;
    cf. *ascent*)
as·sert
as·ser·tion
as·ser·tive
as·sess
as·sess·able
as·sess·ment
as·ses·sor
as·set
as·sev·er·ate
as·sev·er·a·tion
as·si·du·ity
**as·sid·u·ous**
as·sign
as·sign·able

as·sig·nat
as·sig·na·tion
as·sign·ee
as·sign·er
as·sign·ment
as·sim·i·la·ble
as·sim·i·late
as·sim·i·lat·ing
as·sim·i·la·tion
as·sim·i·la·tive
as·sim·i·la·to·ry
as·sist
as·sis·tance (help;
    cf. *assistants*)
as·sis·tant
as·sis·tants (helpers;
    cf. *assistance*)
as·size
as·so·ciate n.
as·so·ci·ate v.
as·so·ci·at·ing
as·so·ci·a·tion
as·so·cia·tive
as·so·nance
as·so·nant
as·sort
as·sort·ment
as·suage
as·suag·ing
as·sume
as·sum·ing
as·sump·tion
as·sur·ance
as·sure
as·sured
as·sur·ing

as·ter
as·ter·isk
as·ter·oid
as·the·nia
asth·ma
as·tig·mat·ic
astig·ma·tism
as·ton·ish
as·ton·ish·ment
as·tound
as·tra·khan
as·tral
astride
as·trin·gen·cy
as·trin·gent
as·tro·dome
as·tro·labe
as·trol·o·ger
as·trol·o·gy
as·tro·naut
as·tro·nau·ti·cal
as·tro·nau·tics
as·tron·o·mer
as·tro·nom·ic
as·tro·nom·i·cal
as·tron·o·my
as·tute
asun·der
asy·lum
asym·met·ric
at·a·rac·tic
at·a·vism
ate·lier
athe·ism
athe·ist
athe·is·tic

ath·e·nae·um
ath·lete
ath·let·ic
ath·let·ics
athwart
At·lan·tic
at·las
at·mo·sphere
at·mo·spher·ic
at·om
atom·ic
at·om·ize
at·om·iz·er
aton·al
atone·ment
aton·ing
atri·um
atro·cious
atroc·i·ty
at·ro·phied
at·ro·phy
at·tach
at·ta·ché
at·ta·ché case
at·tached
at·tach·ment
at·tack
at·tain
at·tain·able
at·tain·der
at·tain·ment
at·taint
at·tar
at·tempt
at·tend
at·ten·dance

at·ten·dant
at·ten·tion
at·ten·tive
at·ten·u·ate
at·ten·u·a·tion
at·test
at·tes·ta·tion
at·tic
at·tire
at·ti·tude
at·tor·ney
at·tor·neys
at·tract
at·trac·tion
at·trac·tive
at·trib·ut·able
at·tri·bute n.
at·trib·ute v.
at·tri·bu·tion
at·trib·u·tive
at·tri·tion
at·tune
atyp·i·cal
au·burn
au cou·rant
auc·tion
auc·tion·eer
au·da·cious
au·dac·i·ty
au·di·bil·i·ty
au·di·ble
au·di·bly
au·di·ence
au·dio·phile
au·dio·vi·su·al
au·dit

15

au·di·tion
au·di·tor
au·di·to·ri·um
au·di·to·ry
au fait
au fond
auf Wie·der·
   seh·en
au·ger (tool; cf. *augur*)
aught (slightest
   thing; cf. *ought*)
aug·ment
aug·men·ta·tion
au gra·tin
au·gur (predict;
   cf. *auger*)
au·gu·ry
au·gust (majestic)
Au·gust (month)
au jus
auk
au lait
au na·tu·rel
aunt (relative; cf. *ant*)
au·ra
au·ral (heard; cf. *oral*)
au·re·ate
au·re·ole
Au·re·o·my·cin
au·ri·cle
au·ric·u·lar
au·rif·er·ous
au·ro·ra bo·re·
   al·is
aus·cul·tate
aus·cul·ta·tion

aus·pice
aus·pi·cious
aus·tere
aus·ter·i·ty
Aus·tra·lian
au·then·tic
au·then·ti·cate
au·then·tic·i·ty
au·thor
au·thor·i·tar·i·an
au·thor·i·ta·tive
au·thor·i·ty
au·tho·ri·za·tion
au·tho·rize
au·tho·riz·ing
au·thor·ship
au·to·bahn
au·to·bio·graph·i·
   cal
au·to·bi·og·ra·phy
au·toch·tho·nous
au·toc·ra·cy
au·to·crat
au·to·crat·ic
au·to—da—fé
au·to·gi·ro
au·to·graph
au·to·graph·ic
au·to·hyp·no·sis
au·to·in·fec·tion
au·to·in·tox·i·ca·
   tion
Au·to·mat
au·to·mate
au·to·mat·ic
au·to·ma·tion

au·tom·a·tism
au·tom·a·ti·za·tion
au·tom·a·tize
au·tom·a·ton
au·to·mo·bile
au·to·mo·tive
au·ton·o·mous
au·ton·o·my
au·top·sy
au·to·sug·ges·tion
au·tumn
au·tum·nal
aux·il·ia·ry
avail
avail·abil·i·ty
avail·able
av·a·lanche
avant—garde
av·a·rice
av·a·ri·cious
avenge
av·e·nue
aver
av·er·age
averred
aver·ring
averse (disinclined;
   cf. *adverse*)
aver·sion
avert
avi·ary (for birds;
   cf. *apiary*)
avi·a·tion
avi·a·tor
avi·cul·ture
av·id

avid·ity
av·o·ca·do
av·o·ca·dos
av·o·ca·tion (hobby; cf. *vocation*)
avoid
avoid·able
avoid·ance
av·oir·du·pois
avow
avow·al
avowed
avun·cu·lar
await
awake
awak·en
award
aware
aware·ness
awash
away (absent)
aweigh (of anchor)
awe·some
aw·ful
awhile
awk·ward
awl (tool; cf. *all*)
aw·ning
awoke
awry
ax
ax·i·om
ax·i·om·at·ic
ax·is
ax·le
ax·le·tree

aza·lea
az·i·muth
Az·tec
azure

bab·bitt met·al
bab·ble (chatter; cf. *bauble, bubble*)
bab·bling
ba·bies
ba·boon
ba·bush·ka
ba·by
ba·by·ing
ba·by—sit
ba·by—sit·ter
bac·ca·lau·re·ate
bac·ca·rat
bac·cha·nal
bac·cha·na·lian
bac·chant
bach·e·lor
bach·e·lor's de·gree
ba·cil·li pl.
ba·cil·lus sing.
back·ache
back·bite
back·board

back·bone
back·break·ing
back·cross
back door n.
back·door adj.
back·drop
back·er
back·field
back·fire
back·gam·mon
back·ground
back·hand
back·hand·ed
back·lash
back·log
back·rest
back room n.
back·room adj.
back·scat·ter
back·seat adj., n.
back·set
back·slide
back·spac·er
back·stage
back·stairs
back·stitch
back·stop
back·stretch
back·stroke
back talk
back·track v.
back up v.
back·up adj., n.
back·ward
back·ward·ly
back·ward·ness

back·wash
back·wa·ter
back·woods
back·woods·man
back·yard
ba·con
bac·te·ria pl.
bac·te·ri·al
bac·te·ri·cid·al
bac·te·ri·cide
bac·te·ri·o·log·i·cal
bac·te·ri·ol·o·gist
bac·te·ri·ol·o·gy
bac·te·ri·um sing.
bad (not good)
bade (commanded)
bad·ger
ba·di·nage
bad·lands
bad·min·ton
baf·fle
baf·fle·ment
baf·fling
bag·a·telle
bag·gage
bag·gage·mas·ter
bagged
bag·gi·ly
bag·ging
bag·gy
bag·pipe
ba·guette
bailed (set free; cf. baled)
bail·ee
bai·liff

bai·li·wick
bail·ment
bail·or
bait (a lure; cf. bate)
Ba·ke·lite
bak·er's doz·en
bak·ing
bal·a·lai·ka
bal·ance
bal·anc·ing
bal·co·nies
bal·co·ny
bald (hairless; cf. balled, bawled)
bal·der·dash
baled (packaged; cf. bailed)
bale·ful
bal·ing
balk
bal·kan·iza·tion
bal·kan·ize
balk·line
balky
bal·lad
bal·lad·ry
bal·last
ball bear·ing
balled (in a ball; cf. bald, bawled)
bal·le·ri·na
bal·let
bal·lis·tic
bal·lis·tics
bal·loon
bal·loon·ist

bal·lot
ball—point pen
ball·room
bal·ly·hoo
balm
balm·i·ness
bal·mor·al
balm
bal·sa
bal·sam
Bal·tic
bal·us·trade
bam·boo
bam·boo·zle
ba·nal
ba·nal·i·ty
ba·nana
band (narrow strip; cf. banned)
ban·dage
ban·dag·ing
ban·dan·na
band·box
ban·deau
ban·de·role
ban·dit
band·mas·ter
ban·do·lier
bands (groups; cf. banns, bans)
band saw
band shell
band·stand
ban·dy
ban·dy—legged
bane·ful

ban·gle
ban·ish
ban·ish·ment
ban·is·ter
ban·jo
bank·book
bank  dis·count
bank  draft
bank·er
bank  mon·ey
bank  note
bank  pa·per
bank  rate
bank·roll
bank·rupt
bank·rupt·cy
banned (forbidden;
  cf. *band*)
ban·ner
ban·ner·et
ban·nock
banns (of marriage;
  cf. *bands, bans*)
ban·quet
ban·quette
bans (forbids;
  cf. *bands, banns*)
ban·shee
ban·tam
ban·ter·ing·ly
ban·yan
ban·zai
bao·bab
bap·tism
bap·tist
bap·tis·tery

bap·tize
bar·bar·ian
bar·bar·ic
bar·ba·rism
bar·bar·i·ty
bar·ba·rize
bar·ba·rous
bar·be·cue
bar·bell
bar·ber
bar·ber·shop
bar·bette
bar·bi·tu·rate
bar·ca·role
bar  chart
bard (poet;
  cf. *barred*)
bard·ol·a·ter
bare (uncover;
  cf. *bear*)
bare·back
bare·faced
bare·foot
bare—hand·ed
bare·head·ed
bare·ly
bar·gain
barge·board
barg·ee
barge·man
barge·mas·ter
bari·tone
bar·i·um
bar·keep·er
bar·ken·tine
bark·er

bar·ley
bar·ley·corn
bar·maid
bar·na·cle
barn·storm·er
barn·yard
baro·graph
ba·rom·e·ter
baro·met·ric
bar·on (nobleman;
  cf. *barren*)
bar·on·age
bar·on·ess
bar·on·et
bar·on·et·cy
ba·ro·ni·al
ba·rony
ba·roque
ba·rouche
bar·rack
bar·ra·cu·da
bar·rage
barred (shut out;
  cf. *bard*)
bar·rel
bar·ren (sterile;
  cf. *baron*)
bar·rette
bar·ri·cade
bar·ri·er
bar·ring
bar·ris·ter
bar·room
bar·row
bar·tend·er
bar·ter

bas·al
ba·salt
bas·cule
base (foundation;
　cf. *bass*)
base·ball
base·board
base·born
base burn·er
base·less
base·line
base·ment
base·ness
base pay
ba·ses (pl. of *basis*)
bas·es (pl. of *base*)
bash·ful
ba·sic
ba·si·cal·ly
ba·sil
ba·sil·i·ca
bas·i·lisk
ba·sin
bas·i·net (helmet;
　cf. *bassinet*)
ba·sis (foundation;
　cf. *bases*)
bas·ket
bas·ket·ball
bas·ket·work
bas—re·lief
bass (deep voice;
　cf. *base*)
bas·si·net (cradle;
　cf. *basinet*)
bas·soon

bass·wood
bas·tion
batch
bate (moderate;
　cf. *bait*)
ba·teau
bat·fish
bath
bathe
ba·thet·ic
bath·house
Bath·i·nette
bath·ing
bath mat
ba·thom·e·ter
ba·thos
bath·robe
bath·room
bath·tub
bathy·scaphe
bathy·sphere
ba·tiste
ba·ton
Bat·on Rouge La.
bat·tal·ion
bat·ten
bat·ter
bat·ter·ies
bat·tery
bat·tle
bat·tle—ax
bat·tle cruis·er
bat·tle cry
bat·tle·field
bat·tle flag
bat·tle·ground

bat·tle group
bat·tle·ment
bat·tle—scarred
bat·tle·ship
bau·ble (trifle;
　cf. *babble, bubble*)
baux·ite
Ba·var·i·an
bawled (shouted;
　cf. *bald, balled*)
bay·ber·ry
bay·o·net
Bay·onne N.J.
bay·ou
bay rum
ba·zaar (market;
　cf. *bizarre*)
ba·zoo·ka
beach (shore;
　cf. *beech*)
beach·comb·er
beach·head
bea·con
bea·dle
bead·work
beady
bea·gle
bean·ie
bear (animal; cf. *bare*)
bear·able
beard·ed
bear·er
bear·skin
beat (flog; cf. *beet*)
be·atif·ic
be·at·i·fi·ca·tion

**20**

be·at·i·fy
be·at·i·tude
beat·nik
beau (suitor; cf. *bow*)
beau·te·ous
beau·ti·cian
beau·ties
beau·ti·fied
beau·ti·ful
beau·ti·fy
beau·ti·fy·ing
beau·ty
bea·ver
be·calm
be·cause
beck·on
be·cloud
be·come
be·com·ing·ly
be·daub
be·daz·zle
bed board
bed·bug
bed·clothes
bed·ding
be·deck
be·dev·il
bed·fast
bed·fel·low
be·dight
be·di·zen
bed·lam
bed·ou·in
bed·post
be·drag·gled
bed·rid·den

bed·rock
bed·room
bed·side
bed·sore
bed·spread
bed·stead
bed·time
beech (tree; cf. *beach*)
beech·nut
beef·eat·er
beef·steak
bee·hive
bee·keep·er
bee·line
beer (liquor; cf. *bier*)
bees·wax
beet (vegetable;
    cf. *beat*)
bee·tle
bee·tle—browed
be·fall
be·fit
be·fog
be·fool
be·fore
be·fore·hand
be·fore·time
be·friend
be·fud·dle
beg·gar
beg·gar·li·ness
beg·gar·ly
beg·gar·weed
beg·gary
be·gin
be·gin·ning

be·grime
be·grudge
be·guile
be·gum
be·gun
be·half
be·have
be·hav·ing
be·hav·ior
be·hav·ior·ism
be·head
be·held
be·he·moth
be·hest
be·hind
be·hind·hand
be·hold
be·hoove
beige
be·la·bor
be·lat·ed·ly
be·lay
bel can·to
be·lea·guer
bel·fry
Bel·gian
Be·lial
be·lie
be·lief
be·liev·able
be·lieve
be·liev·ing
be·lit·tle
be·lit·tling
bell (that rings;
    cf. *belle*)

bel·la·don·na
bell·boy
belle (girl; cf. *bell*)
belles let·tres
bell·flow·er
bell·hop
bel·li·cose
bel·lig·er·ence
bel·lig·er·ent
bell jar
bell met·al
bel·lows
bell·pull
bell rope
bell tow·er
bell·weth·er
bel·ly
bel·ly·ache
bel·ly·band
be·long
be·loved
be·low
belt·ing
bel·ve·dere
be·moan
bench mark
bench show
bench war·rant
ben·day
be·neath
ben·e·dict
bene·dic·tion
bene·dic·to·ry
bene·fac·tion
bene·fac·tor
ben·e·fice

be·nef·i·cence
be·nef·i·cent
be·nef·i·cent·ly
ben·e·fi·cial
ben·e·fi·cia·ries
ben·e·fi·cia·ry
ben·e·fit
ben·e·fit·ed
ben·e·fit·ing
be·nev·o·lence
be·nev·o·lent
be·night·ed
be·nig·nant·ly
be·nig·ni·ty
be·nign·ly
ben·i·son
be·queath
be·quest
ber·ceuse
be·reave
be·reave·ment
beri·beri
Berke·ley Calif.
Berk·ley Mich.
ber·lin
ber·ries
ber·ry (fruit; cf. *bury*)
ber·serk
berth (bed; cf. *birth*)
ber·yl
be·ryl·li·um
be·seech
be·set·ting
be·side
be·sides
be·siege

be·smear
be·smirch
be·speak
Bes·se·mer
bes·tial
bes·ti·al·i·ty
best man
be·stow
best—sell·er
best—sell·ing
bet
be·tide
be·times
be·to·ken·ing
be·tray
be·tray·al
be·troth
be·troth·al
bet·ter (good;
    cf. *bettor*)
bet·ter·ment
bet·ting
bet·tor (one who
    wagers; cf. *better*)
be·tween
be·tween·times
be·tween·whiles
be·twixt
bev·el
bev·eled
bev·el·ing
bev·er·age
bev·ies
bevy
be·wail
be·ware

be·wil·der
be·wil·dered
be·wil·der·ment
be·witch
be·wray
be·yond
be·zant
be·zel
bi·an·nu·al (twice
   yearly; cf. biennial)
bi·as
bi·ased
bi·be·lot
bi·ble
bib·li·cal
bib·li·og·ra·pher
bib·li·og·ra·phy
bib·lio·phile
bib·u·lous
bi·cam·er·al
bi·car·bon·ate
bi·cen·te·na·ry
bi·cen·ten·ni·al
bi·ceps
bi·chlo·ride
bi·chro·mate
bi·cus·pid
bi·cy·cle
bi·cy·clist
Bid·de·ford Maine
Bid·e·ford England
bi·en·ni·al (once in
   two years;
   cf. **biannual**)
bier (for funeral;
   cf. beer)

bi·fur·cate
big·a·mist
big·a·mous
big·a·my
Big Ben
bi·gem·i·nal
big·eyed
big game
big·ger
big·gest
big·head·ed
big·heart·ed
big·horn
bight
big·mouthed
big·ot·ed
big·ot·ry
big shot
big time
big top
big·wig
bi·jou
bi·ki·ni
bi·la·bi·al
bi·lat·er·al
bilge
bilge wa·ter
bi·lin·gual
bil·ious
bill·board
billed (charged;
   cf. build)
bil·let
**bil·let—doux**
**bill·fish**
bill·fold

bill·head
bill·hook
bil·liards
bil·lings·gate
bil·lion
bil·lion·aire
bil·lionth
bill of fare
bill of lad·ing
bill of sale
bil·low
bil·lowy
bill·post·er
bil·ly goat
bi·me·tal·lic
bi·met·al·lism
bi·met·al·list
bi·month·ly
bi·na·ry
bind·er
bind·ery
bind·ing
bind·weed
bin·na·cle
bin·oc·u·lar
bi·no·mi·al
bio·chem·is·try
bio·de·grad·able
bi·og·ra·pher
bio·graph·ic
bio·graph·i·cal
bi·og·ra·phy
bi·o·log·i·cal
bi·ol·o·gy
bi·op·sy
bio·sci·ence

bi·par·ti·san
bi·par·tite
bi·ped
bi·plane
bi·po·lar
bird·bath
bird·brain
bird·call
bird dog
bird·house
bird·lime
bird·man
bird·seed
bird's—eye
bi·ret·ta
birth (beginning;
   cf. *berth*)
birth·day
birth·mark
birth·place
birth·rate
birth·right
birth·stone
bis·cuit
bi·sect
bish·op
bish·op·ric
Bis·marck N. Dak.
bis·muth
bi·son
bisque
bis·sex·tile
bit·ing
bit·stock
bit·ter
bit·tern

bit·ter·ness
bit·ter·root
bit·ter·sweet
bit·ter·weed
bi·tu·men
bi·tu·mi·nous
bi·va·lent
bi·valve
biv·ouac
biv·ouacked
bi·zarre (odd;
   cf. *bazaar*)
bi·zon·al
black—and—blue
black·ball
black·ber·ry
black·bird
black·board
black·cap
black·ened
black—eyed
   Su·san
black·head
black·jack
black lead
black light
black·list
black·mail
black·ness
black out v.
black·out n.
black·poll
black sheep
black·smith
black·snake
black·thorn

black·top
blad·der
blam·able
blame·ful
blame·less
blame·wor·thy
blam·ing
blanc·mange
blan·dish
blank
   en·dorse·ment
blan·ket
blar·ney
bla·sé
blas·pheme
blas·phem·ing
blas·phe·mous
blas·phe·my
blast off v.
blast—off n.
bla·tan·cy
bla·tant
blath·er·skite
blaze
blaz·ing
bla·zon
bla·zon·ry
bleach·er
blem·ish
blend·ed
bless·ed·ness
blew (air; cf. *blue*)
blind·er
blind·fish
blind·fold
blind·ing

blind·ly
blink·er
bliss·ful
blis·ter
blithe
blithe·some
blitz·krieg
bliz·zard
bloat·er
bloc (political)
block (of wood)
block·ade
block·head
block·house
blond
blood
blood bank
blood count
blood·cur·dling
blood·ed
blood·hound
blood·i·est
blood·i·ly
blood·i·ness
blood·less
blood·let·ting
blood·mo·bile
blood mon·ey
blood pres·sure
blood·root
blood·shed
blood·shot
blood·stain
blood·stone
blood·suck·er
blood·thirst·i·ness

blood·thirsty
blood ves·sel
blood·wort
bloody
blos·som
blot·ter
blot·ting
blouse
blow·er
blow·fish
blow·fly
blow·gun
blow out v.
blow·out n.
blow·pipe
blow·torch
blow·tube
blub·ber
blub·bery
blu·cher
blud·geon
blue (color; cf. blew)
blue·bell
blue·ber·ry
blue·bird
blue·bon·net
blue book
blue·bot·tle
blue·coat
blue—eyed
blue·fish
blue·grass
blue·jack
blue jay
blue law
blue moon

blue—pen·cil
blue·print
blue·stock·ing
blu·et
bluff
blu·ing
blu·ish
blun·der
blun·der·buss
blunt·ly
blunt·ness
blur
blurred
blur·ring
blurt
blus·ter
blus·ter·ous
boa
boar (animal; cf. bore)
board (wood;
  cf. bored)
board·er (one who
  pays for meals;
  cf. border)
board foot
board·ing·house
board·ing school
board·room
board rule
board·walk
boast·ful
boast·ing·ly
boat hook
boat·house
boat·load
boat·man

boat·swain
boat train
bob·bin
bob·bi·net
bob·cat
bob·o·link
bob·sled
bob·tail
bob·white
bo·cac·cio
bod·ice
bodi·less
bodi·ly
bod·kin
body·guard
Boer
bo·gey
bo·gey·man
bog·gle v.
bo·gle n.
bo·gus
Bo·he·mi·an
boil·er
bois·ter·ous
bold·er (braver;
   cf. *boulder*)
bold·face n.
bold—faced
bold·ly
bold·ness
bole (trunk of tree;
   cf. *boll, bowl*)
bo·le·ro
bo·li·var
boll (of cotton;
   cf. *bole, bowl*)

boll wee·vil
boll·worm
bol·ster
bolt·er
bolt·rope
bo·lus
bomb
bom·bard
bom·bar·dier
bom·bard·ment
bom·bast
bom·bas·tic
bom·ba·zine
bomb·proof
bomb·shell
bomb·sight
bona fide
bo·nan·za
bon·bon
bon·bon·nière
bond·age
bond·hold·er
bond·maid
bond ser·vant
bonds·man
bone meal
bon·fire
bo·ni·to
bon mot
bon·net
bon·ny
bo·nus
bon vi·vant
bonze
boo·by
boo·dle

book
book·bind·er
book·case
book club
book·deal·er
book·end
book·fair
book·ie
book·ish
book·keep·er
book·keep·ing
book·let
book list
book·lore
book·mak·er
book·man
book·mark
book·mo·bile
book·plate
book·rack
book·rest
book re·view
book·sell·er
book·shelf
book·store
book val·ue
book·work
book·worm
boo·mer·ang
boon·dog·gle
boor·ish·ness
boost·er
boot·black
boot·ed
boo·tee
booth

boot·jack
boot·leg
boot·less
boo·ty
booze
boozy
bo·rac·ic
bo·rate
bo·rax
Bor·deaux
bor·der (edge;
   cf. *boarder*)
bor·der line n.
bor·der·line adj.
bore (weary; cf. *boar*)
bo·re·al
Bo·re·as
bored (uninterested;
   cf. *board*)
bore·dom
bor·ing
bo·ron
bor·ough
   (division of city;
   cf. *burro*, *burrow*)
bor·row
bosky
Bos·ni·an
bo·som
boss·i·ness
bossy
bo·tan·i·cal
bot·a·nist
bot·a·nize
bot·a·ny
botch

both
both·er
both·er·some
bot·tle
bot·tle·neck
bot·tler
bot·tling
bot·tom
bot·tom·less
bot·tom·ry
bot·u·lism
bou·doir
bouf·fant
bough (of tree;
   cf. *bow*)
bought
bouil·la·baisse
bouil·lon (soup;
   cf. *bullion*)
boul·der (rock;
   cf. *bolder*)
bou·le·vard
bounce
bounc·er
bounc·ing
bound
bound·aries
bound·ary
bound·en
bound·er
bound·less
boun·te·ous
boun·ti·ful
boun·ty
bou·quet
bour·bon

bour·geois
bour·geoi·sie
bourse
bou·tique
bou·ton·niere
bo·vine
bow (knot; cf. *beau*)
bow (salutation;
   cf. *bough*)
bowd·ler·ize
bow·el
bow·er
bow·ery
bow·fin
bow·knot
bowl (dish;
   cf. *bole*, *boll*)
bowl·er
bow·line
bowl·ing
bow·man
bow·shot
bow·sprit
bow·string
bow tie
bow·yer
box calf
box·car
box coat
box·er
box·ing
box kite
box of·fice
box score
box spring
box·thorn

box·wood
boy (youth; cf. *buoy*)
boy·cott
boy·hood
boy·ish
boy·sen·ber·ry
brace·let
brac·er
brack·et
brack·et·ing
brack·ish
brad·awl
brag
brag·ga·do·cio
brag·gart
bragged
brag·ging
braille
brain·child
brain cor·al
brain·less
brain·pow·er
brain·sick
brain·storm
brain trust
brain·wash·ing
brain wave
brainy
braise (cook slowly; cf. *braze*)
brake (on a car; cf. *break*)
brake·man
bram·ble
brand
bran·died

bran·dish
brand—new
bran·dy
bras·sard
brass·bound
brass hat
brass·ie
bras·siere
brass·i·ness
bra·va·do
brav·ery
brav·est
bra·vo
bra·vu·ra
brawl
brawn·i·est
brawny
braze (solder; cf. *braise*)
bra·zen
bra·zen—faced
bra·zier
Bra·zil·ian
bra·zil·wood
breach (violation; cf. *breech*)
bread (food; cf. *bred*)
bread·board·ing
bread·fruit
bread·root
bread·stuff
breadth (size; cf. *breath*)
bread·win·ner
break (shatter; cf. *brake*)

break·able
break·age
break·down n.
break down v.
break·er
break·fast
break·neck
break·through n.
break·wa·ter
breast
breast·bone
breast·stroke
breath (of air; cf. *breadth*)
breathe
breath·er
breath·ing
breath·less
breath·tak·ing
bred (produced; cf. *bread*)
breech (rear; cf. *breach*)
breech·es
breech·load·er
breech—load·ing
breed
breed·ing
breeze
breeze·way
breezy
breth·ren
bre·vet
bre·via·ry
brev·i·ty
brew
brew·ery

brew·ing
brews (ferments;
   cf. *bruise*)
bribe
brib·ery
brib·ing
bric—a—brac
brick
brick·bat
brick·kiln
brick·lay·er
brick red
brick·work
brick·yard
brid·al (wedding;
   cf. *bridle*)
bride
bride·groom
brides·maid
bride·well
bridge
bridge·head
bridge·work
bri·dle (harness;
   cf. *bridal*)
brief
brief·case
brief·less
bri·er
bri·er·root
bri·er·wood
brig
bri·gade
brig·a·dier
brig·and
brig·an·tine

bright
bright·en
bright·ly
bright·ness
bright·work
bril·liance
bril·lian·cy
bril·liant
bril·lian·tine
bril·liant·ly
brim
brim·ful
brimmed
brim·mer
brim·ming
brim·stone
brin·dle
bring
brink
brink·man·ship
briny
bri·quette
brisk
bris·ket
bris·tle
bris·tle·tail
bris·tling
bris·tol (cardboard)
Brit·ain (country;
   cf. *Briton*)
Bri·tan·nia
Bri·tan·nic
Brit·ish
Brit·ish·er
Brit·on (person;
   cf. *Britain*)

brit·tle
broach (open;
   cf. *brooch*)
broad
broad·ax
broad·cast
broad·cloth
broad·en
broad jump
broad·leaf adj.
broad—leaved adj.
broad·loom
broad·ly
broad—mind·ed
broad—mind·ed-
   ness
broad·side
broad·sword
broad·tail
bro·cade
broc·co·li
bro·chette
bro·chure
brogue
broil
broil·er
broke
bro·ken
bro·ken·heart·ed
bro·ker
bro·ker·age
bro·mate
bro·mide
bro·mine
bron·chi·al
bron·chi·tis

bron·cho- (medical prefix; cf. *bronco*)
bron·cho·scope
bron·co (horse; cf. *broncho*)
bronze
brooch (pin; cf. *broach*)
brood
brood·er
brook
brook·let
Brook·line Mass.
Brook·lyn N.Y.
broom·stick
broth
broth·er
broth·er·hood
broth·er—in—law
broth·er·ly
brougham
brought
brow
brow·beat
brown bread
brown·ish
brown·out
brown·stone
brown sug·ar
browse
bru·in
bruise (crush; cf. *brews*)
bruis·er
bru·net *or* bru·nette

brunt
brush
brush—off n.
brush up v.
brush·up n.
brush·wood
brush·work
brusque
bru·tal
bru·tal·i·ty
bru·tal·iza·tion
bru·tal·ize
brute
brut·ish
bub·ble (soap; cf. *babble, bauble*)
bub·bly
bu·bon·ic
buc·ca·neer
Bu·ceph·a·lus
buck·board
buck·et
buck·eye
buck·hound
buck·le
buck·ler
buck·ling
buck·ram
buck·saw
buck·shot
buck·skin
buck·thorn
buck·wheat
bu·col·ic
Bud·dha
Bud·dhism

bud·ding
bud·get
bud·get·ary
buf·fa·lo sing. (pl.: *buffalo* or *buffaloes*)
buff·er
buf·fet
buf·foon
buf·foon·ery
bug·bear
bu·gle
bu·gling
build (construct; cf. *billed*)
build·er
build·ing
build·up n.
bul·bous
Bul·gar·i·an
bulge
bulg·ing
bulk·head
bulky
bull·dog
bull·doze
bull·doz·er
bul·let
bul·le·tin
bul·let·proof
bull·fight
bull·finch
bull·frog
bull·head
bul·lion (gold or silver; cf. *bouillon*)

bull·ock
bull pen
bull·pout
bull's—eye
bull·ter·ri·er
bull·whip
bul·ly
bul·ly·rag
bul·rush
bul·wark
bum·ble·bee
bum·boat
bump·er
bump·kin
bumpy
bunch
bun·dle
bun·ga·low
bun·gle
bun·gling
bun·ion
bunk
bun·ker
bun·kum
    or bun·combe
bun·ting
buoy (signal; cf. boy)
buoy·an·cy
buoy·ant
bur·den
bur·den·some
bur·dock
bu·reau
bu·reau·cra·cy
bu·reau·crat
bu·rette

bur·geon
bur·gher
bur·glar
bur·glar·ies
bur·glar·i·ous
bur·glar·ize
bur·glar·proof
bur·glary
bur·go·mas·ter
Bur·gun·dy
buri·al
bur·ied
bur·ies
bur·lap
bur·lesque
bur·ly
Bur·mese
burn
burned
burn·er
bur·nish
bur·noose
burn·sides
burnt
burr
bur·ro (donkey;
    cf. borough, burrow)
bur·ros
bur·row (dig;
    cf. borough, burro)
bur·sar
bur·sa·ry
bur·si·tis
burst
bury (conceal;
    cf. berry)

bury·ing
bus·boy
bush·el
bush·rang·er
bush·whack·er
bus·ied
busi·er
busi·est
busi·ly
busi·ness (enter-
    prise; cf. busyness)
busi·ness·like
busi·ness·man
bus·kin
bus·tle
bus·tling
busy
busy·ness (busy
    state; cf. business)
busy·work
but (conjunction;
    cf. butt)
butch·er
butch·ery
butt (end; cf. but)
butte
but·ter
but·ter·cup
but·ter·fat
but·ter·fish
but·ter·fly
but·ter·milk
but·ter·nut
but·ter·scotch
but·ter·weed
but·tery

but·tock
but·ton
but·ton·hole
but·ton·hook
but·ton·wood
but·tress
bux·om
buy·er
buy·ing
buzz
buz·zard
buzz·er
buzz saw
by—elec·tion
by·gone
by·law
by—line
by·pass
by·path
by·play
by—prod·uct
by·road
bys·sus
by·stand·er
by·way
by·word
Byz·an·tine

ca·bal
cab·a·lis·tic

ca·bana
cab·a·ret
cab·bage
cab·in
cab·i·net
cab·i·net·mak·er
cab·i·net·work
ca·ble
ca·ble·gram
ca·bling
cab·man
cab·o·chon
ca·boose
cab·ri·o·let
cab·stand
ca·cao
cach·a·lot
cache
ca·chet
cach·in·na·tion
ca·cique
cack·le
ca·coph·o·ny
cac·tus (pl.:
    *cacti* or *cactuses*)
ca·dav·er
ca·dav·er·ous
ca·dence
ca·den·za
ca·det
cad·mi·um
ca·du·ceus
Cae·sar
cae·su·ra
caf·e·te·ria
caf·feine

cairn·gorm
cais·son
cai·tiff
ca·jole
ca·jol·ery
cake·walk
cal·a·bash
cal·a·boose
ca·lam·i·tous
ca·lam·i·ty
cal·car·e·ous
cal·cif·er·ous
cal·ci·fi·ca·tion
cal·ci·fy
cal·ci·mine
cal·ci·na·tion
cal·cine
cal·ci·um
cal·cu·la·ble
cal·cu·late
cal·cu·lat·ing
cal·cu·la·tion
cal·cu·la·tor
cal·cu·lus (pl.:
    *calculi*)
cal·dron
cal·en·dar (for dates)
cal·en·der (machine)
calf (pl.: *calves*)
calf·skin
cal·i·ber
cal·i·brate
cal·i·co
Cal·i·for·nia
cal·i·per
ca·liph

cal·is·then·ics
calk
calk·er
call·able
cal·lig·ra·pher
cal·lig·ra·phy
call·ing
cal·los·i·ty
cal·lous (hardened;
   cf. *callus*)
cal·low
cal·lus (hardened
   surface; cf. *callous*)
calm
calm·ly
calm·ness
cal·o·mel
ca·lor·ic
cal·o·rie
cal·o·ries
cal·o·rim·e·ter
ca·lum·ni·ate
ca·lum·ni·a·tion
ca·lum·ni·a·tor
cal·um·nies
ca·lum·ni·ous
cal·um·ny
cal·va·ry
Cal·vin·ism
Cal·vin·ist
Cal·vin·is·tic
ca·lyp·so
ca·lyx
ca·ma·ra·de·rie
cam·ber
cam·bi·um

cam·bric
cam·el
ca·mel·lia
ca·mel·o·pard
Cam·em·bert
cam·eo
cam·eos
cam·era
cam·era·man
cam·i·sole
cam·ou·flage
cam·paign
cam·pa·nile
camp·er
camp·fire
camp·ground
cam·phor
cam·pus
cam·shaft
cam wheel
Can·a·da
Ca·na·di·an
ca·naille
ca·nal
can·a·li·za·tion
can·a·pé
ca·nard
ca·nar·ies
ca·nary
can·cel
can·celed
can·cel·er
can·cel·ing
can·cel·la·tion
can·cer
can·cer·ous

can·de·la·bra
can·did
can·di·da·cy
can·di·date
can·did·ly
can·did·ness
can·died
can·dies
can·dle
can·dle·ber·ry
can·dle·fish
can·dle·light
can·dle·nut
can·dle·pin
can·dle·pow·er
can·dle·stick
can·dle·wick
can·dle·wood
can·dor
can·dy
cane·brake
ca·nine
can·is·ter
can·ker
can·ker·ous
can·ker·worm
can·na
can·nery
can·ni·bal
can·ni·bal·ism
can·ni·bal·ize
can·ni·ly
can·ni·ness
can·ning
can·non (gun;
   cf. *canon, canyon*)

can·non·ade
can·non·eer
can·not
can·ny
ca·noe
ca·noe·ing
ca·noes
can·on (rule;
  cf. *cannon, canyon*)
ca·non·i·cal
can·on·ize
can·o·pies
can·o·py
can·ta·bi·le
can·ta·loupe
can·tan·ker·ous
can·ta·ta
can·ta·trice
can·teen
can·ter
can·ti·cle
can·ti·le·ver
can·to
can·ton
can·ton·al
Can·ton·ese
can·ton·ment
can·tor
can·vas n. (cloth)
can·vass v. (solicit)
can·yon (ravine;
  cf. *cannon, canon*)
ca·pa·bil·i·ties
ca·pa·bil·i·ty
ca·pa·ble
ca·pa·bly

ca·pa·cious
ca·pac·i·tor
ca·pac·i·ty
cap—a—pie
ca·par·i·son
ca·per
cap·il·lar·i·ty
cap·il·lary
cap·i·tal (city,
  property; cf. *capitol*)
cap·i·tal·ism
cap·i·tal·ist
cap·i·tal·iza·tion
cap·i·tal·ize
cap·i·tol (building;
  cf. *capital*)
ca·pit·u·late
ca·pit·u·la·tion
ca·price
ca·pri·cious
cap·size
cap·stan
cap·stone
cap·sule
cap·tain
cap·tion
cap·tious
cap·ti·vate
cap·ti·va·tion
cap·tive
cap·tiv·i·ty
cap·tor
cap·ture
cap·tur·ing
car·a·cole
car·a·cul

car·a·mel
car·a·mel·ize
car·at *or* kar·at
  (weight; cf. *caret,
  carrot*)
car·a·van
car·a·van·sa·ry
car·a·vel
car·a·way
car·bide
car·bine
car·bo·hy·drate
car·bol·ic
car·bon
car·bo·na·ceous
car·bon·ate
car·bon·ic
car·bon·if·er·ous
Car·bo·run·dum
car·box·yl
car·boy
car·bun·cle
car·bu·re·tor
car·cass
car·cin·o·gen
car·ci·no·ma
card cat·a·log
car·da·mom
card·board
card·hold·er
car·di·ac
car·di·gan
car·di·nal
car·di·nal·ate
car·dio·gram
car·dio·graph

car·di·ol·o·gist
car·dio·vas·cu·lar
card ta·ble
ca·reen
ca·reer
care·ful
care·ful·ly
care·less
ca·ress
car·et (a symbol;
 cf. *carat, carrot*)
care·worn
car·fare
car·go sing.
car·goes pl.
car·hop
Ca·rib·be·an
car·i·bou
car·i·ca·ture
car·ies
car·il·lon
ca·ri·o·ca
car·line
car·load
car·mi·na·tive
car·mine
car·nage
car·nal
car·nal·i·ty
car·na·tion
car·ne·lian
car·ni·val
car·niv·o·rous
car·ol
car·om
ca·rot·id

ca·rous·al
ca·rouse
car·pen·ter
car·pen·try
car·pet
car·pet·bag
car·pet·bag·ger
car·pet·ing
car·port
car·riage
car·ri·er
car·ri·on
car·rot (vegetable;
 cf. *carat, caret*)
car·rou·sel
car·ry
car·ry·all
car·ry—over n.
cart·age
carte blanche
car·tel
car·ti·lage
car·ti·lag·i·nous
car·tog·ra·pher
car·tog·ra·phy
car·ton (box)
car·toon (picture)
car·toon·ist
car·touche
car·tridge
carve
cary·at·id
ca·sa·ba
cas·cade
case hard·en
ca·sein

case knife
case·mate
case·ment
ca·sern
case·work
cash·book
ca·shew
cash·ier
cash·mere
ca·si·no
cas·ket
casque
cas·se·role
cas·sia
cas·sock
cas·so·wary
cast (throw; cf. *caste*)
cas·ta·net
cast·away
caste (social class;
 cf. *cast*)
cas·tel·lat·ed
cas·ti·gate
cas·ti·ga·tion
Cas·til·ian
cast iron
cas·tle
cast·off n.
cas·tor
ca·su·al
ca·su·al·ty
ca·su·ist
ca·su·ist·ry
cat·a·clysm
cat·a·comb
cat·a·falque

Cat·a·lan
cat·a·lep·sy
cat·a·lep·tic
cat·a·log
ca·tal·pa
ca·tal·y·sis
cat·a·lyst
cat·a·lyt·ic
cat·a·ma·ran
cat·a·mount
cat·a·pult
cat·a·ract
ca·tarrh
ca·tarrh·al
ca·tas·ta·sis
ca·tas·tro·phe
cat·a·stroph·ic
Ca·taw·ba
cat·bird
cat·boat
cat·call
catch·all
catch·er
catch·pen·ny
catch·word
cat·e·che·sis
cat·e·chism
cat·e·chist
cat·e·chu·men
cat·e·gor·i·cal
cat·e·go·rize
cat·e·go·ry
cat·e·nary
cat·er—cor·nered
ca·ter·er
cat·er·pil·lar

cat·er·waul
cat·fish
cat·gut
ca·thar·sis
ca·thar·tic
ca·the·dral
cath·e·ter
cath·ode
cath·o·lic
Ca·thol·i·cism
cath·o·lic·i·ty
ca·thol·i·cize
cat·like
cat·nip
cat—o'—nine—
    tails
cat's—eye
cat's—paw
cat·sup
cat·tail
cat·tle
cat·walk
Cau·ca·sian
cau·cus
cau·dal
cau·li·flow·er
caulk
caus·al
cau·sal·i·ty
cau·sa·tion
caus·ative
cau·se·rie
cause·way
caus·ing
caus·tic
cau·ter·i·za·tion

cau·ter·ize
cau·tery
cau·tion
cau·tion·ary
cau·tious
cav·al·cade
cav·a·lier
cav·a·lier·ly
cav·al·ry
cav·a·ti·na
ca·ve·at emp·tor
cav·ern
cav·ern·ous
cav·i·ar
cav·il
cav·iled
cav·i·ties
cav·i·ty
ca·vort
cease
ceased
cease·less
ce·dar
cede (yield; cf. *seed*)
ce·dil·la
ceil
ceil·ing
cel·e·brant
cel·e·brate
cel·e·brat·ed
cel·e·bra·tion
cel·e·bra·tor
ce·leb·ri·ty
ce·ler·i·ty
cel·ery
ce·les·ta

ce·les·tial
cel·i·ba·cy
cel·i·bate
cel·lar (underground
    storeroom; cf. *seller*)
cel·lar·age
cel·lar·er
cel·lar·ette
cel·list
cel·lo
cel·lo·phane
cel·lu·lar
cel·lu·loid
cel·lu·lose
Cel·sius
ce·ment
ce·men·ta·tion
cem·e·ter·ies
cem·e·tery
cen·o·bite
ceno·taph
cen·ser (for incense)
cen·sor (examiner)
cen·so·ri·al
cen·so·ri·ous
cen·sor·ship
cen·sur·able
cen·sure
cen·sur·ing
cen·sus (count;
    cf. *senses*)
cent (penny;
    cf. *scent, sent*)
cen·taur
cen·ta·vo
cen·te·na·ry

cen·ten·ni·al
cen·ter·board
cen·ter·piece
cen·ti·grade
cen·ti·gram
cen·ti·li·ter
cen·time
cen·ti·me·ter
cen·ti·pede
cen·tral
cen·tral·iza·tion
cen·tral·ize
cen·trif·u·gal
cen·tri·fuge
cen·trip·e·tal
cen·trist
cen·tu·ri·on
cen·tu·ry
ce·phal·ic
ce·ram·ic
Cer·ber·us
ce·re·al (grain;
    cf. *serial*)
cer·e·bel·lum
ce·re·bral
ce·re·bro·spi·nal
cer·e·mo·ni·al
cer·e·mo·nies
cer·e·mo·ni·ous
cer·e·mo·ny
Ce·res
ce·rise
ce·ri·um
cer·tain
cer·tain·ly
cer·tain·ties

cer·tain·ty
cer·ti·fi·able
cer·tif·i·cate
cer·ti·fi·ca·tion
cer·ti·fies
cer·ti·fy
cer·tio·ra·ri
cer·ti·tude
ce·ru·le·an
cer·vi·cal
cer·vix
ce·si·um
ces·sa·tion
ces·sion (yielding;
    cf. *session*)
cess·pit
cess·pool
chafe (irritate)
chaff (banter)
chaf·finch
cha·grin
cha·grined
chain   gang
chain   mail
chain   saw
chain   stitch
chair·man
chair·per·son
chaise   longue
chal·ced·o·ny
cha·let
chal·ice
chalky
chal·lenge
chal·lis
cham·ber

cham·ber·lain
cham·ber·maid
cha·me·leon
cham·fer
cham·ois
cham·pagne (wine)
cham·paign (plain)
cham·per·ty
cham·pi·on
cham·pi·on·ship
chance·ful
chan·cel
chan·cel·lery
chan·cel·lor
chan·cery
chan·de·lier
chan·dler
chan·dlery
change·abil·i·ty
change·able
change·less
change·ling
chang·ing
chan·nel
chan·neled
chan·nel·ing
chan·son
chan·te·relle
chan·teuse
chan·ti·cleer
cha·os
cha·ot·ic
chap·ar·ral
chap·book
cha·peau (pl.: *chapeaus*)

cha·pel
chap·er·on
chap·fall·en
chap·lain
chap·let
chap·ter
char·ac·ter
char·ac·ter·is·tic
char·ac·ter·iza·tion
char·ac·ter·ize
cha·rade
char·coal
charge·able
charge ac·count
charge—a—plate
char·gé d'af·faires
charg·ing
char·i·ot
char·i·o·teer
cha·ris·ma
char·i·ta·ble
char·i·ta·bly
char·i·ties
char·i·ty
char·la·tan
Charles·ton
   S.C., W. Va.
Charles·town Mass.
char·ley horse
char·nel
char·ter
char·treuse
char·wom·an
Cha·ryb·dis
chased (pursued; cf. *chaste*)

chasm
chasse·pot
chas·sis
chaste (virtuous; cf. *chased*)
chas·ten
chas·tise
chas·tise·ment
chas·ti·ty
cha·su·ble
châ·teau (pl.: *châteaus*)
chat·e·laine
chat·tel
chat·ter
chat·ter·box
chat·ter·er
chat·ting
chauf·feur
chau·tau·qua
chau·vin·ism
cheap·en
cheap·ened
cheap·skate
check·book
check·er·ber·ry
check·er·board
check·ered
check in v.
check—in n.
check·list
check mark
check·mate
check off v.
check·off n.
check out v.

check·out n.
check·point
check·rein
check·room
check up v.
check·up n.
check·writ·er
cheek·bone
cheek·i·ly
cheek·i·ness
cheeky
cheer·ful
cheer·ful·ness
cheer·i·ly
cheer·less
cheery
cheese·burg·er
cheese·cake
cheese·cloth
cheese·par·ing
chef
chef d'oeu·vre
chem·i·cal
che·mise
chem·ist
chem·is·try
che·nille
cher·ish
Cher·o·kee
che·root
cher·ries
cher·ry
cher·ub (pl.:
  *cherubim* or *cherubs*)
chess·board
chess·man

ches·ter·field
chest·nut
che·va·lier
chev·i·ot
chev·ron
Chi·an·ti
chiar·oscu·ro
chi·ca·nery
chick·a·dee
chick·a·ree
chick·en
chick·en·heart·ed
chick·en pox
chick—pea
chick·weed
chi·cle
chic·o·ry
chief·ly
chief·tain
chif·fon
chif·fo·nier
chi·gnon
chil·blain
child·bed
child·birth
child·hood
child·ish
child·less
child·like
child·proof
chil·dren
chill
chill·ing·ly
chill·i·ness
chilly
chi·me·ra

chi·me·ri·cal
chim·ney
chim·neys
chim·pan·zee
chi·na·ber·ry
Chi·na·town
chi·na·ware
chin·chil·la
Chi·nese
Chi·nook
chintz
chip·munk
chip·ping
chi·rog·ra·phy
chi·rop·o·dist
chi·ro·prac·tor
chis·el
chis·eled
chis·el·er
chis·el·ing
chit·chat
chi·val·ric
chiv·al·rous
chiv·al·ry
chlo·ral
chlo·rate
chlor·dane
chlo·ric
chlo·ride
chlo·ri·nate
chlo·rine
chlo·rite
chlo·ro·form
chlo·ro·phyll
chlo·rous
chock—full

choc·o·late
Choc·taw
choir (singers;
   cf. *quire*)
choke·ber·ry
choke·cher·ry
choke·damp
chok·er
cho·ler
chol·era
cho·ler·ic
choose (select;
   cf. *chose*)
choos·ing
chop·house
chop·per
chop·ping
chop·stick
chop su·ey
cho·ral (of a chorus;
   cf. *chorale, coral,*
   *corral*)
cho·rale (sacred song;
   cf. *choral, coral,*
   *corral*)
chord (music;
   cf. *cord*)
chore
cho·rea
cho·re·og·ra·phy
cho·ris·ter
chor·tle
chorus
chose (selected;
   cf. *choose*)
cho·sen

chow·der
chrism
chris·ten
Chris·ten·dom
Chris·tian
Chris·tian·i·ty
Chris·tian·ize
Christ·like
Christ·ly
Christ·mas
Christ·mas·tide
chro·mate
chro·mat·ic
chrome
chro·mite
chro·mi·um
chro·mo·some
chron·ic
chron·i·cle
chro·no·graph
chro·no·log·i·cal
chro·nol·o·gy
chro·nom·e·ter
chro·no·met·ric
chrys·a·lis
chry·san·the·mum
chryso·ber·yl
chrys·o·lite
chrys·o·prase
chuck·le
chuck·le·head
chuk·ker
chum
chum·mi·ness
chum·my
chump

chunk
church·go·er
church·man
church·war·den
church·yard
churl
churl·ish
churn
chute (slide; cf. *shoot*)
chut·ney
chyle
chyme
ci·bo·ri·um
ci·ca·da
ci·ca·la
ci·ca·trix
ci·der
ci—de·vant
ci·gar
cig·a·rette
Cim·me·ri·an
cin·cho·na
Cin·cin·nati Ohio
cinc·ture
cin·der
Cin·der·el·la
cin·e·ma
cin·e·mat·o·graph
cin·na·bar
cin·na·mon
cin·que·cen·to
cin·que·foil
ci·pher
Cir·cas·sian
Cir·ce
cir·cle

cir·clet
cir·cling
cir·cuit
cir·cu·itous
cir·cuit·ry
cir·cu·lar
cir·cu·lar·iza·tion
cir·cu·lar·ize
cir·cu·late
cir·cu·la·tion
cir·cu·la·tive
cir·cu·la·tor
cir·cu·la·to·ry
cir·cum·am·bi·ent
cir·cum·cise
cir·cum·ci·sion
cir·cum·fer·ence
cir·cum·flex
cir·cum·lo·cu·tion
cir·cum·nav·i·gate
cir·cum·scribe
cir·cum·scrip·tion
cir·cum·spect
cir·cum·spec·tion
cir·cum·stance
cir·cum·stan·tial
cir·cum·stan·ti·al·
  i·ty
cir·cum·stan·tial·ly
cir·cum·stan·ti·ate
cir·cum·vent
cir·cum·ven·tion
cir·cus
cir·rho·sis
cir·ro·cu·mu·lus
cir·ro·stra·tus

cis·tern
cit·a·del
ci·ta·tion
cite (quote;
  cf. *sight, site*)
cit·ing
cit·i·zen
cit·i·zen·ry
cit·i·zen·ship
ci·trate
cit·ric
cit·ron
cit·ro·nel·la
cit·rus
city
civ·et
civ·ic
civ·il
ci·vil·ian
ci·vil·i·ty
civ·i·li·za·tion
civ·i·lize
civ·il·ly
claim·ant
clair·voy·ance
clair·voy·ant
cla·mant
clam·bake
clam·ber (climb;
  cf. *clamor*)
clam·mi·ness
clam·my
clam·or (outcry;
  cf. *clamber*)
clam·or·ous
clam·shell

clan·des·tine
clan·gor
clan·gor·ous·ly
clan·nish
clans·man
clap·board
clap·per
clap·ping
clap·trap
claque
clar·et
clar·i·fi·ca·tion
clar·i·fied
clar·i·fy
clar·i·net
clar·i·on
clar·i·ty
clas·sic
clas·si·cal
clas·si·cism
clas·si·cist
clas·si·fi·able
clas·si·fi·ca·tion
clas·si·fied
clas·si·fy
class·mate
class·room
clat·ter
clause (grammatical;
  cf. *claws*)
claus·tro·pho·bia
clav·i·chord
clav·i·cle
cla·vier
claws (animal's nails;
  cf. *clause*)

clay·bank
clay·more
clean—cut
clean·er
clean·hand·ed
clean—limbed
clean·li·ness
clean·ly
clean·ness
cleanse
cleans·er
cleans·ing
clear·ance
clear—cut
clear—eyed
clear·head·ed
clear·ing·house
clear—sight·ed
cleav·age
cleav·er
cle·ma·tis
clem·en·cy
clem·ent
clep·sy·dra
clere·sto·ry
cler·gy
cler·gy·man
cler·ic
cler·i·cal
cler·i·cal·ism
clev·er
clew *or* clue
cli·ché
cli·ent
cli·en·tele
cliff—hang·er

cli·mac·ter·ic
cli·mac·tic (of a
    climax; cf. *climatic*)
cli·mate
cli·mat·ic (of cli-
    mate; cf. *climactic*)
cli·max
cling·stone
clin·ic
clin·i·cal
cli·ni·cian
clin·ker
clip·per
clip·ping
clique
clo·aca
cloak—and—
    dag·ger
clob·ber
clock·wise
clock·work
clod·hop·per
clog·ging
clois·ter
closed—end
close—fist·ed
close—hauled
close·ness
clos·et
close—up n.
clo·sure
cloth n.
clothe v.
clothes·pin
cloth·ier
cloth·ing

clo·ture
cloud·burst
cloud·i·ly
cloud·i·ness
cloud·less
clout
clo·ven—foot·ed
clo·ver
clo·ver·leaf
club·bing
club car
club chair
club·foot
club·house
club steak
clum·si·er
clum·si·est
clum·si·ly
clum·si·ness
clum·sy
clus·ter
clutch
clut·ter
coach dog
coach·man
co·ad·ju·tor
co·ag·u·late
co·ag·u·la·tion
co·alesce
co·ales·cence
co·ales·cent
coal gas
co·ali·tion
coal tar
coarse (rough;
    cf. *corse, course*)

coars·en
coast·al
coast·er
coast guard
coast·line
coast·wise
coat·tail
co·au·thor
coax
co·ax·i·al
co·balt
cob·bler
cob·ble·stone
CO·BOL
co·bra
cob·web
co·caine
coc·cyx
Co·chin Chi·na
co·chi·neal
cock·ade
cock·a·too
cock·a·trice
cock·boat
cock·cha·fer
cock·crow
cock·le·bur
cock·le·shell
cock·ney
cock·pit
cock·roach
cock·sure
cock·tail
co·coa
co·co·nut
co·coon

co·de·fen·dant
co·deine
co·dex
cod·fish
cod·i·cil
cod·i·fi·ca·tion
cod·i·fied
cod·i·fy
co·ed
co·ed·u·ca·tion
co·ef·fi·cient
coel·acanth
co·erce
co·er·cion
co·er·cive
co·eval
co·ex·is·tence
cof·fee
cof·fee·house
cof·fee·pot
cof·fee shop
cof·fee ta·ble
cof·fer
cof·fer·dam
cof·fin
co·gen·cy
co·gent
cog·i·tate
cog·i·ta·tion
cog·i·ta·tive
co·gnac
cog·nate
cog·ni·zance
cog·ni·zant
cog·no·men
cog·wheel

co·hab·it
co·heir
co·here
co·her·ence
co·her·en·cy
co·her·ent
co·he·sion
co·he·sive
co·hort
coif·feur (person)
coif·fure (style)
coign (position;
   cf. *coin, quoin*)
coin (money;
   cf. *coign, quoin*)
coin·age
co·in·cide
co·in·ci·dence
co·in·ci·den·tal
co·in·sur·ance
co·in·sure
co·ition
col·an·der
cold—blood·ed
cold chis·el
cold cream
cold cuts
cold frame
cold front
cold sore
cold sweat
cold war
cold wave
co·le·op·ter·ous
cole·slaw
col·ic

43

col·ic·root
col·ic·weed
col·i·se·um
co·li·tis
col·lab·o·rate
col·lab·o·ra·tion
col·lab·o·ra·tor
col·lage
col·lapse
col·lapsed
col·laps·ible
col·lar
col·lar·bone
col·late
col·lat·er·al
col·la·tion
col·league
col·lect
col·lect·ed
col·lect·ible
col·lec·tion
col·lec·tive
col·lec·tive·ly
col·lec·tiv·ism
col·lec·tiv·ize
col·lec·tor
col·lege
col·le·gial
col·le·gi·al·i·ty
col·le·gian
col·le·giate
col·le·gi·um
col·lide
col·lie (dog;
  cf. *coolie, coolly*)
col·lier

col·liery
col·li·sion (crash;
  cf. *collusion*)
col·lo·ca·tion
col·lo·di·on
col·loid
col·lop
col·lo·qui·al
col·lo·qui·al·ism
col·lo·qui·al·ly
col·lo·quies
col·lo·qui·um
col·lo·quy
col·lu·sion (secret
  agreement;
  cf. *collision*)
col·lu·sive
co·logne
co·lon
col·o·nel (officer;
  cf. *kernel*)
col·o·nel·cy
co·lo·nial
co·lo·nial·ism
col·o·nies
col·o·nist
col·o·ni·za·tion
col·o·nize
col·on·nade
col·o·ny
col·o·phon
col·or
Col·o·ra·do
col·or·ation
col·or·a·tu·ra
col·or—blind

col·ored
col·or·fast
col·or·ful
col·or guard
col·or·less
co·los·sal
co·los·se·um
co·los·sus
col·umn
co·lum·nar
col·um·nist
co·ma (insensibility;
  cf. *comma*)
co·ma·tose
com·bat
com·bat·ant
com·bat·ed
com·bat·ing
com·bat·ive
com·bi·na·tion
com·bine
com·bus·ti·ble
com·bus·tion
come·back n.
co·me·di·an (mas.)
co·me·di·enne (fem.)
com·e·dy
come·li·ness
come·ly
come—on n.
co·mes·ti·ble
com·et
com·fit
com·fort
com·fort·able
com·fort·er

com·ic
com·i·cal
com·ing
co·mi·ty
com·ma (punctuation; cf. *coma*)
com·mand (order; cf. *commend*)
com·man·dant
com·man·deer
com·mand·er
com·mand·ment
com·man·do
com·man·dos
com·mem·o·rate
com·mem·o·ra·tion
com·mem·o·ra·tive
com·mence
com·mence·ment
com·menc·ing
com·mend (praise; cf. *command*)
com·mend·able
com·men·da·tion
com·men·da·to·ry
com·men·su·ra·bil·i·ty
com·men·su·ra·ble
com·men·su·rate
com·men·su·rate·ly
com·ment
com·men·tary
com·men·ta·tor
com·merce
com·mer·cial

com·mer·cial·ism
com·mer·cial·iza·tion
com·mer·cial·ize
com·min·gle
com·mi·nu·tion
com·mis·er·ate
com·mis·er·a·tion
com·mis·sar
com·mis·sar·i·at
com·mis·sary
com·mis·sion
com·mis·sion·aire
com·mis·sion·er
com·mit
com·mit·ment
com·mit·ted
com·mit·tee
com·mit·ting
com·mode
com·mo·di·ous
com·mod·i·ties
com·mod·i·ty
com·mo·dore
com·mon
com·mon·al·ty
com·mon·er
com·mon·place
com·mon sense n.
com·mon·sense adj.
com·mon·wealth
com·mo·tion
com·mu·nal
com·mune
com·mu·ni·ca·ble
com·mu·ni·cant

com·mu·ni·cate
com·mu·ni·ca·tion
com·mu·ni·ca·tive
com·mu·ni·ca·tor
com·mu·nion
com·mu·ni·qué
com·mu·nism
com·mu·nist
com·mu·ni·ties
com·mu·ni·ty
com·mu·ta·tion
com·mu·ta·tor
com·mute
com·mut·er
com·pact
com·pan·ion
com·pan·ion·able
com·pan·ion·ship
com·pan·ion·way
com·pa·nies
com·pa·ny
com·pa·ra·ble
com·par·a·tive
com·pare
com·par·i·son
com·part·ment
com·pass
com·pas·sion
com·pas·sion·ate
com·pat·i·bil·i·ty
com·pat·i·ble
com·pa·tri·ot
com·peer
com·pel
com·pelled
com·pel·ling

com·pen·di·ous
com·pen·di·um
com·pen·sate
com·pen·sa·tion
com·pen·sa·tive
com·pen·sa·to·ry
com·pete
com·pe·tence
com·pe·ten·cy
com·pe·tent
com·pe·ti·tion
com·pet·i·tive
com·pet·i·tor
com·pi·la·tion
com·pile
com·pil·er
com·pla·cence
com·pla·cen·cy
com·pla·cent (self-
   satisfied;
   cf. *complaisant*)
com·plain
com·plain·ant
com·plaint
com·plai·sance
com·plai·sant
   (obliging;
   cf. *complacent*)
com·ple·ment (full
   quantity;
   cf. *compliment*)
com·ple·men·tal
com·ple·men·ta·ry
com·plete
com·ple·tion
com·plex

com·plex·ion
com·plex·ioned
com·plex·i·ty
com·pli·an·cy
com·pli·ant
com·pli·cate
com·pli·cat·ed
com·pli·ca·tion
com·plic·i·ty
com·plied
com·pli·ment (flat-
   ter; cf. *complement*)
com·pli·men·ta·ry
com·ply
com·po·nent
com·port
com·port·ment
com·pose
com·posed
com·pos·er
com·pos·ite
com·pos·ite·ly
com·po·si·tion
com·pos·i·tor
com·post
com·po·sure
com·pound
com·pre·hend
com·pre·hen·si·ble
com·pre·hen·sion
com·pre·hen·sive
com·press
com·pressed
com·press·ible
com·pres·sion
com·pres·sor

com·prise
com·pro·mise
comp·trol·ler
com·pul·sion
com·pul·so·ry
com·punc·tion
com·put·able
com·pu·ta·tion
com·pute
com·put·er
com·put·er·ize
com·rade
con·cat·e·na·tion
con·cave
con·cav·i·ty
con·ceal
con·ceal·ment
con·cede
con·ced·ed·ly
con·ceit
con·ceit·ed
con·ceiv·able
con·ceive
con·cen·trate
con·cen·tra·tion
con·cen·tra·tor
con·cen·tric
con·cept
con·cep·tion
con·cep·tu·al
con·cern
con·cert
con·cer·ti·na
con·cert·mas·ter
con·cer·to
con·ces·sion

con·ces·sion·aire
conch
con·cierge
con·cil·i·ate
con·cil·i·a·tion
con·cil·ia·to·ry
con·cise
con·clave
con·clude
con·clu·sion
con·clu·sive
con·coct
con·coc·tion
con·com·i·tant
con·cord
con·cor·dance
con·cor·dat
con·course
con·crete
con·crete·ly
con·cu·bine
con·cur
con·curred
con·cur·rence
con·cur·rent
con·cur·ring
con·cus·sion
con·demn
con·dem·na·tion
con·dem·na·tory
con·demned
con·den·sa·tion
con·dense
con·dens·er
con·de·scend
con·de·scend·ing·ly

con·de·scen·sion
con·dign
con·di·ment
con·di·tion
con·di·tion·al
con·di·tioned
con·dole
con·do·lence
con·do·min·i·um
con·do·na·tion
con·done
con·dor
con·duce
con·du·cive
con·duct
con·duc·tion
con·duc·tor
con·duit
con·el·rad
con·fab·u·late
con·fec·tion
con·fec·tion·er
con·fec·tion·ery
con·fed·er·a·cy
con·fed·er·ate
con·fed·er·a·tion
con·fer
con·fer·ee
con·fer·ence
con·ferred
con·fer·ring
con·fess
con·fessed·ly
con·fes·sion
con·fes·sion·al
con·fes·sor

con·fet·ti
con·fi·dant (friend;
   cf. *confident*)
con·fide
con·fi·dence
con·fi·dent (sure;
   cf. *confidant*)
con·fi·den·tial
con·fid·ing
con·fig·u·ra·tion
con·fine
con·fine·ment
con·firm
con·fir·ma·tion
con·firmed
con·fis·cate
con·fis·ca·tion
con·fis·ca·to·ry
con·fi·ture
con·fla·gra·tion
con·flict
con·flic·tion
con·flu·ence
con·form
con·form·able
con·for·ma·tion
con·form·ist
con·for·mi·ty
con·found
con·found·ed·ly
con·fra·ter·ni·ty
con·front
con·fron·ta·tion
Con·fu·cian
con·fuse
con·fused·ly

con·fus·ing
con·fu·sion
con·fu·ta·tion
con·fute
con·ga
con·gé
con·geal
con·ge·ner
con·ge·nial
con·ge·nial·i·ty
con·gen·i·tal
con·ger eel
con·gest
con·ges·tion
con·glom·er·ate
con·glom·er·a·tion
con·grat·u·late
con·grat·u·la·tion
con·grat·u·la·to·ry
con·gre·gate
con·gre·ga·tion
con·gre·ga·tion·al
con·gress
con·gres·sio·nal
con·gress·man
con·gru·ence
con·gru·ent
con·gru·ity
con·gru·ous
con·ic
con·i·cal
co·ni·fer
co·nif·er·ous
con·jec·tur·al
con·jec·ture
con·ju·gal

con·ju·gate
con·ju·ga·tion
con·junc·tion
con·junc·ti·va
con·junc·ture
con·jure
con·jur·er
con·nect
con·nect·ed·ly
Con·nect·i·cut
con·nec·tion
con·nec·tive
con·niv·ance
con·nive
con·nois·seur
con·no·ta·tion
con·no·ta·tive
con·note
con·nu·bi·al
con·quer
con·quered
con·quer·ing
con·quer·or
con·quest
con·san·guin·e·ous
con·san·guin·i·ty
con·science
con·sci·en·tious
con·scious
con·scious·ness
con·script
con·scrip·tion
con·se·crate
con·se·cra·tion
con·sec·u·tive
con·sen·sus

con·sent
con·se·quence
con·se·quent
con·se·quen·tial
con·se·quent·ly
con·ser·va·tion
con·ser·va·tism
con·ser·va·tive
con·ser·va·to·ry
con·serve
con·sid·er
con·sid·er·able
con·sid·er·ate
con·sid·er·a·tion
con·sid·ered
con·sign
con·sign·ee
con·sign·ment
con·sign·or
con·sist
con·sis·ten·cy
con·sis·tent
con·sis·to·ry
con·so·la·tion
con·so·la·to·ry
con·sole
con·sol·i·date
con·sol·i·da·tion
con·som·mé
con·so·nance
con·so·nant
con·so·nan·tal
con·sort
con·spec·tus
con·spic·u·ous
con·spir·a·cy

con·spir·a·tor
con·spire
con·sta·ble
con·stab·u·lary
con·stan·cy
con·stant
con·stel·la·tion
con·ster·na·tion
con·sti·pate
con·stit·u·en·cy
con·stit·u·ent
con·sti·tute
con·sti·tu·tion
con·sti·tu·tion·al
con·sti·tu·tion·al·i·ty
con·sti·tu·tion·al·ly
con·strain
con·straint
con·strict
con·stric·tion
con·stric·tor
con·struct
con·struc·tion
con·struc·tion·ist
con·struc·tive
con·strue
con·strued
con·stru·ing
con·sul (government official; cf. *council*, *counsel*)
con·sul·ar
con·sul·ate
con·sult
con·sul·tant

con·sul·ta·tion
con·sul·ta·tive
con·sume
con·sum·ed·ly
con·sum·mate
con·sum·ma·tion
con·sump·tion
con·sump·tive
con·tact
con·ta·gion
con·ta·gious
con·tain·er
con·tain·ment
con·tam·i·nate
con·tam·i·na·tion
con·tem·plate
con·tem·pla·tion
con·tem·pla·tive
con·tem·po·ra·ne·ous
con·tem·po·rary
con·tempt
con·tempt·ible
con·temp·tu·ous
con·tend
con·ten·tion
con·ten·tious
con·tent·ment
con·test
con·tes·tant
con·tes·ta·tion
con·text
con·tex·tu·al
con·tex·ture
con·ti·gu·ity
con·tig·u·ous

con·ti·nence
con·ti·nent
con·ti·nen·tal
con·tin·gen·cy
con·tin·gent
con·tin·u·al
con·tin·u·ance
con·tin·u·a·tion
con·tin·ue
con·tinu·ing
con·ti·nu·ity
con·tin·u·ous
con·tort
con·tor·tion
con·tor·tion·ist
con·tour
con·tra·band
con·tra·bass
con·tract
con·trac·tion
con·trac·tor
con·tra·dict
con·tra·dic·tion
con·tra·dic·to·ri·ly
con·tra·dic·to·ry
con·tra·dis·tinc·tion
con·tra·in·di·cate
con·tral·to
con·trap·tion
con·tra·pun·tal
con·trari·ness
con·trari·wise
con·trary
con·trast
con·tra·vene

con·tra·ven·tion
con·tre·danse
con·tre·temps
con·trib·ute
con·tri·bu·tion
con·trib·u·tor
con·trib·u·to·ry
con·trite
con·tri·tion
con·triv·ance
con·trive
con·trol
con·trolled
con·trol·ler
con·trol·ling
con·tro·ver·sial
con·tro·ver·sy
con·tro·vert
con·tu·ma·cious
con·tu·ma·cy
con·tu·me·li·ous
con·tume·ly
con·tuse
con·tu·sion
co·nun·drum
con·va·lesce
con·va·les·cence
con·va·les·cent
con·va·lesc·ing
con·vec·tion
con·vene
con·ve·nience
con·ve·nient
con·vent
con·ven·ti·cle
con·ven·tion

con·ven·tion·al
con·ven·tion·al·i·ty
con·ven·tu·al
con·verge
con·ver·gence
con·ver·sant
con·ver·sa·tion
con·ver·sa·tion·al
con·ver·sa·tion·al-
     ist
con·verse
con·ver·sion
con·vert
con·vert·er
con·vert·ibil·i·ty
con·vert·ible
con·vex
con·vex·i·ty
con·vey
con·vey·ance
con·vict
con·vic·tion
con·vince
con·vinc·ing·ly
con·viv·ial
con·viv·i·al·i·ty
con·vo·ca·tion
con·voke
con·vo·lu·tion
con·vol·vu·lus
con·voy
con·voy·ing
con·vulse
con·vul·sion
con·vul·sive
cook·ery

cook·out n.
cool·er
coo·lie (laborer;
     cf. *collie, coolly*)
cool·ly (coldly;
     cf. *collie, coolie*)
co—op
coo·per
coo·per·age
co·op·er·ate
co·op·er·a·tion
co·op·er·a·tive
co—opt
co·or·di·nate
Co·per·ni·can
copi·er
co·pi·lot
co·pi·ous
cop·per
cop·per·as
cop·per·head
cop·per·plate
cop·per·smith
cop·pice
co·pra
cop·u·late
copy·book
copy·cat
copy·hold·er
copy·ing
copy·ist
copy·right
co·que·try
co·quette
cor·al (pink; cf. *choral,
     chorale, corral*)

cor·al·line

cord (string;
cf. *chord*)

cord·age

cor·dial

cor·dial·i·ty

cord·ite

cor·don

cor·do·van

cor·du·roy

core (center;
cf. *corps, corpse*)

co·re·spon·dent
(legal term;
cf. *correspondent*)

co·ri·an·der

Co·rin·thi·an

cork·screw

cork·wood

cor·mo·rant

corn bor·er

corn bread

corn·cob

corn·crib

cor·nea

cor·ner

cor·ner·stone

cor·ner·wise

cor·net

cor·net·ist

corn—fed

corn·field

corn·flakes

corn·flow·er

cor·nice

corn·meal

corn pone

corn·stalk

corn·starch

corn sug·ar

cor·nu·co·pia

co·rol·la

co·rol·lary

co·ro·na

cor·o·nach

cor·o·nary

cor·o·na·tion

cor·o·ner

cor·o·net

cor·po·ral

cor·po·rate

cor·po·ra·tion

cor·po·ra·tive

cor·po·re·al

corps (group of
people;
cf. *core, corpse*)

corpse (body;
cf. *core, corps*)

cor·pu·lence

cor·pu·lent

cor·pus

cor·pus·cle

cor·rade

cor·ral (animal pen;
cf. *choral, chorale,
coral*)

cor·rect

cor·rec·tion

cor·rec·tive

cor·rec·tor

cor·re·late

cor·re·la·tion

cor·rel·a·tive

cor·re·spond

cor·re·spon·dence
(letters;
cf. *correspondents*)

cor·re·spon·dent
(writer of letters;
cf. *corespondent*)

cor·re·spon·dents
(writers of letters;
cf. *correspondence*)

cor·ri·dor

cor·rob·o·rate

cor·rob·o·ra·tion

cor·rob·o·ra·tive

cor·rode

cor·ro·sion

cor·ro·sive

cor·ru·gate

cor·ru·ga·tion

cor·rupt

cor·rupt·ible

cor·rup·tion

cor·sage

cor·sair

corse (corpse;
cf. *coarse, course*)

corse·let

cor·set

cor·tege

cor·ti·sone

co·run·dum

cor·us·cate

cor·us·ca·tion

cor·vette

co·ry·za
cos·met·ic
cos·me·tol·o·gist
cos·me·tol·o·gy
cos·mic
cos·mog·o·ny
cos·mol·o·gy
cos·mo·naut
cos·mo·pol·i·tan
cos·mop·o·lite
cos·mos
cos·sack
cost·li·ness
cost—plus
cos·tume
cos·tum·er
co·te·rie
co·ter·mi·nous
co·til·lion
cot·tage
cot·ton
cot·ton·tail
cot·ton·wood
cou·gar
cou·lomb
coun·cil (assembly;
    cf. *consul, counsel*)
coun·cil·man
coun·cil·or
coun·sel (advice;
    cf. *consul, council*)
coun·seled
coun·sel·ing
coun·sel·or
count·down n.
coun·te·nance

count·er
coun·ter·act
coun·ter·bal·ance
coun·ter·claim
coun·ter·clock-
    wise
coun·ter·feit
coun·ter·feit·er
coun·ter·foil
coun·ter·ir·ri·tant
coun·ter·mand
coun·ter·march
coun·ter·mea·sure
coun·ter·mine
coun·ter·pane
coun·ter·part
coun·ter·point
coun·ter·rev·o·lu-
    tion
coun·ter·sign
coun·ter·spy
coun·ter·ten·or
coun·ter·weight
count·ess
count·ing·house
coun·try
coun·try·man
coun·try·seat
coun·try·side
coun·ty
coup d'etat
cou·pé *or* coupe
cou·ple
cou·pler
cou·plet
cou·pling

cou·pon
cour·age
cou·ra·geous
cou·ri·er
course (way;
    cf. *coarse, corse*)
cour·te·ous
cour·te·san
cour·te·sy
court·house
court·ier
court·li·ness
court·ly
court—mar·tial
court·room
court·ship
court·yard
cous·in
cous·in—ger·man
cou·tu·ri·er
cov·e·nant
Cov·en·try
cov·er
cov·er·age
cov·er·all
cov·er charge
cov·er·let
co·vert
cov·er·ture
cov·et·ous
cov·ey
cow·ard (frightened;
    cf. *cowered*)
cow·ard·ice
cow·ard·li·ness
cow·ard·ly

**52**

cow·bell
cow·boy
cow·catch·er
cow·ered (crouched;
   cf. *coward*)
cow·girl
cow·hand
cow·hide
cow·lick
cowl·ing
co—work·er
cow·pea
cow·pox
cow·punch·er
cow·slip
cox·comb
cox·swain
coy·ly
coy·ote
co·zi·ly
co·zi·ness
co·zy
crab ap·ple
crabbed
crab·bing
crab·grass
crack·brained
crack down v.
crack·down n.
crack·er
crack·er·jack
crack·le
crack·le·ware
crack·pot
cracks·man
cra·dle

craft·i·ly
crafts·man
cram
crammed
cram·ming
cran·ber·ry
cra·ni·al
cra·ni·um
crank·i·ness
crank·shaft
cranky
cran·ny
cra·ter
cra·vat
cra·ven
craw·fish
cray·on
cra·zi·ly
cra·zi·ness
cra·zy
creak (sound;
   cf. *creek, crick*)
cream·ery
cream·i·ness
cream puff
cre·ate
cre·ation
cre·ative
cre·ator
crea·ture
cre·dence
cre·den·tial
cred·i·bil·i·ty
cred·i·ble (believable;
   cf. *creditable,*
   *credulous*)

cred·it
cred·it·able
   (estimable; cf.
   *credible, credulous*)
cred·it card
cred·i·tor
cred·it rat·ing
cre·do
cred·u·lous (gullible;
   cf. *credible,*
   *creditable*)
creek (water;
   cf. *creak, crick*)
creep·i·ness
creepy
cre·mate
cre·ma·tion
cre·ma·to·ry
Cre·mo·na
cre·ole
cre·o·sote
crepe
cre·pus·cu·lar
cre·scen·do
cres·cent
crest·fall·en
cre·tin
cre·tonne
cre·vasse
crev·ice
crews (sailors;
   cf. *cruise, cruse*)
crib
crib·bage
cribbed
crib·bing

crick (cramp;
  cf. *creak, creek*)
crick·et
cried
cri·er
Cri·me·an
crim·i·nal
crim·i·nal·i·ty
crim·i·nal·ly
crim·i·nol·o·gy
crim·son
cringe
cring·ing
crin·kle
crin·o·line
crip·ple
crip·pled
crip·pling
cri·ses pl.
cri·sis sing.
criss·cross
cri·te·ria pl.
cri·te·ri·on sing.
crit·ic
crit·i·cal
crit·i·cism
crit·i·cize
cri·tique
cro·chet
crock·ery
croc·o·dile
cro·cus
crook·ed·ness
croon·er
crop
cropped

crop·ping
cro·quet (game)
cro·quette (food)
cro·sier
cross·bar
cross·bow
cross·cut
cross—ex·am·ine
cross—eyed
cross—grained
cross hair
cross·hatch
cross·ing
cross·over
cross—ques·tion
cross—ref·er·ence
cross·road
cross sec·tion
cross—stitch
cross·walk
cross·wise
cross·word
  puz·zle
crotch·et
crotch·ety
crou·pi·er
crou·ton
crow·bar
cru·cial
cru·ci·ble
cru·ci·fix
cru·ci·fix·ion
cru·ci·form
cru·ci·fy
cru·di·ty
cru·el

cru·el·ly
cru·el·ty
cru·et
cruise (sail;
  cf. *crews, cruse*)
cruis·er
crul·ler
crum·ble (break;
  cf. *crumple*)
crum·bling
crum·pet
crum·ple (wrinkle;
  cf. *crumble*)
crum·pling
crup·per
cru·sade
cruse (small cup;
  cf. *crews, cruise*)
crus·ta·ceous
crux
cry (*cried, cries*)
cry·ing
cryo·bi·ol·o·gy
cryo·gen
cryo·gen·ics
crypt
crypt·anal·y·sis
cryp·tic
cryp·to·gram
crys·tal
crys·tal·line
crys·tal·li·za·tion
crys·tal·lize
cu·bic
cu·bi·cal adj.
cu·bi·cle n.

cu·bit
cuck·old
cuck·oo
cu·cum·ber
cud·dle
cud·gel
cud·geled
cud·gel·ing
cue (signal; cf. *queue*)
cui·rass
cui·sine
cu·li·nary
cul·mi·nate
cul·mi·na·tion
cul·pa·bil·i·ty
cul·pa·ble
cul·prit
cul·ti·vate
cul·ti·va·tion
cul·ti·va·tor
cul·tur·al
cul·ture
cul·vert
cum·ber·some
cum·brous
cum·mer·bund
cu·mu·la·tive
cu·mu·lus
cu·ne·i·form
cun·ning·ly
cup·bear·er
cup·board
cu·pel
cup·ful
cu·pid·i·ty
cu·po·la

cur·able
cu·ra·cao
cu·ra·re
cu·rate
cu·ra·tive
cu·ra·tor
curb·stone
cur·dle
cu·rette
cur·few
cu·rio
cu·ri·os·i·ty
cu·ri·ous
curli·cue
curl·i·ness
cur·rant (berry)
cur·rent (prevalent)
cur·ric·u·lum
cur·ried
cur·ry
cur·ry·comb
cur·sive
cur·so·ri·ly
cur·so·ry
cur·tail
cur·tain
cur·tain call
cur·va·ture
curve
cur·vi·lin·ear
cush·ion
cus·pi·dor
cus·tard
cus·to·di·an
cus·to·dy
cus·tom

cus·tom·ary
cus·tom·er
cus·tom·house
cut·away
cu·ti·cle
cut·lass
cut·lery
cut·let
cut off v.
cut·off n.
cut·out n., adj.
cut·purse
cut—rate
cut·throat
cut·ting
cut·tle·fish
cut up v.
cut·up n.
cut·wa·ter
cut·worm
cy·an·a·mide
cy·an·ic
cy·a·nide
cy·ano·gen
cy·a·no·sis
cy·ber·net·ics
cy·cla·mate
cy·cle
cy·cli·cal
cy·cloid
cy·clone
cy·clo·pe·dia
cy·clops
cy·clo·ra·ma
cy·clo·tron
cyg·net

cyl·in·der
cy·lin·dri·cal
cym·bal (musical;
   cf. *symbol*)
cyn·ic
cyn·i·cal
cyn·i·cism
cy·no·sure
cy·press
cyst
cys·tic
cys·toid
czar
cza·ri·na
Czech

dab·ble
da ca·po
dachs·hund
Da·cron
dac·tyl
daf·fo·dil
dag·ger
da·guerre·o·type
dahl·ia
dai·lies
dai·ly
dain·ti·ly
dain·ti·ness

dain·ty
dairy (for milk;
   cf. *diary*)
dairy·maid
dairy·man
da·is
dai·sy
dal·li·ance
dal·ma·tian
dam·age
dam·a·scene
dam·ask
dammed (blocked;
   cf. *damned*)
dam·ming
dam·na·ble
dam·na·tion
damned (cursed;
   cf. *dammed*)
damned·est
damn·ing
Dam·o·cles
damp·en
damp·er
dam·sel
dance
dan·de·li·on
dan·dle
dan·dling
dan·druff
dan·ger
dan·ger·ous
dan·gle
Dan·ish
dan·seuse
dare·dev·il

dark·en
dark horse
dar·kle
dark·ness
dark·room
dar·ling
Dar·win·ian
dash·board
das·tard·ly
da·ta pl. (sing.: *datum*)
date
dat·ing
da·tum (pl.: *data*)
daugh·ter
daugh·ter—in—law
daunt·less·ly
dau·phin
dav·en·port
da·vit
daw·dle
daw·dling
day·bed
day·book
day·break
day camp
day coach
day·dream
day·flow·er
day la·bor
day·light
day·room
day school
day·star
day·time
daz·zle
daz·zling

dea·con
dead·beat
dead·en
dead·eye
dead·fall
dead·head
dead heat
dead·light
dead·line
dead·li·ness
dead·lock
dead·weight
dead·wood
deaf—mute
deal
dealt
dear (beloved; cf. *deer*)
dearth
death·bed
death ben·e·fit
death·blow
death·less
death·ly
death mask
death's—head
death war·rant
death·watch
de·ba·cle
de·bar·ka·tion
de·base
de·bat·able
de·bate
de·bauch
de·bauch·ery
de·ben·ture
de·bil·i·tate

de·bil·i·ty
deb·it (bookkeeping
    entry; cf. *debt*)
deb·o·nair
de·brief·ing
de·bris
debt (obligation;
    cf. *debit*)
debt·or
de·but
deb·u·tante
de·cade
de·ca·dence
de·ca·dent
deca·gon
de·cal·co·ma·nia
deca·logue
de·camp
de·cant
de·cant·er
de·cap·i·tate
de·cath·lon
de·cay
de·cease
de·ceased (dead;
    cf. *diseased*)
de·ce·dent
de·ceit·ful
de·ceive
De·cem·ber
de·cem·vir
de·cen·cy
de·cent (proper;
    cf. *descent, dissent*)
de·cen·tral·ize
de·cep·tion

de·cep·tive
deci·bel
de·cide
de·cid·ed
de·cid·u·ous
de·ci·mal
dec·i·mate
deci·me·ter
de·ci·pher
de·ci·sion
de·ci·sive
deck chair
de·claim
dec·la·ma·tion
de·clam·a·to·ry
dec·la·ra·tion
de·clar·a·tive
de·clare
de·clen·sion
dec·li·na·tion
de·cline
de·cliv·i·ty
de·coc·tion
dé·col·le·té
de·com·pose
de·com·po·si·tion
de·con·tam·i·nate
dec·o·rate
dec·o·ra·tion
dec·o·ra·tive
dec·o·ra·tor
de·co·rous
de·co·rum
de·coy
de·coyed
de·coy·ing

de·crease
de·cree (law;
   cf. *degree*)
de·cree·ing
de·crep·it
de·cre·scen·do
de·cry
ded·i·cate
ded·i·ca·tion
de·duce
de·duc·ible
de·duc·ing
de·duct·ible
de·duc·tion
de·duc·tive
deep·en
deep—root·ed
deep—seat·ed
deer (animal; cf. *dear*)
deer·hound
deer·skin
de·face
de fac·to
de·fal·cate
de·fal·ca·tion
def·a·ma·tion
de·fam·a·to·ry
de·fame
de·fault·er
de·feat
de·fect
de·fec·tion
de·fec·tive
de·fec·tor
de·fend
de·fen·dant

de·fense
de·fen·si·ble
de·fen·sive
de·fer
def·er·ence (respect;
   cf. *difference*)
def·er·en·tial
   (respectful;
   cf. *differential*)
de·fer·ment
de·fer·ra·ble
de·ferred
de·fer·ring
de·fi·ance
de·fi·ant
de·fi·cien·cy
de·fi·cient
def·i·cit
de·fied
de·file
de·fin·able
de·fine
de·fine·ment
def·i·nite (clear;
   cf. *definitive*)
def·i·ni·tion
de·fin·i·tive (final;
   cf. *definite*)
de·flate
de·flect
de·flec·tion
de·fo·li·ant
de·fo·li·ate
de·fo·li·a·tion
de·form
de·for·ma·tion

de·for·mi·ty
de·fraud
de·fray
de·frayed
de·funct
de·fy
de·fy·ing
de·gen·er·a·cy
de·gen·er·ate
de·gen·er·a·tion
deg·ra·da·tion
de·grade
de·gree (from
   college; cf. *decree*)
de·gree—day
de·hu·mid·i·fy
de·hy·drate
de·i·fi·ca·tion
deign
de·ist
de·i·ty
de·ject·ed
de·jec·tion
de ju·re
deka·gram
Del·a·ware
de·lay
de·layed
de·lay·ing
de·lec·ta·ble
de·lec·ta·tion
del·e·gate
del·e·ga·tion
de·lete
del·e·te·ri·ous
de·le·tion

delft·ware
de·lib·er·ate
de·lib·er·a·tion
de·lib·er·a·tive
del·i·ca·cies
del·i·ca·cy
del·i·cate
del·i·ca·tes·sen
de·li·cious
de·light
de·light·ful
de·lin·e·ate
de·lin·e·a·tion
de·lin·e·a·tor
de·lin·quen·cy
de·lin·quent
del·i·quesce
del·i·ques·cent
de·lir·i·ous
de·lir·i·um
de·liv·er
de·liv·er·ance
de·liv·er·ies
de·liv·ery
de·lude
del·uge
de·lu·sion
de·luxe
delve
de·mag·ne·tize
dem·a·gogue
de·mand
de·mar·ca·tion
de·mean
de·mea·nor
de·ment·ed

de·men·tia
de·mer·it
de·mesne
demi·god
demi·john
de·mil·i·ta·rize
demi·monde
de·mise
demi·tasse
de·mo·bi·lize
de·moc·ra·cy
dem·o·crat
dem·o·crat·ic
de·mog·ra·pher
de·mo·graph·ic
de·mog·ra·phy
de·mol·ish
de·mo·li·tion
de·mon
de·mon·e·ti·za·tion
de·mon·e·tize
de·mon·stra·ble
dem·on·strate
dem·on·stra·tion
de·mon·stra·tive
dem·on·stra·tor
de·mor·al·ize
de·mount·able
de·mur  (delay)
de·mure  (modest)
de·mur·rage
de·murred
de·mur·rer
de·mur·ring
de·na·ture
de·ni·al

de·nied
den·im
den·i·zen
de·nom·i·na·tion
de·nom·i·na·tor
de·note
de·noue·ment
de·nounce
den·si·ty
den·tal
den·ti·frice
den·tist
den·tist·ry
den·ture
de·nude
de·nun·ci·a·tion
de·nun·ci·a·to·ry
de·ny
de·odor·ant
de·odor·ize
de·part
de·part·ment
de·part·men·tal
de·par·ture
de·pend·able
de·pen·den·cy
de·pen·dent
de·pict
de·pic·tion
de·pil·a·to·ry
de·plane
de·plete
de·ple·tion
de·plor·able
de·plore
de·ploy

de·po·nent
de·pop·u·late
de·port·able
de·por·ta·tion
de·port·ment
de·pose
de·pos·it
de·pos·i·tary
de·po·si·tion
de·pos·i·to·ry
de·pot
de·pra·va·tion
   (corruption;
   cf. *deprivation*)
de·prave
de·prav·i·ty
dep·re·cate
dep·re·ca·tion
dep·re·ca·to·ry
de·pre·ci·ate
de·pre·ci·a·tion
dep·re·da·tion
de·press
de·pressed
de·pres·sion
de·pri·va·tion (loss;
   cf. *depravation*)
de·prive
dep·u·ta·tion
de·pute
dep·u·tize
dep·u·ty
de·rail
de·range
de·range·ment
der·e·lict

der·e·lic·tion
de·ride
de·ri·sion
de·ri·sive
de·ri·so·ry
der·i·va·tion
de·riv·a·tive
de·rive
der·ma·tol·o·gist
der·ma·tol·o·gy
der·o·ga·tion
de·rog·a·to·ry
der·rick
der·vish
des·cant
de·scend
de·scen·dant
de·scent (going
   down; cf. *decent,*
   *dissent*)
de·scrib·able
de·scribe
de·scrip·tion
de·scrip·tive
des·e·crate
des·e·cra·tion
de·seg·re·gate
de·sen·si·tize
des·ert n. (dry
   country; cf. *dessert*)
de·sert v. (leave;
   cf. *dessert*)
de·ser·tion
de·serve
de·served·ly
de·serv·ing

des·ic·cate
des·ic·ca·tion
des·ic·ca·tor
de·sid·er·a·ta pl.
de·sid·er·a·tum sing.
de·sign
des·ig·nate
des·ig·na·tion
de·sign·ed·ly
de·sign·er
de·sir·abil·i·ty
de·sir·able
de·sire
de·sir·ous
de·sist
Des Moines Iowa
des·o·late
des·o·la·tion
de·spair
des·per·a·do sing.
des·per·a·does pl.
des·per·ate
   (hopeless;
   cf. *disparate*)
des·per·a·tion
de·spi·ca·ble
de·spise
de·spite
de·spoil
de·spond
de·spon·den·cy
de·spon·dent
des·pot
des·pot·ic
des·pot·i·cal·ly
des·po·tism

des·sert (food;
   cf. *desert*)
des·sert·spoon
des·ti·na·tion
des·tine v.
des·ti·nies
des·ti·ny
des·ti·tute
des·ti·tu·tion
de·stroy
de·struc·ti·ble
de·struc·tion
de·struc·tive
de·sue·tude
des·ul·to·ry
de·tach
de·tach·ment
de·tail
de·tain
de·tect
de·tec·tion
de·tec·tive
de·tec·tor
de·ten·tion
de·ter
de·ter·gent
de·te·ri·o·rate
de·te·ri·o·ra·tion
de·ter·min·able
de·ter·mi·nant
de·ter·mi·nate
de·ter·mi·na·tion
de·ter·mine
de·ter·min·ism
de·terred
de·ter·rent

de·ter·ring
de·test
de·test·able
de·tes·ta·tion
de·throne
det·i·nue
det·o·nate
det·o·na·tion
det·o·na·tor
de·tract
de·trac·tion
det·ri·ment
det·ri·men·tal
dev·as·tate
dev·as·ta·tion
de·vel·op
de·vel·oped
de·vel·op·ing
de·vel·op·ment
de·vi·ate
de·vi·a·tion
de·vice n. (invention;
   cf. *devise*)
dev·il·fish
dev·il·ish
dev·il·ment
de·vi·ous
de·vise v. (invent;
   cf. *device*)
de·void
de·volve
de·vote
dev·o·tee
de·vo·tion
de·vo·tion·al
de·vour

de·vout
dew·ber·ry
dew·drop
dew·lap
dew point
dewy
dex·ter
dex·ter·i·ty
dex·ter·ous
dex·trose
dhow
di·a·be·tes
di·a·bet·ic
di·a·ble·rie
di·a·bol·ic
di·a·bol·i·cal
di·ab·o·lism
di·a·crit·i·cal
di·a·dem
di·aer·e·sis
di·ag·nose
di·ag·no·sis
di·ag·nos·tic
di·ag·nos·ti·cian
di·ag·o·nal
di·a·gram
di·al
di·a·lect
di·a·lec·tic
di·a·lec·ti·cal
di·aled
di·al·ing
di·a·logue
di·am·e·ter
di·a·met·ric
di·a·mond

di·a·per
di·aph·a·nous
di·a·phragm
di·ar·rhea
di·a·ry (journal;
  cf. *dairy*)
dia·ton·ic
di·a·tribe
di·chot·o·my
dic·ta (sing.: *dictum*)
Dic·ta·phone
dic·tate
dic·ta·tion
dic·ta·tor
dic·ta·to·ri·al
dic·tion
dic·tio·nar·ies
dic·tio·nary
dic·tum (pl.: *dicta*)
di·dac·tic
died (perished;
  cf. *dyed*)
die·hard n.
die—hard adj.
di·elec·tric
di·er·e·sis
die·mak·er
die·sel
die·sink·er
di·et
di·etary
di·etet·ic
di·etet·ics
dif·fer
dif·fer·ence (unlike-
  ness; cf. *deference*)

dif·fer·ent
dif·fer·en·tial
  (change;
  cf. *deferential*)
dif·fer·en·ti·ate
dif·fer·en·ti·a·tion
dif·fi·cult
dif·fi·cul·ties
dif·fi·cul·ty
dif·fi·dence
dif·fi·dent
dif·frac·tion
dif·fuse
dif·fu·sion
di·gest
di·gest·ible
di·ges·tion
di·ges·tive
dig·it
dig·i·tal
dig·i·tal·is
dig·ni·fied
dig·ni·fy
dig·ni·tary
dig·ni·ty
di·gress
di·gres·sion
di·lap·i·date
di·lap·i·dat·ed
di·lap·i·da·tion
di·la·ta·tion
di·late
di·la·tion
dil·a·to·ri·ness
dil·a·to·ry
di·lem·ma

dil·et·tante
dil·i·gence
dil·i·gent
di·lute
di·lu·tion
di·men·sion
di·min·ish
di·min·u·en·do
di·min·u·tion
di·min·u·tive
dim·i·ty
dim·mer
dim·ness
dim·out
dim·ple
dim·wit n.
dim—wit·ted adj.
di·nar (coin)
din·er (eater)
di·nette
din·ghy (boat)
din·gy (dull)
din·ner
din·ner bell
din·ner cloth
din·ner fork
din·ner jack·et
din·ner ta·ble
din·ner·ware
di·no·saur
di·oc·e·san
di·o·cese
di·ode
di·ora·ma
diph·the·ria
diph·thong

di·plo·ma
di·plo·ma·cy
dip·lo·mat
dip·lo·mat·ic
dip·per
dip·so·ma·nia
di·rect
di·rec·tion
di·rect·ly
di·rec·tor
di·rec·tor·ate
di·rec·to·ry
dire·ful
dirge
di·ri·gi·ble
dirndl
dirt·i·ly
dirt·i·ness
dirty
dis·abil·i·ty
dis·able
dis·abuse
dis·ad·van·tage
dis·ad·van·ta-
  geous
dis·af·fect·ed
dis·af·fec·tion
dis·agree
dis·agree·able
dis·agree·ment
dis·al·low
dis·ap·pear
dis·ap·pear·ance
dis·ap·point
dis·ap·point·ment
dis·ap·pro·ba·tion

dis·ap·prov·al
dis·ap·prove
dis·ar·ma·ment
dis·ar·range
dis·ar·tic·u·late
dis·as·sem·ble
  (take apart;
  cf. *dissemble*)
dis·as·so·ci·ate
di·sas·ter
di·sas·trous
dis·avow
dis·avow·al
dis·band
dis·bar
dis·bar·ring
dis·be·lief
dis·be·lieve
dis·be·liev·er
dis·burse (pay out;
  cf. *disperse*)
dis·burse·ment
dis·card
dis·cern
dis·cern·ible
dis·cern·ment
dis·charge
dis·ci·ple
dis·ci·pli·nar·i·an
dis·ci·plin·ary
dis·ci·pline
dis·claim
dis·claim·er
dis·close
dis·clo·sure
dis·cog·ra·phy

dis·col·or
dis·col·or·ation
dis·com·fit  (balk;
  cf. *discomfort*)
dis·com·fi·ture
dis·com·fort
  (uneasiness;
  cf. *discomfit*)
dis·com·pose
dis·com·po·sure
dis·con·cert
dis·con·nect
dis·con·so·late
dis·con·tent
dis·con·tent·ment
dis·con·tinu·ance
dis·con·tin·ue
dis·con·tin·u·ous
dis·cord
dis·cor·dance
dis·cor·dant
dis·co·theque
dis·count
dis·cour·age
dis·cour·age·ment
dis·course
dis·cour·te·ous
dis·cour·te·sy
dis·cov·er
dis·cov·er·er
dis·cov·ery
dis·cred·it
dis·cred·it·able
dis·creet  (prudent;
  cf. *discrete*)
dis·crep·an·cy

dis·crete (separate;
   cf. *discreet*)
dis·cre·tion
dis·cre·tion·ar·y
dis·crim·i·nate
dis·crim·i·na·tion
dis·cur·sive
dis·cus (athletic term)
dis·cuss (talk about)
dis·cus·sion
dis·dain
dis·dain·ful
dis·ease
dis·eased (sick;
   cf. *deceased*)
dis·em·bar·ka·tion
dis·em·bar·rass
dis·em·bow·el
dis·en·chant·ment
dis·en·gage
dis·en·tan·gle
dis·es·teem
dis·fa·vor
dis·fig·ure
dis·fig·ure·ment
dis·fran·chise
dis·gorge
dis·grace
dis·grace·ful
dis·grun·tle
dis·guise
dis·gust
dis·ha·bille
dis·har·mon·ic
dish·cloth
dis·heart·en

di·shev·el
di·shev·el·ling
dish·mop
dis·hon·est
dis·hon·or
dis·hon·or·able
dish·pan
dish·rag
dish tow·el
dish·wash·er
dish·wa·ter
dis·il·lu·sion
dis·in·cli·na·tion
dis·in·fect
dis·in·fec·tant
dis·in·fes·ta·tion
dis·in·gen·u·ous
dis·in·her·it
dis·in·te·grate
dis·in·te·gra·tion
dis·in·ter·est·ed
dis·join
dis·junc·tion
dis·junc·tive
dis·like
dis·lo·cate
dis·lo·ca·tion
dis·lodge
dis·loy·al
dis·loy·al·ty
dis·mal
dis·man·tle
dis·man·tling
dis·mast
dis·may
dis·mem·ber

dis·miss
dis·miss·al
dis·mount
dis·obe·di·ence
dis·obe·di·ent
dis·obey
dis·obeyed
dis·oblige
dis·or·der
dis·or·dered
dis·or·der·ly
dis·or·ga·ni·za·tion
dis·or·ga·nize
dis·own
dis·par·age
dis·par·age·ment
dis·pa·rate (differ-
   ent; cf. *desperate*)
dis·par·i·ty
dis·pas·sion·ate
dis·patch
dis·pel
dis·pelled
dis·pel·ling
dis·pen·sa·ry
dis·pen·sa·tion
dis·pense
dis·pers·al
dis·perse (scatter;
   cf. *disburse*)
dis·pers·ible
dis·per·sion
dispir·it
dis·place
dis·place·ment
dis·play

dis·please
dis·plea·sure
disport
dis·pos·able
dis·pos·al
dis·pose
dis·po·si·tion
dis·pos·sess
dis·proof
dis·pro·por·tion
dis·pro·por·tion·ate
dis·prove
dis·pu·ta·ble
dis·pu·tant
dis·pu·ta·tion
dis·pu·ta·tious
dis·pute
dis·qual·i·fi·ca·tion
dis·qual·i·fy
dis·qui·si·tion
dis·re·gard
dis·re·pair
dis·rep·u·ta·ble
dis·re·pute
dis·re·spect
dis·re·spect·ful
dis·robe
dis·rupt
dis·sat·is·fac·tion
dis·sat·is·fied
dis·sect
dis·sec·tion
dis·sem·ble
　(disguise;
　cf. *disassemble*)
dis·sem·i·nate

dis·sen·sion
dis·sent
　(disagreement;
　cf. *decent, descent*)
dis·sent·er
dis·sen·tient
dis·ser·ta·tion
dis·ser·vice
dis·si·dence
dis·si·dent
dis·sim·i·lar
dis·sim·i·lar·i·ty
dis·sim·i·la·tion
dis·sim·u·late
dis·si·pate
dis·si·pat·ed
dis·si·pa·tion
dis·so·ci·ate
dis·so·ci·a·tion
dis·sol·u·ble
dis·so·lute
dis·so·lu·tion
dis·solve
dis·so·nance
dis·so·nant
dis·suade
dis·sua·sion
dis·taff
dis·tance
dis·tant
dis·taste
dis·taste·ful
dis·tem·per
dis·tend
dis·ten·sion
dis·tich

dis·till
dis·til·late
dis·til·la·tion
dis·till·er
dis·till·ery
dis·tinct
dis·tinc·tion
dis·tinc·tive
dis·tinc·tive·ly
dis·tinc·tive·ness
dis·tin·guish
dis·tort
dis·tor·tion
dis·tract
dis·trac·tion
dis·traught
dis·tress
dis·trib·ute
dis·tri·bu·tion
dis·trib·u·tor
dis·trict
dis·trust
dis·trust·ful
dis·turb
dis·tur·bance
dis·union
dis·use
dit·to
di·ur·nal
di·va
di·van
div·er
di·verge
di·ver·gence
di·ver·gent
di·vers (various)

di·verse (different)
di·ver·si·fi·ca·tion
di·ver·si·fy
di·ver·sion
di·ver·si·ty
di·vert
di·vest
di·vide
div·i·dend
div·i·na·tion
di·vine
di·vin·i·ty
di·vis·i·bil·i·ty
di·vi·sion
di·vorce
div·ot
di·vulge
diz·zi·ly
diz·zi·ness
diz·zy
doc·ile
do·cil·i·ty
dock·et
dock·hand
dock·side
dock·yard
doc·tor
doc·tor·al
doc·tor·ate
doc·tri·naire
doc·tri·nal
doc·trine
doc·u·ment
doc·u·men·ta·ry
doc·u·men·ta·tion
dodge

doe (deer; cf. *dough*)
doe·skin
dog·ber·ry
dog·cart
dog·catch·er
dog  col·lar
dog  days
doge
dog—eared
dog·fight
dog·fish
dog·ged
dog·ger·el
dog·house
dog·ma
dog·mat·ic
dog·mat·i·cal
dog·ma·tism
dog·ma·tize
do—good·er
dog  pad·dle n.
dog—pad·dle v.
dog  rose
dog  tag
dog·tooth
dog·trot
dog·watch
dog·wood
doi·lies
doi·ly
dol·drums
dole·ful
dol·lar
dol·man (cloak)
dol·men (monument)
do·lor

do·lor·ous
dol·phin
do·main
Domes·day  Book
do·mes·tic
do·mes·ti·cate
do·mes·tic·i·ty
do·mi·cile
dom·i·nant
dom·i·nate
dom·i·na·tion
dom·i·neer·ing
Do·min·i·can
do·mi·nie
do·min·ion
dom·i·no sing.
dom·i·noes pl.
do·nate
do·na·tion
done (finished;
  cf. *dun*)
don·jon
don·key
don·key·work
do·nor
don't
dooms·day
door·jamb
door·keep·er
door·knob
door·man
door·mat
door·nail
door·plate
door  prize
door·sill

door·step
door·stop
door·way
door·yard
dor·mant
dor·mer
dor·mi·to·ry
dor·mouse
dor·sal
dos·age
dos·sier
dot·age
dot·ard
dou·ble
dou·ble—deal·er
dou·ble—deal·ing
dou·ble—deck·er
dou·ble—en·try adj.
dou·ble en·try n.
dou·ble—faced
dou·ble—park
dou·ble—quick
dou·blet
dou·ble take
dou·ble—talk n.
dou·ble·think
dou·ble time n.
dou·ble—time v.
dou·bloon
doubt·ful
doubt·less
dough (bread; cf. doe)
dough·boy
dough·nut
dove·cote
dove·tail

dow·a·ger
dowd·i·ness
dowdy
dow·el
dow·eled
dow·el·ing
dow·er
down—and—out
   adj.
down—and—out-
   er n.
down·beat
down·cast
down·fall
down·grade
down·heart·ed
down·hill
down·pour
down·range
down·right
down·stage
down·stairs
down·state
down·stream
down·stroke
down·swing
down·time
down—to—earth
down·town
down·trend
down·trod·den
down·turn
down·ward
down·wind
downy
dow·ry

dox·ol·o·gy
doy·en
doz·en
drab
drab·ber
drab·best
drach·ma
dra·co·ni·an
draft (draw;
   cf. draught, drought)
draft horse
draft·i·ness
drafts·man
drag
dragged
drag·ging
drag·line
drag·net
drag·o·man
drag·on
drag·on·et
drag·on·fly
dra·goon
drag·rope
drain·age
drain·er
drain·pipe
dra·mat·ic
dra·ma·tist
dra·ma·tize
dra·ma·tur·gy
drap·ery
dras·tic
draught (drink;
   cf. draft, drought)
draw·back n.

draw·bar
draw·bridge
draw·ee
draw·er
drawn·work
draw·string
dray·age
dray·man
dread·ful
dread·nought
dream·i·ly
dream·i·ness
dream·land
dreamy
drea·ri·ly
drea·ri·ness
drea·ry
dress·er
dress·i·ness
dress·ing room
dress·mak·er
drib·ble
drib·bling
drift·wood
drill
dril·ling
drill·mas·ter
drill press
drink·able
drip
drip—dry adj., v.
dripped
drip·ping
drive—in n.
driv·el
driv·er

drive·way
driz·zle
droll·ery
drom·e·dary
drop
dropped
drop·ping
drop cur·tain
drop·head
drop·kick n.
drop—kick v.
drop leaf
drop let·ter n.
drop·light
drop·out n.
drop·per
drop·sy
drought (dryness;
    cf. *draft, draught*)
drowsy
drudg·ery
drug
drugged
drug·ging
drug·gist
drug·store
drum
drum·beat
drum·fire
drum ma·jor·ette
drummed
drum·mer
drum·ming
drum·roll
drum·stick
drunk·ard

drunk·en
drunk·o·me·ter
dry (dried, dries)
dry·ad
dry cell
dry—clean v.
dry clean·ing n.
dry dock n.
dry—dock v.
dry goods
dry ice
dry·ly
dry·ness
dry·point
dry rot n.
dry—rot v.
dry run
dry—shod
du·al (twofold;
    cf. *duel*)
du·bi·ety
du·bi·ous
du·cal
duc·at
duch·ess
duchy
duck·board
duck·ling
duck·pin
duck soup
duc·tile
dud·geon
du·el (combat;
    cf. *dual*)
du·eled
du·el·ing

du·el·ist
du·et
du·gong
dug·out
duke·dom
dul·cet
dul·ci·mer
dull·ard
dull·ness
dul·ly
dumb·bell
dumb·wait·er
dum·my
dump·ling
dun (demand for payment; cf. *done*)
dune bug·gy
dun·ga·ree
dun·geon
dun·nage
duo·dec·i·mal
duo·dec·i·mo
du·o·de·nal
du·o·de·num
du·plex
du·pli·cate
du·pli·ca·tion
du·pli·ca·tor
du·plic·i·ty
du·ra·bil·i·ty
du·ra·ble
du·rance
du·ra·tion
dur·bar
du·ress
dur·ing

dusky
dust·bin
dust bowl
dust·cloth
dust·cov·er
dust·heap
dust·i·ness
dust jack·et
dust·less
dust·man
dust mop
dust·pan
dust·proof
dust·rag
dust storm
dust·up
dusty
Dutch ov·en
Dutch treat
du·te·ous
du·ti·able
du·ti·ful
du·ty
dwarf·ish
dwell·ing
dwin·dle
dwin·dling
dyed (colored; cf. *died*)
dye·ing (coloring)
dye·stuff
dye·wood
dy·ing (expiring)
dy·nam·ic
dy·na·mite
dy·na·mo

dy·na·mom·e·ter
dy·nast
dy·nas·tic
dy·nas·ty
Dy·nel
dys·en·tery
dys·func·tion
dys·lex·ia
dys·pep·sia
dys·pep·tic
dys·pho·ria
dys·tro·phy
dys·uria

ea·ger
ea·gle
ea·gre
ear·ache
ear·drop
ear·drum
ear·li·er
ear·li·est
ear·ly
ear·mark
earn (gain; cf. *urn*)
ear·nest
earn·ings
ear·phone
ear·ring

ear·shot
ear·split·ting
earth·born
earth·bound
earth·en·ware
earth·li·ness
earth·ly
earth·quake
earth·ward
earth·work
earth·worm
ear·wax
ear·wig
ea·sel
ease·ment
eas·i·er
eas·i·est
eas·i·ly
Eas·ter
east·ern
east·ward
easy·go·ing
eat·able
ebb
ebbed
ebb·ing
eb·o·ny
ebul·lient
eb·ul·li·tion
ec·cen·tric
ec·cen·tric·i·ty
ec·chy·mo·sis
ec·cle·si·as·ti·cal
ech·e·lon
echo
ech·oes

éclair
eclec·tic
eclipse
eco·log·i·cal
ecol·o·gist
ecol·o·gy
eco·nom·ic
eco·nom·i·cal
econ·o·mist
econ·o·mize
econ·o·my
ec·sta·sy
ec·stat·ic
ec·u·men·i·cal
ec·ze·ma
ed·dy
edel·weiss
ede·ma
edge·ways
edg·i·ness
edg·ing
ed·i·ble
edict
ed·i·fi·ca·tion
ed·i·fice
ed·i·fy
Ed·in·burg Tex.
Ed·in·burgh Scotland
ed·it
edi·tion (printing;
    cf. *addition*)
ed·i·tor
ed·i·to·ri·al
ed·i·to·ri·al·ize
ed·u·ca·ble
ed·u·cate

ed·u·ca·tion·al
ed·u·ca·tive
ed·u·ca·tor
ef·face
ef·face·ment
ef·fect (result;
    cf. *affect*)
ef·fec·tive
ef·fec·tu·al
ef·fec·tu·ate
ef·fem·i·nate
ef·fer·vesce
ef·fer·ves·cent
ef·fete
ef·fi·ca·cious
ef·fi·ca·cy
ef·fi·cien·cy
ef·fi·cient
ef·fi·gy
ef·flo·res·cent
ef·flu·vi·um
ef·fort
ef·fron·tery
ef·ful·gence
ef·fu·sion
ef·fu·sive
egg·head
egg·nog
egg·plant
ego
ego·ism
ego·ist
ego·tism
ego·tist
egre·gious
egress

ei·der
eight
ei·ther
ejac·u·late
ejac·u·la·tion
ejac·u·la·to·ry
eject
ejec·tion
elab·o·rate
elab·o·ra·tion
élan
elapse (pass;
    cf. *lapse*)
elas·tic
elas·tic·i·ty
elat·ed·ly
ela·tion
el·bow·room
el·der
el·der·ber·ry
el·dest
elect
elec·tion
elec·tion·eer
elec·tive
elec·tor
elec·tor·al
elec·tor·ate
elec·tric
elec·tri·cal
elec·tri·cian
elec·tric·i·ty
elec·tri·fi·ca·tion
elec·tri·fied
elec·tri·fy
elec·tro·cute

elec·trode
elec·trol·y·sis
elec·tro·lyte
elec·tro·mag·net
elec·tron
elec·tro·plate
elec·tro·scope
elec·tro·type
el·ee·mos·y·nary
el·e·gance
el·e·gant
ele·gi·ac
el·e·gy
el·e·ment
el·e·men·tal
el·e·men·ta·ry
el·e·phant
el·e·phan·ti·a·sis
el·e·phan·tine
el·e·vate
el·e·va·tor
elf (pl.: *elves*)
elic·it (draw out;
    cf. *illicit*)
elide
el·i·gi·bil·i·ty
el·i·gi·ble (qualified;
    cf. *illegible*)
elim·i·nate
elim·i·na·tion
eli·sion
elite
elix·ir
Eliz·a·be·than
el·lipse
el·lip·sis

el·lip·tic
el·lip·ti·cal
el·o·cu·tion
el·o·cu·tion·ist
elon·gate
elon·ga·tion
elope
el·o·quence
el·o·quent
else·where
elu·ci·date
elu·ci·da·tion
elude (escape;
    cf. *allude*)
elu·sive (evasive;
    cf. *illusive*)
elves (sing.: *elf*)
ema·ci·ate
ema·ci·a·tion
em·a·nate
em·a·na·tion
eman·ci·pate
eman·ci·pa·tion
eman·ci·pa·tor
emas·cu·late
em·balm
em·bank·ment
em·bar·go
em·bar·goes
em·bar·rass
em·bar·rass·ment
em·bas·sy
em·bel·lish
em·bez·zle
em·bit·ter
em·bla·zon

em·blem
em·blem·at·ic
em·bod·i·ment
em·body
em·bold·en
em·bo·lism
em·boss
em·bou·chure
em·brace
em·bra·sure
em·broi·dery
em·broil
em·bryo
em·bry·on·ic
emend (correct;
  cf. *amend*)
emen·da·tion
em·er·ald
emerge
emer·gence
emer·gen·cy
emer·i·tus
emet·ic
em·i·grant (outgoing;
  cf. *immigrant*)
em·i·grate
em·i·gra·tion
émi·gré
em·i·nence
em·i·nent (promi-
  nent; cf. *imminent*)
emir
em·is·sary
emis·sion
emit
emit·ted

emit·ting
emol·lient
emol·u·ment
emo·tion
emo·tion·al
em·per·or
em·pha·ses pl.
em·pha·sis sing.
em·pha·size
em·phat·ic
em·pire
em·pir·ic
em·pir·i·cal
em·ploy
em·ploy·abil·i·ty
em·ploy·able
em·ploy·ee
em·ploy·er
em·ploy·ment
em·po·ri·um
em·pow·er
em·press n.
emp·ty
emp·ty—head·ed
em·py·ema
em·py·re·an
emu
em·u·late
em·u·la·tion
em·u·lous
emul·si·fy
emul·sion
en·able
en·act
en·act·ment
enam·el

enam·eled
enam·el·ing
enam·el·ware
en·am·or
en·camp·ment
en·caus·tic
en·ceinte
en·chant·er
en·chant·ing
en·chant·ment
en·chant·ress
en·cir·cle
en·clave
en·clit·ic
en·close
en·clo·sure
en·co·mi·as·tic
en·co·mi·um
en·com·pass
en·core
en·coun·ter
en·cour·age
en·cour·age·ment
en·cour·ag·ing
en·croach
en·croach·ment
en·cum·ber
en·cum·brance
en·cyc·li·cal
en·cy·clo·pe·dia
en·dan·ger
en·dear
en·dear·ment
en·deav·or
en·dem·ic
end·ing

en·dive
end·less
end·long
end man
end·most
en·dorse
en·dorse·ment
en·dow
en·dow·ment
end ta·ble
en·dur·able
en·dur·ance
en·dure
en·dur·ing
end·ways
en·e·ma
en·e·mies pl.
en·e·my sing.
en·er·get·ic
en·er·gize
en·er·giz·er
en·er·gy
en·er·vate v.
ener·vate adj.
en·er·va·tion
en·fee·ble
en·fet·ter
en·fold
en·force
en·force·able
en·force·ment
en·forc·er
en·fran·chise
en·fran·chise·ment
en·gage
en·gaged

en·gage·ment
en·gag·ing
en·gen·der
en·gine
en·gi·neer
en·gi·neer·ing
En·glish
En·glish·man
En·glish·wom·an
en·graft
en·grave
en·grav·er
en·grav·ing
en·gross
en·gross·ing
en·gross·ment
en·gulf
en·hance
en·hance·ment
enig·ma
enig·mat·ic
en·join
en·joy
en·joy·ably
en·joy·ment
en·lace
en·large
en·large·ment
en·light·en
en·light·en·ment
en·list
en·list·ment
en·liv·en
en·mi·ty
en·nui
enor·mi·ty

enor·mous
enough
en·rage
en·rap·ture
en·rich
en·rich·ment
en·robe
en·roll
en·rolled
en·roll·ing
en·roll·ment
en route
en·sconce
en·shrine
en·shroud
en·sign
en·slave
en·slave·ment
en·snare
en·sue
en·sure
en·tab·la·ture
en·tail
en·tail·ment
en·tan·gle
en·tan·gle·ment
en·ter
en·ter·prise
en·ter·pris·ing
en·ter·tain
en·ter·tain·er
en·ter·tain·ment
en·thrall
en·throne
en·thuse
en·thu·si·asm

en·thu·si·ast
en·thu·si·as·tic
en·thu·si·as·ti·cal·ly
en·tice
en·tice·ment
en·tire
en·tire·ty
en·ti·tle
en·ti·ty
en·tomb
en·tomb·ment
en·to·mol·o·gy
  (insects;
  cf. *etymology*)
en·tou·rage
en·trails
en·train
en·trance
en·trant
en·trap
en·treat
en·treat·ies
en·treaty
en·tre·pre·neur
en·try·way
en·twine
enu·mer·ate
enu·mer·a·tion
enu·mer·a·tor
enun·ci·ate
enun·ci·a·tion
enun·ci·a·tor
en·vel·op v.
en·ve·lope n.
en·vel·oped
en·vel·op·ment

en·ven·om
en·vi·able
en·vi·ably
en·vied
en·vi·ous
en·vi·ron
en·vi·ron·ment
en·vi·ron·men·tal·ly
en·vis·age
en·vi·sion
en·voy
en·vy
en·zyme
Eo·lith·ic
ep·au·let
ephem·er·al
ep·ic (poem; cf.
  *epoch*)
ep·i·cal
ep·i·cure
ep·i·cu·re·an
ep·i·dem·ic
epi·der·mal
epi·der·mic
epi·der·mis
ep·i·gram (witty
  saying; cf. *epigraph*,
  *epitaph*, *epithet*)
ep·i·graph (motto;
  cf. *epigram*,
  *epitaph*, *epithet*)
ep·i·graph·ic
ep·i·lep·sy
ep·i·lep·tic
ep·i·logue

epiph·a·ny
epis·co·pal
Epis·co·pa·lian
ep·i·sode
ep·i·sod·ic
ep·i·sod·i·cal
epis·tle
epis·to·lary
ep·i·taph (inscrip-
  tion; cf. *epigram*,
  *epigraph*, *epithet*)
ep·i·thet (curse;
  cf. *epigram*,
  *epigraph*; *epitaph*)
epit·o·me
epit·o·mize
ep·och (era; cf. *epic*)
ep·och·al
ep·oxy
equa·bil·i·ty
equa·ble
equal
equaled
equal·ing
equal·i·ty
equal·ize
equal·iz·er
equal·ly
equa·nim·i·ty
equa·tion
equa·tor
equa·to·ri·al
eques·tri·an
equi·an·gu·lar
equi·dis·tance
equi·dis·tant

equi·lat·er·al
equi·lib·ri·um
equi·noc·tial
equi·nox
equip
equip·ment
equipped
equip·ping
eq·ui·ta·ble
eq·ui·ty
equiv·a·lence
equiv·a·lent
equiv·o·cal
equiv·o·cate
equiv·o·ca·tion
equiv·o·ca·tor
era
erad·i·ca·ble
erad·i·cate
erad·i·ca·tion
erad·i·ca·tive
erad·i·ca·tor
eras·able (can be
   erased; cf. *irascible*)
erase
eras·er
era·sure
erect
erec·tile
erec·tion
er·go
er·mine
ero·sion
ero·sive
erot·ic
err

er·rand
er·rant
er·rant·ry
er·ra·ta pl.
er·rat·ic
er·ra·tum sing.
er·ro·ne·ous
er·ror
erst·while
eruct
eruc·ta·tion
er·u·dite
er·u·di·tion
erupt (break out;
   cf. *irrupt*)
erup·tion
erup·tive
er·y·sip·e·las
es·ca·late
es·ca·la·tor
es·ca·pade
es·cape
es·cape·ment
es·cap·ism
es·ca·role
es·cheat
es·chew
es·chew·al
es·cort
es·cri·toire
es·crow
es·cutch·eon
Es·ki·mo
esoph·a·gus
es·o·ter·ic
es·pe·cial

Es·pe·ran·to
es·pi·o·nage
es·pla·nade
es·pous·al
es·pouse
espres·so
es·prit
es·py
es·quire
es·say (try; cf. *assay*)
es·say·ist
es·sence
es·sen·tial
es·sen·ti·al·i·ty
es·tab·lish
es·tab·lish·ment
es·tate
es·teem
es·ti·ma·ble
es·ti·mate
es·ti·ma·tion
es·top
es·topped
es·top·pel
es·trange
es·trange·ment
es·tu·ary
et cet·era
etch·ing
eter·nal
eter·ni·ty
ether
ethe·re·al
ethe·re·al·ize
ether·iza·tion
eth·i·cal

eth·ics
Ethi·o·pi·an
eth·nic
eth·ni·cal
eth·yl
eth·yl·ene
et·i·quette
et·y·mo·log·i·cal
et·y·mol·o·gy (words;
   cf. *entomology*)
eu·chre
eu·clid·e·an
eu·lo·gies
eu·lo·gize
eu·lo·gy
eu·phe·mism
eu·phe·mis·tic
eu·phe·mize
eu·pho·ni·ous
eu·pho·ny
Eu·ro·pe·an
eu·tro·phi·ca·tion
evac·u·ate
evac·u·a·tion
evade
eval·u·ate
eval·u·a·tion
ev·a·nes·cence
evan·gel·i·cal
evan·ge·lism
evan·ge·list
evan·ge·lis·tic
evan·ge·lize
evap·o·rate
evap·o·ra·tion
evap·o·ra·tive

eva·sion
eva·sive
even
even·fall
even·hand·ed
eve·ning (time)
even·ing (smoothing)
even·ness
even·song
event
event·ful
even·tide
even·tu·al
even·tu·al·i·ty
even·tu·al·ly
even·tu·ate
ev·er·green
ev·er·last·ing
ev·er·more
evert
ev·ery·body
ev·ery·day
ev·ery·thing
ev·ery·where
evict
evic·tion
ev·i·dence
ev·i·dent
ev·i·den·tial
evil·ly
evince
evis·cer·ate
evo·ca·ble
evo·ca·tion
evoc·a·tive
evo·ca·tor

evoke
evo·lu·tion
evo·lu·tion·ary
evolve
evul·sion
ewe (sheep;
   cf. *yew, you*)
ex·ac·er·bate
ex·ac·er·ba·tion
ex·act
ex·act·ing
ex·ac·ti·tude
ex·act·ly
exact·ness
ex·ag·ger·ate
ex·ag·ger·a·tion
ex·ag·ger·a·tor
ex·alt
ex·al·ta·tion
ex·am·i·na·tion
ex·am·ine
ex·am·ple
ex·as·per·ate
ex·as·per·a·tion
Ex·cal·i·bur
ex·ca·vate
ex·ca·va·tion
ex·ca·va·tor
ex·ceed (surpass;
   cf. *accede*)
ex·ceed·ing
ex·cel
ex·celled
ex·cel·lence
ex·cel·len·cy
ex·cel·lent

ex·cel·ling
ex·cel·si·or
ex·cept (exclude; cf. *accept*)
ex·cept·ing
ex·cep·tion
ex·cep·tion·able
ex·cep·tion·al
ex·cerpt
ex·cess (surplus; cf. *access*)
ex·ces·sive
ex·change
ex·che·quer
ex·cis·able
ex·cise
ex·ci·sion
ex·cit·abil·i·ty
ex·cit·able
ex·ci·ta·tion
ex·cite
ex·cite·ment
ex·cit·ing
ex·claim
ex·cla·ma·tion
ex·clam·a·to·ry
ex·clude
ex·clu·sion
ex·clu·sive
ex·com·mu·ni·cate
ex·com·mu·ni·ca·tion
ex·co·ri·ate
ex·crete
ex·cre·tion
ex·cru·ci·ate

ex·cru·ci·a·tion
ex·cul·pate
ex·cul·pa·tion
ex·cul·pa·to·ry
ex·cur·sion
ex·cur·sive
ex·cus·able
ex·cuse
ex·e·crate
ex·e·cra·tion
ex·e·cute
ex·e·cu·tion
ex·e·cu·tion·er
ex·ec·u·tive
ex·ec·u·tor
ex·ec·u·trix fem.
ex·e·ge·sis
ex·em·plar
ex·em·pla·ry
ex·em·pli·fi·ca·tion
ex·em·pli·fy
ex·empt
ex·emp·tion
ex·er·cise (exertion; cf. *exorcise*)
ex·ert (exercise; cf. *exsert*)
ex·er·tion
ex·e·unt
ex·hal·ant
ex·ha·la·tion
ex·hale
ex·haust
ex·haust·er
ex·haust·ible
ex·haus·tion

ex·haus·tive
ex·hib·it
ex·hi·bi·tion
ex·hi·bi·tion·er
ex·hib·i·tive
ex·hib·i·tor
ex·hib·i·to·ry
ex·hil·a·rant
ex·hil·a·rate
ex·hil·a·ra·tion
ex·hil·a·ra·tive
ex·hort
ex·hor·ta·tion
ex·hu·ma·tion
ex·hume
ex·i·gen·cies
ex·i·gen·cy
ex·ile
ex·ist
ex·is·tence
ex·is·tent
ex·is·ten·tial·ism
ex·it
ex·o·dus
ex·on·er·ate
ex·on·er·a·tion
ex·on·er·a·tive
ex·o·ra·ble
ex·or·bi·tant
ex·or·cise (expel; cf. *exercise*)
ex·o·ter·ic
ex·ot·ic
ex·pand
ex·panse
ex·pan·si·ble

ex·pan·sion
ex·pan·sive
ex par·te
ex·pa·ti·ate
ex·pa·tri·ate
ex·pa·tri·a·tion
ex·pect
ex·pec·tan·cy
ex·pec·tant
ex·pec·ta·tion
ex·pec·to·rant
ex·pec·to·rate
ex·pec·to·ra·tion
ex·pe·di·en·cy
ex·pe·di·ent
ex·pe·di·ent·ly
ex·pe·dite
ex·pe·di·tion
ex·pe·di·tion·ary
ex·pe·di·tious
ex·pel
ex·pelled
ex·pel·ling
ex·pend·able
ex·pen·di·ture
ex·pense
ex·pen·sive
ex·pe·ri·ence
ex·pe·ri·enced
ex·per·i·ment
ex·per·i·men·tal
ex·per·i·men·ta·tion
ex·pert·ly
ex·pert·ness
ex·pi·a·ble
ex·pi·ate

ex·pi·a·tion
ex·pi·a·to·ry
ex·pi·ra·tion
ex·pire
ex·plain·able
ex·pla·na·tion
ex·plan·a·to·ry
ex·ple·tive
ex·pli·ca·ble
ex·plic·it
ex·plode
ex·ploit
ex·ploi·ta·tion
ex·plo·ra·tion
ex·plor·a·to·ry
ex·plore
ex·plor·er
ex·plo·sion
ex·plo·sive
ex·po·nent
ex·port
ex·port·able
ex·por·ta·tion
ex·port·er
ex·pose v.
ex·po·sé n.
ex·posed
ex·pos·er
ex·po·si·tion
ex·pos·i·tive
ex·pos·i·to·ry
ex post fac·to
ex·pos·tu·la·tion
ex·po·sure
ex·pound
ex·press

ex·press·age
ex·press·ible
ex·pres·sion
ex·pres·sive
ex·press·ly
ex·press·man
ex·press·way
ex·pul·sion
ex·pul·sive
ex·punge
ex·pur·gate
ex·pur·ga·tion
ex·pur·ga·to·ry
ex·qui·site
ex·sert (protrude; cf. *exert*)
ex·sert·ed
ex·tant (existing; cf. *extent*)
ex·tem·po·ra·ne·ous
ex·tem·po·rary
ex·tem·po·re
ex·tem·po·rize
ex·tend
ex·ten·si·ble
ex·ten·sion
ex·ten·sive
ex·tent (degree; cf. *extant*)
ex·ten·u·ate
ex·ten·u·a·tion
ex·te·ri·or
ex·ter·mi·nate
ex·ter·mi·na·tion
ex·ter·mi·na·tor

ex·ter·mi·na·to·ry
ex·ter·nal
ex·ter·nal·ize
ex·ter·nal·ly
ex·tinct
ex·tinc·tion
ex·tin·guish·able
ex·tir·pate
ex·tol
ex·tolled
ex·tol·ling
ex·tort
ex·tor·tion
ex·tra
ex·tract
ex·tract·able
ex·trac·tion
ex·trac·tive
ex·trac·tor
ex·tra·cur·ric·u·lar
ex·tra·dit·able
ex·tra·dite
ex·tra·di·tion
ex·tral·i·ty
ex·tra·mar·i·tal
ex·tra·mu·ral
ex·tra·ne·ous
ex·traor·di·nari·ly
ex·traor·di·nary
ex·trap·o·late
ex·tra·sen·so·ry
ex·tra·ter·ri·to·ri·al·i·ty
ex·trav·a·gance
ex·trav·a·gant
ex·trav·a·gan·za

ex·trav·a·sa·tion
ex·treme
ex·trem·ist
ex·trem·i·ty
ex·tri·ca·ble
ex·tri·cate
ex·tri·ca·tion
ex·trin·sic
ex·tro·vert
ex·trude
ex·tru·sion
ex·u·ber·ance
ex·u·ber·ant
ex·u·da·tion
ex·ude
ex·ult
ex·ul·ta·tion
eye·ball
eye·bright
eye·brow
eye·cup
eyed
eye·drop·per
eye·ful
eye·glass
eye·hole
eye·ing
eye·lash
eye·let (decorative hole; cf. *islet*)
eye·le·teer
eye·lid
eye—open·er
eye·piece
eye·sight
eye·sore

eye·spot
eye·strain
eye·strings
eye·tooth
eye·wash
eye·wink
eye·wit·ness
ey·rie

fa·ble
fa·bled
fab·ric
fab·ri·cate
fab·ri·ca·tion
fab·u·lous
fa·cade
face·down adv.
face—hard·en
face—lift·ing
fac·er
fac·et (of diamond; cf. *faucet*)
fa·ce·tious
fa·cial
fac·ile
fa·cil·i·tate
fa·cil·i·ties
fa·cil·i·ty
fac·ing

79

fac·sim·i·le
fac·tion
fac·tion·al
fac·tious (partisan;
    cf. *factitious*,
    *fictitious*)
fac·ti·tious (arti-
    ficial; cf. *factious*,
    *fictitious*)
fac·tor
fac·to·ri·al
fac·tor·ize
fac·to·ry
fac·tu·al
fac·ul·ta·tive
fac·ul·ties
fac·ul·ty
fad
fade
fag·ot
fag·ot·ing
Fahr·en·heit
fa·ience
fail·ure
faint (weak; cf. *feint*)
faint·heart·ed
faint·ish
faint·ly
fair (just; cf. *fare*)
fair·ground
fair·ly
fair—mind·ed
fair·ness
fair—spok·en
fair  trade n.
fair—trade v.

fair·way
fair—weath·er adj.
fairy
fairy·land
fairy  tale n.
fairy—tale adj.
faith·ful
faith·less
fak·er
fa·kir
fal·con
fal·la·cious
fal·la·cy
fal—lal
fall·en
fal·li·bil·i·ty
fal·li·ble
fall·ing
fall  out v.
fall·out n.
fal·low
false·hood
false·ly
false·ness
fal·set·to
fal·si·fi·ca·tion
fal·si·fi·er
fal·si·fy
fal·si·ty
fal·ter
fa·mil·iar
fa·mil·iar·i·ty
fa·mil·iar·ize
fa·mil·iar·ly
fam·i·lies
fam·i·ly

fam·ine
fam·ish
fa·mous
fa·nat·ic
fa·nat·i·cal
fa·nat·i·cism
fan·ci·er
fan·ci·ful
fan·cy
fan·cy—free
fan·cy·work
fan·fare
fan·light
fanned
fan·ning
fan·light
fan·tail
fan·ta·sia
fan·tas·tic
fan·tas·ti·cal
fan·ta·sy
far·ad
far·a·day
far·away
farce
far·ci·cal
fare (price; cf. *fair*)
fare·well
far·fetched
fa·ri·na
far·i·na·ceous
farm·er
farm·hand
farm·house
farm·ing
farm·land

farm·stead
farm·yard
far—off
far—out
far·ra·go
far—reach·ing
far·row
far·see·ing
far·sight·ed
far·ther (at greater
    distance; cf. *further*)
far·ther·most
far·thest
far·thing
fas·ci·nate
fas·ci·na·tion
fas·ci·na·tor
fas·cism
fash·ion·able
fas·ten·er
fas·ten·ing
fas·tid·i·ous
fas·tig·i·ate
fas·tig·i·at·ed
fast·ness
fa·tal·ist
fa·tal·is·tic
fa·tal·i·ty
fa·tal·ly
fate (destiny; cf. *fete*)
fat·ed
fate·ful
fa·ther
fa·ther·hood
fa·ther—in—law
fa·ther·land

fa·ther·less
fa·ther·like
fa·ther·ly
fath·om
fath·om·able
fath·om·less
fa·tigue
fat·ten
fat·ty
fa·tu·i·ty
fat·u·ous
fau·cet (for water;
    cf. *facet*)
fault·i·ly
fault·i·ness
fault·less
faulty
faun (deity; cf. *fawn*)
faux pas
fa·vor·able
fa·vored
fa·vor·er
fa·vor·ite
fa·vor·it·ism
fawn (deer; cf. *faun*)
faze
fe·al·ty
fear·ful
fear·less
fear·some
fea·si·bil·i·ty
fea·si·ble
feat (deed; cf. *feet*)
feath·er·bed·ding
feath·er·brained
feath·ered

feath·er·edge
feath·er·head·ed
feath·er·stitch
feath·er·weight
feath·ery
fea·ture
fea·tured
fea·ture·less
feb·ri·fuge
Feb·ru·ary
fe·cund
fe·cun·di·ty
fed·er·al·ism
fed·er·al·ist
fed·er·al·iza·tion
fed·er·al·ize
fed·er·ate
fed·er·a·tion
fee·ble
fee·ble·mind·ed
feed·back
feed·er
feed·stuff
feel·er
feel·ing
feet (pl. of *foot*;
    cf. *feat*)
feign
feigned
feint (trick; cf. *faint*)
feld·spar
fe·lic·i·tate
fe·lic·i·ta·tion
fe·lic·i·tous
fe·lic·i·ty
fe·line

fel·low·ship
fel·on
fe·lo·ni·ous
fel·o·ny
felt·ing
fe·male
fem·i·nine
fem·i·nin·i·ty
fem·i·nism
fem·i·ni·za·tion
fe·mur
fence
fence·less
fenc·er
fenc·ing
fend·er
fen·es·tra·tion
fer·ment
fer·ment·able
fer·men·ta·tion
fern·ery
fe·ro·cious
fe·roc·i·ty
fer·ret
fer·ri·age
fer·ried
Fer·ris wheel
fer·rous
fer·rule (metal ring; cf. *ferule*)
fer·ry·boat
fer·tile
fer·til·i·ty
fer·til·iza·tion
fer·til·ize
fer·til·iz·er

fer·ule (rod; cf. *ferrule*)
fer·vent
fer·vid
fer·vor
fes·cue
fes·tal
fes·ter
fes·ti·val
fes·tive
fes·tiv·i·ty
fes·toon
fetch·ing
fete (festival; cf. *fate*)
fe·tish·ism
fet·lock
fet·ter
fet·tle
fe·tus
feu·dal·ism
feu·dal·ize
feu·dal·ly
feu·da·to·ry
feud·ist
feuil·le·ton
fe·ver
fe·ver·ish
fe·ver·weed
fey
fi·an·cé mas.
fi·an·cée fem.
fi·as·co
fi·at
fi·ber·board
fi·ber·glass
fi·brous

fib·u·la
fick·le
fic·tion
fic·tion·al
fic·ti·tious (imaginary; cf. *factious, factitious*)
fid·dle
fid·dler
fid·dle·stick
fi·del·i·ty
fid·gety
fi·du·cia·ry
field corn
field day
field·er
field glass
field goal
field house
field·piece
fiend·ish
fierce
fi·ery
fi·es·ta
fif·teen
fif·ti·eth
fif·ty
fig·ment
fig·u·ra·tive
fig·ure
fig·ured
fig·ure·head
fig·u·rine
fil·a·ment
fil·a·ture
fil·bert

fil·ial
fil·i·bus·ter
fil·i·gree
fil·ing
Fil·i·pi·no
fill·er
fil·let
fill·ing
film·strip
fil·ter (strainer;
  cf. *philter*)
filth·i·ness
filthy
fi·nal
fi·na·le
fi·nal·ist
fi·nal·i·ty
fi·nal·ly
fi·nance
fi·nan·cial
fi·nan·cier
find·er
find·ing
fine·ly
fine·ness
fin·ery
fine·spun
fi·nesse
fin·ger
fin·ger bowl
fin·ger·print
fin·ger·tip
fin·i·cal
fin·icky
fi·nis
fin·ish

fin·ished
fin·ish·er
fi·nite
fir (tree; cf. *fur*)
fire ant
fire·arm
fire·ball
fire·bird
fire blight
fire·boat
fire·box
fire·brand
fire·break
fire·brick
fire·bug
fire·clay
fire·crack·er
fire—cured
fire·damp
fire·dog
fire—eat·er
fire fight·er
fire·fly
fire·house
fire irons
fire·light
fire·man
fire·place
fire·plug
fire·pow·er
fire·proof
fire sale
fire screen
fire·side
fire·stone
fire tow·er

fire·trap
fire wall
fire·wa·ter
fire·wood
fire·work
fir·ing
fir·kin
firm·ly
firm·ness
first·born
first class n.
first—class adj., adv.
first·hand
first—rate
fis·cal (financial;
  cf. *physical*)
fish·er
fish·er·man
fish·ery
fish·hook
fish·ing
fish·mong·er
fish·plate
fish stick
fish sto·ry
fish·tail
fishy
fis·sion
fis·sion·able
fis·sure
fist·ic
fist·i·cuffs
fit·ful
fit·ness
fit·ted
fit·ting

five·fold
fix·able
fix·ate
fix·a·tion
fix·a·tive
fixed
fix·ing
fix·ture
fiz·zle
flab·ber·gast
flab·bi·ness
flab·by
flac·cid
fla·con
flag·el·late
flag·el·la·tion
flag·ging
flag·man
flag·on
flag·pole
fla·gran·cy
fla·grant
flag·ship
flag·staff
flag·stone
flail
flair (aptitude; cf. *flare*)
flaky
flam·boy·ant
flame·out
flame·proof
fla·min·go
flam·ma·ble
fla·neur
flan·nel
flan·nel·ette

flap·jack
flapped
flap·per
flap·ping
flare (torch; cf. *flair*)
flare—up
flash·back
flash·board
flash·bulb
flash card
flash flood
flash·i·ly
flash·i·ness
flash·ing
flash·light
flash point
flashy
flat·boat
flat·car
flat·foot n.
flat—foot·ed
flat·iron
flat·ten
flat·ter
flat·ter·er
flat·tery
flat·top
flat·u·lent
flat·ware
flat·work
flaunt
fla·vor·ful
fla·vor·ing
flax·seed
flaxy
flea (insect; cf. *flee*)

flea·bite
flea—bit·ten
fledg·ling
flee (escape; cf. *flea*)
flee·ing
flesh·i·ness
flesh·ly
flesh·pots
fleshy
flew (did fly; cf. *flu, flue*)
flex·i·bil·i·ty
flex·i·ble
flick·er
fli·er
flight deck
flight·i·ness
flight pay
flim·flam
flim·si·ly
flim·si·ness
flim·sy
flin·ders
flint glass
flint·i·ness
flinty
flip—flop
flip·pan·cy
flip·pant
flipped
flip·per
flip·ping
flir·ta·tion
flir·ta·tious
flitch
flit·ter

fliv·ver
float·ing
floc·cu·lent
floe (ice; cf. *flow*)
flood·gate
flood·light
flood·wa·ter
floor·board
floor·ing
floor lamp
floor·walk·er
flop·house
flop·ping
flop·py
flo·ral
flo·res·cence
flo·res·cent
flo·ri·cul·ture
flor·id
Flor·i·da
flo·rin
flo·ta·tion
flo·til·la
flot·sam
flounce
flounc·ing
floun·der
flour (bread;
    cf. *flower*)
flour·ish
floury
flow (of water; cf. *floe*)
flow·chart
flow·er (blossom;
    cf. *flour*)
flow·er·pot

flow·ery
flown
flu (influenza;
    cf. *flew*, *flue*)
fluc·tu·ate
fluc·tu·a·tion
flue (chimney;
    cf. *flew*, *flu*)
flu·en·cy
flu·ent
fluff·i·ness
fluffy
flu·id
flu·id·ex·tract
flu·id·i·ty
flu·id·ounce
flu·o·res·cent
flu·o·ri·date
flu·o·ri·da·tion
flu·o·ride
flu·o·rine
flu·o·ro·scope
flur·ry
flut·ter
flut·tery
flux
fly·blown
fly—boy
fly·by
fly—by—night
fly·catch·er
fly·er
fly·ing
fly·leaf
fly·pa·per
fly·speck

fly·wheel
foamy
fo·cal
fo·cal·ize
fo·ci pl.
fo·cus sing.
fo·cused
fo·cus·es
fo·cus·ing
fod·der
fog·bound
fog·gy (weather)
fog·horn
fo·gy (person)
fold·er
fold·ing
fo·liage
fo·li·ate
fo·li·at·ed
fo·li·a·tion
fo·lio
folk·lore
folks·i·ness
folksy
folk·tale
folk·way
fol·low
fol·low·er
fol·low·ing
fol·low up v.
fol·low—up n., adj.
fol·ly
fo·ment
fo·men·ta·tion
fon·dant
fon·dle

fon·dler
fond·ly
fond·ness
food·stuff
fool·ery
fool·har·di·ness
fool·har·dy
fool·ish
fool·proof
fools·cap
foot·ball
foot·bath
foot·board
foot brake
foot·bridge
foot·can·dle
foot·ed
foot·fall
foot fault n.
foot·fault v.
foot·gear
foot·hill
foot·hold
foot·ing
foot·less
foot·lights
foot·lock·er
foot·loose
foot·man
foot·mark
foot·note
foot·pace
foot·pad
foot·path
foot—pound
foot·print

foot·race
foot·rest
foot rule
foot·sore
foot·step
foot·stool
foot—ton
foot·walk
foot·way
foot·wear
foot·work
for·age
for·ay
for·bade
for·bear (be patient;
   cf. *forebear*)
for·bear·ance
for·bid
for·bid·den
for·bid·der
for·bid·ding
for·bore
forced
force·ful
force ma·jeure
for·ceps
forc·ible
fore·arm
fore·bear (ancestor;
   cf. *forbear*)
fore·bode
fore·bod·ing
fore·cast
fore·cast·er
fore·cas·tle
fore·close

fore·clo·sure
fore·doom
fore·fa·ther
fore·fin·ger
fore·foot
fore·front
fore·go
fore·go·ing
fore·gone
fore·ground
fore·hand
fore·hand·ed
fore·head
for·eign
for·eign·er
fore·judge
fore·knowl·edge
fore·lock
fore·man
fore·mast
fore·most
fore·name
fore·noon
fo·ren·sic
fore·or·dain
fore·part
fore·quar·ter
fore·run
fore·run·ner
fore·see
fore·see·a·ble
fore·shad·ow
fore·short·en
fore·sight
for·est
fore·stall

for·es·ta·tion
for·est·er
for·est·ry
fore·tell
fore·thought
for·ev·er
fore·warn
fore·word (preface; cf. *forward*)
for·feit
for·fei·ture
for·gave
forg·er
forg·ery
for·get·ful
for·get—me—not
for·get·ta·ble
for·get·ting
for·give·ness
for·giv·ing
for·go
for·got
for·lorn
for·mal
form·al·de·hyde
for·mal·i·ty
for·mal·ize
for·mal·ly (ceremonially; cf. *formerly*)
for·mat
for·ma·tion
for·ma·tive
for·mer adj.
form·er n.
for·mer·ly (previously; cf. *formally*)

form·mi·da·ble
form·less
for·mu·la
for·mu·la·rize
for·mu·late
for·mu·la·tion
for·sake
for·sooth
for·swear
for·sworn
for·syth·ia
fort (stronghold; cf. *forte*)
forte (talent; cf. *fort*)
forth (forward; cf. *fourth*)
forth·com·ing
forth·right
forth·with
for·ti·eth
for·ti·fi·ca·tion
for·ti·fi·er
for·ti·fy
for·tis·si·mo
for·ti·tude
fort·night
FOR·TRAN
for·tress
for·tu·i·tous
for·tu·i·ty
for·tu·nate
for·tune
for·tune—tell·er
for·ty
for·ty—nin·er
fo·rum

for·ward (ahead; cf. *foreword*)
for·ward·er
for·ward·ly
for·ward·ness
for·wards
fos·sil
fos·sil·if·er·ous
fos·ter
foul (bad; cf. *fowl*)
foul·mouthed
foul·ness
foun·da·tion
found·er n.
foun·der v.
found·ling
found·ry
foun·tain
foun·tain·head
four—flush·er
four—in—hand
four·score
four·some
four·teen
four·teenth
fourth (next after third; cf. *forth*)
fowl (poultry; cf. *foul*)
fox·hole
fox·hound
fox·i·ness
fox ter·ri·er
fox—trot
foy·er
fra·cas
frac·tion

frac·tion·al
frac·tious
frac·ture
frag·ile
fra·gil·i·ty
frag·ment
frag·men·tary
fra·grance
fra·grant
frail·ty
fram·er
frame—up
frame·work
fram·ing
franc (money;
   cf. *frank*)
fran·chise
Fran·cis·can
frank (candid;
   cf. *franc*)
frank·furt·er
frank·in·cense
frank·ly
frank·ness
fran·tic
fra·ter·nal
fra·ter·ni·ty
frat·er·nize
frat·ri·cide
fraud·u·lence
fraud·u·lent
freak·ish
freck·le
free·board
free·born
freed·man

free·dom
free—for—all
free·hand
free·hold
free lance n.
free—lance adj., v.
free·ly
free·man
Free·ma·son
free·ma·son·ry
free·stone
free·think·er
free·way
freeze (from cold;
   cf. *frieze*)
freeze—dry
freez·er
freight·er
fre·net·ic
fren·zy
Fre·on
fre·quen·cy
fre·quent
fres·co
fresh·en
fresh·ly
fresh·ness
fresh·wa·ter
fret·ful
fret·work
fri·a·ble
fri·ar
fric·as·see
fric·tion
fric·tion·al
Fri·day

friend·less
friend·li·ness
friend·ly
friend·ship
frieze (ornament;
   cf. *freeze*)
frig·ate
fright
fright·en
fright·ened
fright·ful
frig·id
fri·gid·i·ty
frip·pery
frit·ter
fri·vol·i·ty
friv·o·lous
frog·man
frol·ic
frol·ic·some
frol·icked
frol·ick·ing
front·age
fron·tal
fron·tier
fron·tiers·man
fron·tis·piece
front·less
front man
front mat·ter
frost·bite
frost·i·ness
frost·ing
fro·ward
froze
fro·zen

fru·gal
fru·gal·i·ty
fru·gal·ly
fruit·cake
fruit·er·er
fruit fly
fruit·ful
fru·ition
fruit·less
frus·trate
frus·tra·tion
fud·dy—dud·dy
fu·el
fuel cell
fu·eled
fu·el·ing
fu·gi·tive
ful·crum
ful·fill
ful·fill·ing
ful·fill·ment
full·back
full—blood·ed
full—blown
full—bod·ied
full dress n.
full—dress adj.
full—fledged
full—length
full·ness
full—scale
full time n.
full—time adj.
ful·ly
ful·mi·nate
ful·some

fum·ble
fu·mi·gate
fu·mi·ga·tion
fu·mi·ga·tor
func·tion
func·tion·al
func·tion·ary
fun·da·men·tal·ism
fu·ner·al (burial)
fu·ner·ary
fu·ne·re·al (solemn)
fun·gi (sing.: *fungus*)
fun·gi·ble
fun·gi·cide
fun·gous adj.
fun·gus n. (pl.: *fungi*)
fu·nic·u·lar
fun·nel
fun·neled
fun·nel·ing
fun·ny
fur (hair; cf. *fir*)
fur·be·low
fur·bish
fu·ri·ous
fur·long
fur·lough
fur·nace
fur·nish
fur·ni·ture
fu·ror
fur·ri·er
fur·ring
fur·row
fur·ry (with fur;
    cf. *fury*)

fur·ther (in addition;
    cf. *farther*)
fur·ther·ance
fur·ther·more
fur·ther·most
fur·thest
fur·tive
fu·ry (rage; cf. *furry*)
furze
fu·se·lage
fus·i·bil·i·ty
fus·ible
fu·sion
fuss·bud·get
fuss·i·ly
fuss·i·ness
fussy
fu·tile
fu·til·i·ty
fu·ture
fu·tu·ri·ty
fuzz·i·ness
fuzzy

ga·ble
gad·about
gad·fly
gad·get
ga·droon
Gael·ic

gag rule
gai·ety
gain·er
gain·ful
gain·say
gait (manner of
    walking; cf. *gate*)
gai·ter
gal·axy
gal·lant
gal·lant·ry
gal·le·on
gal·lery
gal·ley
gal·leys
gal·li·cism
gal·lon
gal·lop
gal·lop·ing
gal·loped
gal·lows
gall·stone
gal·van·ic
gal·va·ni·za·tion
gal·va·nize
gam·bit
gam·ble (bet;
    cf. *gambol*)
gam·bler
gam·bling
gam·bol (play;
    cf. *gamble*)
gam·boled
gam·bol·ing
gam·brel
game·keep·er

game·ness
games·man·ship
game·ster
Gan·dhi·an
gan·gli·on
gang·plank
gan·grene
gang·ster
gang·way
gant·let
ga·rage
gar·bage
gar·den
gar·den·er
gar·de·nia
Gar·di·ner Maine
Gard·ner Mass.
gar·gle
gar·goyle
gar·land
gar·lic
gar·ment
gar·ner
gar·net
gar·nish
gar·nish·ee
gar·nish·ment
gar·ri·son
gar·ru·li·ty
gar·ru·lous
gar·ter
gas·bag
gas cham·ber
gas·eous
gas·es
gas fit·ter

gas·house
gas·ket
gas·light
gas log
gas mask
gas·o·line
gassed
gas·si·ness
gas·sing
gas sta·tion
gas·sy
gas·tight
gas·tric
gas·tri·tis
gas·tro·nom·ic
gas·tron·o·my
gas·works
gate (door; cf. *gait*)
gate·way
gath·er·ing
gauge
gaunt·let
gauze
gav·el
gay·ness
ga·ze·bo
ga·zelle
ga·zette
gear·ing
gel·a·tin
ge·la·ti·nize
ge·lat·i·nous
gen·darme
ge·ne·al·o·gy
gen·er·al
gen·er·a·lis·si·mo

gen·er·al·i·ty
gen·er·al·iza·tion
gen·er·al·ize
gen·er·al·ly
gen·er·al·ship
gen·er·ate
gen·er·a·tion
gen·er·a·tive
gen·er·a·tor
ge·ner·ic
gen·er·os·i·ty
gen·er·ous
gen·e·sis
ge·nial
ge·nial·i·ty
ge·nial·ly
gen·i·tal
gen·i·tive
ge·nius (greatly
   gifted; cf. *genus*)
gen·teel
gen·tile
gen·til·i·ty
gen·tle
gen·tle·man
gen·tle·ness
gent·ly
gen·try
gen·u·flect
gen·u·flec·tion
gen·u·ine
ge·nus (pl.: *genera*;
   classification;
   cf. *genius*)
geo·det·ic
ge·og·ra·pher

geo·graph·ic
geo·graph·i·cal
ge·og·ra·phy
geo·log·ic
geo·log·i·cal
ge·ol·o·gist
ge·ol·o·gy
ge·om·e·ter
geo·met·ric
geo·met·ri·cal
geo·me·tri·cian
ge·om·e·try
Geor·gia
ge·ra·ni·um
ger·i·at·rics
Ger·man
ger·mane
ger·mi·cide
ger·mi·nate
ger·mi·na·tion
germ·proof
ger·ry·man·der
ger·und
ge·sta·po
ges·tate
ges·ta·tion
ges·tic·u·late
ges·tic·u·la·tion
ges·tic·u·la·to·ry
ges·ture
get·at·able
get·away n.
get—to·geth·er n.
get·up n.
get up v.
gey·ser

ghast·li·ness
ghast·ly
gher·kin
ghet·to
ghost·like
ghost·ly
ghoul (demon;
   cf. *goal*)
gi·ant
gib·ber·ish
gibe (taunt; cf. *jibe*)
gib·let
Gi·bral·tar
gid·di·ly
gid·di·ness
gid·dy
gi·gan·tic
gig·gle
gig·o·lo
gild (decorate with
   gold; cf. *guild*)
gilt—edged
gim·crack
gim·let
gim·mick
gin·ger
gin·ger ale
gin·ger·bread
gin·ger·ly
gin·ger·snap
ging·ham
gink·go
gi·raffe
gird·er
gir·dle
gir·dling

girl·hood
girl·ish
girth
gist (essence; cf. *jest*)
giv·en
giv·ing
giz·zard
gla·cial
gla·cial·ly
gla·cier (ice; cf. *glazier*)
glad·den
glad·i·a·tor
glad·i·a·to·ri·al
gla·di·o·lus
glad·ly
glad·ness
glam·or·ize
glam·or·ous
glam·our
glance
glanc·ing
glan·du·lar
glar·ing
glass·blow·er
glass·ful
glass·i·ly
glass·ine
glass·i·ness
glass·ware
glass wool
glassy
glaze
gla·zier (glassworker; cf. *glacier*)
gleamy

glean·ings
glee·ful
glid·er
glim·mer·ing
glimpse
glis·ten
glit·ter
glit·tery
gloam·ing
glob·al·ly
glob·u·lar
glock·en·spiel
gloom·i·ly
gloom·i·ness
gloomy
glo·ri·fi·ca·tion
glo·ri·fi·er
glo·ri·fy
glo·ri·ous
glo·ry
glos·sa·ry
gloss·i·ly
gloss·i·ness
glossy
glow·er
glow·worm
glu·cose
glue
glued
glu·ey
glu·i·er
glu·i·est
glu·ing
glum·ly
glum·mer
glum·mest

glum·ness
glu·ten
glu·ten·ous
glut·ton
glut·ton·ous
glut·tony
glyc·er·in
gnarl
gnarled
gnash
gnat
gnaw
gneiss
gnome
gno·mon
gnu (animal; cf. *knew, new*)
goal (objective; cf. *ghoul*)
goal·post
gob·ble
gob·bler
gob·let
gob·lin
go—cart
god·child
god·daugh·ter
god·dess
god·fa·ther
god·head
god·less
god·like
god·li·ness
god·ly
god·moth·er
god·par·ent

god·send
god·son
God·speed
gog·gle
go·ing
goi·ter
gold·brick
gold·en
gold·en·rod
gold·field
gold—filled
gold·fish
gold  foil
gold  leaf
gold·smith
golf
Go·li·ath
gon·do·la
gon·do·lier
goo
good—bye
good—heart·ed
good·hu·mored
good·ly
good—na·tured
good·ness
good—tem·pered
good·will
goo·ey
goof·i·ness
goo·gol
goo·i·er
goo·i·est
goose·ber·ry
goose·flesh
goose·neck

goose  step n.
goose—step v.
go·pher
gorge
gor·geous
Gor·gon·zo·la
go·ril·la (animal;
     cf. *guerrilla*)
gor·man·dize
gos·pel
gos·sa·mer
gos·sip
gos·sip·ing
Goth·ic
gou·lash
gourd
gour·mand (big eater)
gour·met (epicure)
gout
gov·ern
gov·ern·able
gov·ern·ess
gov·ern·ment
gov·ern·men·tal
gov·er·nor—
     gen·er·al
gov·er·nor·ship
grab
grabbed
grab·bing
grace·ful
grace·less
gra·cious
gra·da·tion
gra·di·ent
grad·u·al

grad·u·ate
grad·u·a·tion
graft·er
gram·mar
gram·mar·i·an
gram·mat·i·cal
gram·o·phone
gra·na·ry
grand·aunt
grand·child
grand·daugh·ter
gran·deur
grand·fa·ther
gran·dil·o·quence
gran·dil·o·quent
gran·di·ose
gran·di·o·so
grand·moth·er
grand·neph·ew
grand·niece
grand·sire
grand·son
grand·stand
grand·un·cle
grang·er
gran·ite
gran·ite·ware
grant·ee
grant·er
grant—in—aid
gran·u·lar
gran·u·late
gran·u·la·tion
gran·u·la·tor
grape·fruit
grape·shot

grape·vine
graph·ic
graph·i·cal
graph·ite
grap·nel
grap·ple
grasp·ing
grass·hop·per
grassy
grate (fireplace;
  cf. *great*)
grate·ful
grat·i·fi·ca·tion
grat·i·fy
grat·i·fy·ing
grat·ing
gra·tis
grat·i·tude
gra·tu·i·tous
gra·tu·i·ty
gra·va·men
grave·clothes
grav·el
grave·ness
grave·stone
grave·yard
grav·i·tate
grav·i·ta·tion
grav·i·ta·tive
grav·i·ty
gra·vy
gray·beard
gray·ish
gra·zier
greas·er
grease·wood

greasy
great (large; cf. *grate*)
great·coat
great—heart·ed
greed·i·ly
greedy
green·back
green·ery
green—eyed
green·gage
green·gro·cer
green·horn
green·house
green·ing
green·ish
green·room
greet·ing
gre·gar·i·ous
Gre·go·ri·an
grem·lin
gre·nade
gren·a·dier
gren·a·dine
grey·hound
grid·dle    cake
grid·iron
griev·ance
griev·ous
grif·fin
grill (broil)
grille (grating)
grill·room
grill·work
gri·mace
grim·ly
grim·ness

grin
grind·stone
grinned
grin·ning
grip (grasp;
  cf. *gripe, grippe*)
gripe (complain;
  cf. *grip, grippe*)
grippe (sickness;
  cf. *grip, gripe*)
grip·ping (grasping)
gris·ly (ghastly;
  cf. *gristly, grizzly*)
gris·tle
gris·tly (full of gristle;
  cf. *grisly, grizzly*)
grist·mill
grit
grit·ted
grit·ting
grit·ty
griz·zle
griz·zled
griz·zly (bear;
  cf. *grisly, gristly*)
groan (moan;
  cf. *grown*)
gro·cer·ies
gro·cery
grog·gy
groove (rut; cf. *grove*)
gross·ly
gro·tesque
ground·hog
ground·less
ground·ling

ground·wa·ter
ground·work
grove (trees;
  cf. *groove*)
grov·el
grov·eled
grov·el·ing
grow·er
growl·er
grown (matured;
  cf. *groan*)
grub
grubbed
grub·bing
grub·stake
grudge
grudg·ing·ly
gru·el
gru·el·ing
grue·some
grum·ble
grumpy
guar·an·tee (to secure;
  cf. *guaranty*)
guar·an·tor
guar·an·ty (a pledge;
  cf. *guarantee*)
guard·house
guard·ian
guard·ian·ship
guards·man
gu·ber·na·to·ri·al
guern·sey
guer·ril·la (soldier;
  cf. *gorilla*)
guess·ti·mate

guess·work
guid·ance
guide·line
guild (association;
  cf. *gild*)
guild·hall
guile·less·ness
guil·lo·tine
guilt·i·ly
guilt·i·ness
guilt·less
guilty
guimpe
guin·ea
gui·tar
gull·ibil·i·ty
gull·ible
gul·lies
gul·ly
gum·drop
gummed
gum·my
gump·tion
gun·boat
gun·cot·ton
gun·fire
gun·flint
gun·lock
gun·man
gun·met·al
gun·nery
gun·pow·der
gun room
gun·run·ner
gun·shot
gun·wale

gup·py
gur·gle
Gur·kha
gush·er
gus·to
gut·ta—per·cha
Gut·ten·berg N.J.
gut·ter
gut·ter·snipe
gut·tur·al
guz·zle
gym·na·si·um
gym·nast
gym·nas·tic
gym·nas·tics
gy·ne·col·o·gy
gyp·sum
gyp·sy
gy·rate
gy·ra·tion
gy·ro·com·pass
gy·ro·scope
gy·ro·sta·bi·liz·er

ha·be·as cor·pus
hab·er·dash·er
hab·er·dash·ery
ha·bil·i·tate
hab·it

hab·it·able
ha·bi·tant
hab·i·tat
hab·i·ta·tion
ha·bit·u·al
ha·bit·u·ate
hab·i·tude
ha·ci·en·da
hack·ie
hack·man
hack·ney
hack·neyed
hack·saw
had·dock
hag·gard
hag·gle
ha·gi·og·ra·phy
hail (ice; cf. *hale*)
hail·stone
hail·storm
hair (fur; cf. *hare*)
hair·breadth
hair·brush
hair·cut
hair·do
hair·dress·er
hair·i·ness
hair·line
hair·net
hair·piece
hair·pin
hair—rais·ing
hair shirt
hair·split·ter
hair·split·ting
hair·spring

hairy
Hai·tian
hal·cy·on
hale (healthy; cf. *hail*)
half-back
half—baked
half—breed
half broth·er
half gain·er
half·heart·ed
half—life n.
half—mast
half—moon
half note
half·pen·ny
half sole n.
half—sole v.
half step
half ti·tle
half·tone
half—track
half—truth
half·way
hal·i·but
hal·i·to·sis
hall (room; cf. *haul*)
hall·mark
hal·low
Hal·low·een
hal·lu·ci·nate
hal·lu·ci·na·tion
hal·lu·ci·na·to·ry
hall·way
hal·ter
halve (divide in half;
    cf. *have*)

halves
Ham·burg
ham·burg·er
Ham·il·to·ni·an
ham·let
ham·mer
ham·mock
ham·per
ham·ster
ham·string
Ham·tramck Mich.
hand·bag
hand·ball
hand·bill
hand·book
hand·car
hand·cart
hand·clasp
hand·cuff
hand·ed·ness
hand·ful
hand·grip
hand·hold
hand·i·cap
hand·i·capped
hand·i·cap·ping
hand·i·craft
hand·i·ly
hand·i·work
hand·ker·chief
han·dle
han·dle·bar
han·dled
han·dler
hand—let·ter v.
han·dling

hand·list
hand·made adj.
hand·maid·en n.
hand—me—down
hand or·gan
hand·out n.
hand·pick
hand·rail
hand·saw
hands down adv.
hands—down adj.
hand·set
hand·shake
hand·some
hand·spike
hand·spring
hand·stamp n., v.
hand·stand
hand truck
hand·work
hand·wo·ven
hand·writ·ing
handy·man
han·gar (shed; cf. *hanger*)
hang·dog adj.
hang·er (for clothes; cf. *hangar*)
hang·er—on
hang·ing
hang·man
hang·nail
hang out v.
hang·out n.
hang·over
han·ker

han·ky—pan·ky
han·som
hap·haz·ard
hap·less
hap·ly
hap·pen
hap·pen·ing
hap·pen·stance
hap·pi·ly
hap·pi·ness
hap·py
hap·py—go—lucky
Haps·burg
ha·rangue
ha·rass
ha·rass·ing
har·bin·ger
har·bor
har·bor·age
hard—bit·ten
hard—boiled
hard·en
hard·fist·ed
hard·head·ed
hard·heart·ed
har·di·hood
har·di·ly
har·di·ness
hard·ly
hard·ness
hard·pan
hard sauce
hard·ship
hard·tack
hard·top

hard·ware
hard·wood
hard·work·ing
har·dy
hare (rabbit; cf. *hair*)
hare·brained
hare·lip
har·em
har·le·quin
har·le·quin·ade
harm·ful
harm·less
har·mon·ic
har·mon·i·ca
har·mo·ni·ous
har·mo·ni·za·tion
har·mo·nize
har·mo·ny
har·ness
harp·ist
har·poon
harp·si·chord
har·ri·dan
har·ri·er
har·row
har·ry
hart (deer; cf. *heart*)
har·um—scar·um
har·vest
har·vest·er
has—been n.
ha·sen·pfef·fer
hash·ish
hash mark
has·sle
has·ten

hast·i·ly
hast·i·ness
hasty
hat·band
hat·box
hatch·ery
hatch·et
hatch·ing
hatch·way
hate·ful
hat·er
hat·ful
hat·pin
ha·tred
hat·ter
haugh·ty
haul (pull; cf. *hall*)
haul·age
haunt
Ha·vana
have (possess;
    cf. *halve*)
have·lock
ha·ven
have—not n.
hav·er·sack
hav·oc
Ha·waii
Ha·wai·ian
haw·ser
haw·thorn
hay fe·ver
hay·rack
hay·seed
haz·ard
haz·ard·ous

haze
ha·zel
haz·i·ly
haz·i·ness
haz·ing
hazy
H—bomb
head·ache
head·band
head·board
head·cheese
head cold
head·dress
head·first
head·gear
head·hunt·er
head·i·ly
head·i·ness
head·ing
head·land
head·less
head·light
head·line
head·lock
head·long
head louse
head·man
head·mas·ter
head—on adj.
head·phone
head·piece
head·quar·ters
head·rest
head·set
head·spring
head·stone

head·strong
head·wait·er
head·wa·ter
head·way
head wind
head·work
heal (cure; cf. *heel*)
health·ful
health·i·ly
health·i·ness
healthy
hear (listen; cf. *here*)
heard (past tense of
    hear; cf. *herd*)
hear·ing
hear·ken
hear·say
heart (in body;
    cf. *hart*)
heart·ache
heart·beat
heart block
heart·break
heart·break·ing
heart·bro·ken
heart·burn
heart·en
heart·felt
hearth
hearth·stone
heart·i·ly
heart·i·ness
heart·land
heart·less
heart·rend·ing
heart·sick

heart·string
heart·throb
hearty
heat·er
hea·then
heath·er
heat shield
heave
heav·en
heav·en·ly
heav·en·ward
heavi·ly
heavi·ness
heavy
heavy—du·ty
heavy—foot·ed
heavy—hand·ed
heavy·heart·ed
heavy·set
heavy·weight
He·bra·ic
He·brew
hect·are
hec·tic
hec·to·graph
hec·to·me·ter
hedge·hog
hedge·row
hee·bie—jee·bies
heed·ful
heed·less
heel (of foot; cf. *heal*)
he·ge·mo·ny
he·gi·ra
heif·er
height

height·en
hei·nous
heir (inheritor; cf. *air*)
heir·ess fem.
heir·loom
he·li·cop·ter
he·lio·graph
he·lio·trope
he·li·pad
he·li·port
he·li·um
hell—bent
hel·lion
hel·met
helms·man
help·er
help·ful
help·less
help·mate
hel·ter—skel·ter
Hel·ve·tian
hemi·sphere
hemi·sphe·ric
hemi·sphe·ri·cal
hem·line
hem·lock
he·mo·glo·bin
he·mo·phil·ia
hem·or·rhage
hem·or·rhoid
hem·stitch
hence·forth
hence·for·ward
hench·man
hen·nery
hen·peck

he·pat·ic
he·pat·i·ca
hep·a·ti·tis
hep·ta·gon
her·ald
he·ral·dic
her·ald·ry
herb·age
herb·al
her·biv·o·rous
Her·cu·le·an
Her·cu·les
herd (of animals; cf. *heard*)
herd·er
here (place; cf. *hear*)
here·abouts
here·af·ter
he·red·i·tary
he·red·i·ty
here·in
here·in·af·ter
here·in·be·fore
her·e·sy
her·e·tic
he·ret·i·cal
here·to·fore
here·with
her·i·ta·ble
her·i·tage
Her·mes
her·mit
her·mit·age
her·nia
he·ro
he·roes

99

he·ro·ic
he·ro·ical
her·o·in (drug;
    cf. *heroine*)
her·o·ine (woman;
    cf. *heroin*)
her·o·ism
her·on
her·ring
her·ring·bone
her·self
hes·i·tan·cy
hes·i·tant
hes·i·tate
hes·i·tat·ing·ly
hes·i·ta·tion
het·ero·dox
het·er·o·ge·ne·ity
het·er·o·ge·neous
hew (chop; cf. *hue*)
hexa·gon
hex·ag·o·nal
hey·day
hi·a·tus
Hi·a·wa·tha
hi·ber·nate
hi·ber·na·tion
hi·bis·cus
hic·cup
hick·o·ry
hid·den
hide·away
hide·bound
hid·eous
hide·out
hi·er·arch

hi·er·ar·chi·cal
hi·er·ar·chy
hi·er·at·ic
hi·ero·glyph·ic
hig·gle·dy—
    pig·gle·dy
high·ball
high·born
high·boy
high·bred
high·brow
high chair
high—class adj.
high·er—up n.
high·fa·lu·tin
high·fi·del·i·ty
high—grade adj.
high—hand·ed
high·land
high·land·er
high—lev·el adj.
high·light
high—mind·ed
high·ness
high—pres·sure
high·road
high school
high sea
high—sound·ing
high—spir·it·ed
high—strung
high—ten·sion
high—test
high—toned
high·way
high·way·man

hi·lar·i·ous
hi·lar·i·ty
hill·bil·ly
hill·ock
hill·side
hilly
him (pronoun;
    cf. *hymn*)
Hi·ma·la·yan
him·self
hin·der v.
hind·er adj.
hin·drance
hind·sight
Hin·du
hinge
hing·ing
hin·ter·land
hip·bone
hip·pies pl.
hip·po·drome
hip·po·pot·a·mus
hip·pie sing.
hire·ling
hir·sute
hiss·ing
his·ta·mine
his·to·ri·an
his·tor·ic
his·tor·i·cal
his·to·ry
his·tri·on·ic
hit—and—run adj.
hitch·hike
hith·er
hith·er·to

hoard (amass;
    cf. *horde*)
hoard·ing
hoar·i·ness
hoarse (voice;
    cf. *horse*)
hoary
hoax
hob·ble
hob·by·horse
hob·gob·lin
hob·nail
hob·nob
ho·bo
hock·ey
ho·cus—po·cus
hoe
hoe·cake
hoe·down
hoe·ing
hog
hogged
hog·ging
hog·gish
hogs·head
hog·wash
hoi  pol·loi
hoist·er
hold·back n.
hold·er
hold·fast
hold·ing
hold  over v.
hold·over n.
hold  up v.
hold·up n.

hole (cavity; cf. *whole*)
hole·proof
hol·ey (full of holes;
    cf. *holly, holy,
    wholly*)
hol·i·day
ho·li·ness
hol·lan·daise
hol·low
hol·ly (shrub;
    cf. *holey,
    holy, wholly*)
ho·lo·caust
ho·lo·graph
hol·ster
ho·ly (sacred; cf.
    *holey, holly, wholly*)
hom·age
hom·burg
home·body
home·bred
home·com·ing
home·grown
home·land
home·less
home·like
home·li·ness
home·ly (plain;
    cf. *homey*)
home·made
home·mak·er
ho·meo·path
ho·meo·path·ic
ho·me·op·a·thy
home·own·er
home  plate

Ho·mer·ic
home·room
home  rule
home  run
home·sick
home·site
home·spun
home·stead
home·stretch
home·town
home·ward
home·work
hom·ey (homelike;
    cf. *homely*)
ho·mi·cide
hom·i·lies
hom·i·ly
ho·mo·ge·ne·ity
ho·mo·ge·neous
ho·mog·e·nize
ho·mog·e·nous
ho·mol·o·gous
hom·onym
ho·mo·phone
hon·est
hon·es·ty
hon·ey
hon·ey·bee
hon·ey·comb
hon·ey·dew
hon·eyed
hon·ey·moon
hon·ey·suck·le
hon·ky—tonk
hon·or
hon·or·able

hon·o·rar·i·um
hon·or·ary
hon·or·if·ic
hood·ed
hood·lum
hoo·doo
hood·wink
hoof·er
hoo·kah
hook·up
hook·worm
hoop·skirt
hoose·gow
Hoo·sier
hope·ful
hope·less
hop·per
hop·scotch
horde (crowd;
   cf. *hoard*)
hore·hound
ho·ri·zon
hor·i·zon·tal
hor·mone
hor·net
horn·pipe
horny
horo·scope
hor·ri·ble
hor·rid
hor·ri·fy
hor·ror
hors d'oeuvre
   (pl.: *hors d'oeuvres*)
horse (animal;
   cf. *hoarse*)

horse·back
horse·car
horse·flesh
horse·fly
horse·hair
horse·hide
horse·laugh
horse·man
horse op·era
horse·play
horse·pow·er
horse·rad·ish
horse sense
horse·shoe
horse·whip
hor·ti·cul·tur·al
hor·ti·cul·ture
ho·siery
hos·pice
hos·pi·ta·ble
hos·pi·tal
hos·pi·tal·i·ty
hos·pi·tal·iza·tion
hos·pi·tal·ize
hos·tage
hos·tel·ry
host·ess
hos·tile
hos·til·i·ty
hos·tler
hot
hot air
hot·bed
hot—blood·ed
hot·box
hotch·potch

hot dog
ho·tel
hot·foot
hot·head
hot·head·ed
hot·house
hot plate
hot rod
hot·shot
hot spring
Hot·ten·tot
hot·ter
hot·test
hour (60 minutes;
   cf. *our*)
hour·glass
hour·ly
house·boat
house·break·ing
house·bro·ken
house·clean
house·coat
house·dress
house·fly
house·ful
house·hold
house·hold·er
house·keep·er
house·less
house·lights
house·maid
house·man
house·moth·er
house par·ty
house·room
house·warm·ing

house·wife
house·wives
house·work
hous·ing
hov·el
hov·er
how·ev·er
how·it·zer
howl·er
how·so·ev·er
how—to
hua·ra·che
hub·bub
huck·le·ber·ry
huck·ster
hud·dle
hue (color; cf. *hew*)
huff·i·ly
huff·i·ness
huffy
huge·ness
Hu·gue·not
hulk·ing
hul·la·ba·loo
hu·man
hu·mane
hu·man·ism
hu·man·ist
hu·man·is·tic
hu·man·i·tar·i·an
hu·man·i·ty
hu·man·ize
hu·man·kind
hu·man·ly
hum·ble
hum·ble·ness

hum·bly
hum·bug
hum·drum
hu·mer·us (bone; cf. *humorous*)
hu·mid
hu·mid·i·fy
hu·mid·i·ty
hu·mi·dor
hu·mil·i·ate
hu·mil·i·a·tion
hu·mil·i·ty
hummed
hum·ming
hum·ming·bird
hum·mock
hu·mor
hu·mor·ist
hu·mor·ous (funny; cf. *humerus*)
hump·back
hunch·back
hun·dred
hun·dredth
hun·dred·weight
Hun·gar·i·an
hun·ger
hun·gri·er
hun·gri·ly
hun·gry
hunt·er
Hun·ting·don Pa.
Hun·ting·ton Ind., N.Y., W. Va.
hunts·man
hur·dle

hur·dy—gur·dy
hur·ly—bur·ly
Hu·ron
hur·rah
hur·ri·cane
hur·ried
hur·ry
hurt·ful
hus·band
hus·band·man
hus·band·ry
husk·i·ly
husk·i·ness
husk·ing
hus·ky
hus·sar
hus·tings
hus·tle
hy·a·cinth
hy·brid
Hy·dra
hy·dran·gea
hy·drant
hy·drate
hy·drau·lic
hy·dro·car·bon
hy·dro·chlo·ric
hy·dro·chlo·ride
hy·dro·dy·nam·ics
hy·dro·elec·tric
hy·dro·gen
hy·dro·ly·sis
hy·drom·e·ter
hy·dro·phane
hy·dro·pho·bia
hy·dro·phone

hy·dro·plane
hy·dro·pon·ics
hy·dro·scope
hy·dro·stat·ic
hy·drous
hy·e·na
hy·giene
hy·gien·ic
hy·grom·e·ter
hy·gro·scope
hy·gro·scop·ic
hy·men
hy·me·ne·al
hymn (song; cf. *him*)
hym·nal
hym·nol·o·gy
hy·per·bo·la (curve)
hy·per·bo·le
 (exaggeration)
hy·per·crit·i·cal
 (overcritical;
 cf. *hypocritical*)
hy·per·phys·i·cal
hy·per·ten·sion
hy·phen
hy·phen·ate
hy·phen·at·ed
hyp·no·sis
hyp·not·ic
hyp·no·tism
hyp·no·tist
hyp·no·tize
hy·po·chon·dria
hy·po·chon·dri·ac
hy·po·chon·dri·a·
 cal

hy·poc·ri·sy
hyp·o·crite
hyp·o·crit·i·cal
 (deceitful;
 cf. *hypercritical*)
hy·po·der·mal
hy·po·der·mic
hy·po·der·mis
hy·po·eu·tec·tic
hy·pot·e·nuse
hy·poth·e·cate
hy·poth·e·ses pl.
hy·poth·e·sis sing.
hy·po·thet·i·cal
hy·po·thet·i·cal·ly
hys·sop
hys·ter·e·sis
hys·te·ria
hys·ter·i·cal
hys·ter·ics

iam·bic
iam·bus
Ibe·ri·an
ibex (goat)
ibis (bird)
ice
ice age
ice bag

ice·berg
ice·boat
ice·bound
ice·box
ice·break·er
ice cap
ice—cold
ice cream n.
ice—cream adj.
ice field
ice floe
ice·house
ice·man
ice pack
ice pick
ice plant
ice wa·ter
ici·cle
ic·i·ly
ic·i·ness
ic·ing
icon
icon·ic
icon·o·clast
icy
Ida·ho
ide·al (perfect;
 cf. *idle, idol, idyl*)
ide·al·ism
ide·al·ist
ide·al·is·tic
ide·al·iza·tion
ide·al·ize
ide·al·ly
iden·ti·cal
iden·ti·fi·ca·tion

iden·ti·fied
iden·ti·fy
ideo·gram
ide·ol·o·gy
id·i·o·cy
id·i·om
id·i·om·at·ic
id·io·syn·cra·sy
id·i·ot
id·i·ot·ic
idle (inactive;
  cf. *ideal, idol, idyl*)
idle·ness
idly
idol (object
  of worship;
  cf. *ideal, idle, idyl*)
idol·a·trous
idol·a·try
idol·ize
idyll (of rustic life;
  cf. *ideal, idle, idol*)
idyl·lic
if·fy
ig·loo
ig·ne·ous
ig·nes·cent
ig·nis fat·u·us
ig·nit·able
ig·nite
ig·ni·tion
ig·no·ble
ig·no·min·i·ous
ig·no·mi·ny
ig·no·ra·mus
ig·no·rance

ig·no·rant
ig·nore
igua·na
il·e·um (intestine;
  cf. *ilium*)
il·i·ac
Il·i·ad
il·i·um (pelvic bone;
  cf. *ileum*)
ilk
ill—ad·vised
ill—bred
il·le·gal
il·le·gal·i·ty
il·leg·i·bil·i·ty
il·leg·i·ble
  (unreadable;
  cf. *eligible*)
il·le·git·i·ma·cy
il·le·git·i·mate
ill—fat·ed
ill—fa·vored
il·lib·er·al
il·lic·it (unlawful;
  cf. *elicit*)
il·lim·it·able
Il·li·nois
il·lit·er·a·cy
il·lit·er·ate
il·lit·er·ate·ness
ill—man·nered
ill—na·tured
ill·ness
il·log·i·cal
ill—starred
ill—treat

il·lu·mi·nate
il·lu·mi·na·tion
il·lu·mi·na·tive
il·lu·mi·na·tor
il·lu·mine
il·lu·sion
il·lu·sive (mislead-
  ing; cf. *elusive*)
il·lu·so·ry
il·lus·trate
il·lus·tra·tion
il·lus·tra·tive
il·lus·tra·tor
il·lus·tri·ous
ill will
im·age
im·ag·ery
imag·in·able
imag·i·nary
imag·i·na·tion
imag·i·na·tive
imag·ine
im·bal·ance
im·be·cile
im·be·cil·i·ty
im·bibe
im·bri·cate
im·bri·cat·ed
im·bri·ca·tion
im·bro·glio
im·bue
im·i·ta·ble
im·i·tate
im·i·ta·tion
im·i·ta·tive
im·i·ta·tor

im·mac·u·late
im·ma·nent
im·ma·te·ri·al
im·ma·te·ri·al·i·ty
im·ma·ture
im·mea·sur·able
im·me·di·a·cy
im·me·di·ate
im·me·di·ate·ly
im·me·mo·ri·al
im·mense
im·men·si·ty
im·merge
im·merse
im·mer·sion
im·mi·grant
  (incoming;
  cf. *emigrant*)
im·mi·grate
im·mi·gra·tion
im·mi·nence
im·mi·nent
  (impending;
  cf. *eminent*)
im·mis·ci·ble
im·mo·bile
im·mo·bi·li·za·tion
im·mo·bi·lize
im·mod·er·ate
im·mod·er·a·tion
im·mod·est
im·mo·late
im·mo·la·tion
im·mor·al

im·mo·ral·i·ty
im·mor·tal
im·mor·tal·i·ty
im·mor·tal·ize
im·mov·abil·i·ty
im·mov·able
im·mov·ably
im·mune
im·mu·ni·ty
im·mu·nize
im·mu·nol·o·gy
im·mure
im·mu·ta·bil·i·ty
im·mu·ta·ble
im·pact
im·pair
im·pair·ment
im·pal·pa·ble
im·pan·el
im·par·i·ty
impark
im·part
im·par·tial
im·par·tial·i·ty
im·par·ti·ble
im·pass·abil·i·ty
im·pass·able
im·passe
im·pas·si·bil·i·ty
im·pas·si·ble
im·pas·sion
im·pas·sioned
im·pas·sive
im·pa·tience
im·pa·tient
im·peach

im·peach·ment
im·pec·ca·bil·i·ty
im·pec·ca·ble
im·pe·cu·ni·os·i·ty
im·pe·cu·nious
im·ped·ance
im·pede
im·ped·i·ment
im·ped·i·men·ta
im·pel
im·pelled
im·pel·lent
im·pel·ling
im·pend
im·pend·ing
im·pen·e·tra·bil·i·ty
im·pen·e·tra·ble
im·per·a·tive
im·per·a·tive·ly
im·per·cep·ti·ble
im·per·fect
im·per·fec·tion
im·per·fect·ly
im·per·fect·ness
im·per·fo·rate
im·pe·ri·al
im·pe·ri·al·ism
im·pe·ri·al·ist
im·pe·ri·al·ly
im·per·il
im·pe·ri·ous
im·per·ish·able
im·per·me·able
im·per·son·al
im·per·son·ate

im·per·son·ation
im·per·son·ator
im·per·ti·nence
im·per·ti·nen·cy
im·per·ti·nent
im·per·turb·abil·i·ty
im·per·turb·able
im·per·vi·ous
im·pe·ti·go
im·pet·u·os·i·ty
im·pet·u·ous
im·pe·tus
im·pi·ety
im·pinge
im·pi·ous
imp·ish
im·pla·ca·ble
im·plant
im·ple·ment
im·pli·cate
im·pli·ca·tion
im·pli·ca·tive
im·plic·it
im·plied
im·plore
im·plo·sion
im·ply
im·po·lite
im·pol·i·tic
im·pon·der·a·ble
im·port
im·port·able
im·por·tance
im·por·tant
im·por·ta·tion

im·por·tu·nate
im·por·tune
im·por·tu·ni·ty
im·pose
im·pos·ing
im·po·si·tion
im·pos·si·bil·i·ty
im·pos·si·ble
im·post
im·pos·tor (pretender)
im·pos·ture (fraud)
im·po·tence
im·po·ten·cy
im·po·tent
im·pound
im·pov·er·ish
im·prac·ti·ca·bil·i·ty
im·prac·ti·ca·ble
im·prac·ti·cal
im·pre·cate
im·pre·ca·tion
im·pre·ca·to·ry
im·preg·na·bil·i·ty
im·preg·na·ble
im·preg·nate
im·preg·na·tion
im·pre·sa·rio
im·press
im·press·ible
im·pres·sion
im·pres·sion·able
im·pres·sive
im·pri·mis
im·print
im·pris·on
im·pris·on·ment

im·prob·a·bil·i·ty
im·prob·a·ble
im·promp·tu
im·prop·er
im·pro·pri·ety
im·prov·able
im·prove
im·prove·ment
im·prov·er
im·prov·i·dence
im·prov·i·dent
im·pro·vi·sa·tion
im·pro·vise
im·pru·dence
im·pru·dent
im·pru·dent·ly
im·pu·dence
im·pu·dent
im·pugn
im·pulse
im·pul·sion
im·pul·sive
im·pu·ni·ty
im·pure
im·pu·ri·ty
im·put·able
im·pu·ta·tion
im·pu·ta·tive
im·pute
in·abil·i·ty
in·ac·ces·si·bil·i·ty
in·ac·ces·si·ble
in·ac·cu·ra·cy
in·ac·cu·rate
in·ac·tion
in·ac·tive

in·ac·tiv·i·ty
in·ad·e·qua·cy
in·ad·e·quate
in·ad·mis·si·ble
in·ad·ver·tence
in·ad·ver·tent
in·ad·vis·able
in·alien·able
in·al·ter·able
inane
in·an·i·mate
inan·i·ty
in·ap·peas·able
in·ap·pli·ca·ble
in·ap·po·site
in·ap·pre·cia·ble
in·ap·pre·cia·tive
in·ap·pro·pri·ate
in·apt
in·ar·tic·u·late
in·ar·tis·tic
in·as·much  as
in·at·ten·tion
in·at·ten·tive
in·au·di·ble
in·au·gu·ral
in·au·gu·rate
in·au·gu·ra·tion
in·aus·pi·cious
in·born
in·bound
in·bred
in·cal·cu·la·ble
in·ca·les·cent
in·can·desce
in·can·des·cence

in·can·des·cent
in·can·ta·tion
in·ca·pa·bil·i·ty
in·ca·pa·ble
in·ca·pac·i·tate
in·ca·pac·i·ta·tion
in·ca·pac·i·ty
in·car·cer·ate
in·car·cer·a·tion
in·car·na·tion
in·cau·tious
in·cen·di·ary
in·cense
in·cen·tive
in·cep·tion
in·cep·tive
in·ces·sant
in·cest
in·ces·tu·ous
in·cho·ate
in·ci·dence
in·ci·dent
in·ci·den·tal
in·ci·den·tal·ly
in·cin·er·ate
in·cin·er·a·tion
in·cin·er·a·tor
in·cip·i·ent
in·cise
in·ci·sion
in·ci·sive
in·ci·sor
in·ci·ta·tion
in·cite (stir up;
    cf. *insight*)
in·cite·ment

in·cit·er
in·ci·vil·i·ty
in·clem·en·cy
in·clem·ent
in·cli·na·tion
in·cline
in·clined
in·clin·ing
in·clude
in·clud·ed
in·clu·sion
in·clu·sive
in·co·erc·ible
in·cog·ni·to
in·co·her·ence
in·co·her·ent
in·com·bus·ti·ble
in·come
in·com·ing
in·com·men·su·ra·
    ble
in·com·men·su·rate
in·com·mu·ni·ca·
    ble
in·com·pa·ra·ble
in·com·pat·i·bil·i·ty
in·com·pat·i·ble
in·com·pe·tence
in·com·pe·tent
in·com·plete
in·com·pre·hen·
    si·ble
in·com·press·ible
in·com·put·able
in·con·ceiv·able
in·con·clu·sive

in·con·gru·ity
in·con·gru·ous
in·con·se·quent
in·con·se·quen·tial
in·con·sid·er·able
in·con·sid·er·ate
in·con·sis·ten·cy
in·con·sis·tent
in·con·sol·able
in·con·spic·u·ous
in·con·stant
in·con·test·able
in·con·tro·vert·ible
in·con·ve·nience
in·con·ve·nient
in·con·vert·ible
in·cor·po·rate
in·cor·po·ra·tion
in·cor·po·ra·tor
in·cor·po·re·al
in·cor·rect
in·cor·ri·gi·bil·i·ty
in·cor·ri·gi·ble
in·cor·rupt
in·cor·rupt·ible
in·creas·able
in·crease
in·creas·ing·ly
in·cred·i·bil·i·ty
in·cred·i·ble
   (unbelievable;
   cf. *incredulous*)
in·cre·du·li·ty
in·cred·u·lous
   (unbelieving;
   cf. *incredible*)

in·cre·ment
in·crim·i·nate
in·crim·i·na·to·ry
in·crus·ta·tion
in·cu·bate
in·cu·ba·tion
in·cu·ba·tor
in·cu·bus
in·cul·cate
in·cul·ca·tion
in·cul·pate
in·cul·pa·tion
in·cul·pa·to·ry
in·cum·ben·cy
in·cum·bent
in·cur
in·cur·able
in·cu·ri·ous
in·curred
in·cur·ring
in·cur·sion
in·cur·vate
in·cur·va·tion
in·debt·ed·ness
in·de·cen·cy
in·de·cent
in·de·ci·pher·able
in·de·ci·sion
in·de·ci·sive
in·de·clin·able
in·de·co·rous
in·de·co·rum
in·deed
in·de·fat·i·ga·ble
in·de·fen·si·ble
in·de·fin·able

in·def·i·nite
in·del·i·ble
in·del·i·ca·cy
in·del·i·cate
in·dem·ni·fi·ca·
   tion
in·dem·ni·fied
in·dem·ni·fy
in·dem·ni·ty
in·dent
in·den·ta·tion
in·den·tion
in·den·ture
in·de·pen·dence
in·de·pen·dent
in·de·scrib·able
in·de·struc·ti·ble
in·de·ter·min·able
in·de·ter·mi·nate
in·de·ter·mi·na·
   tion
in·dex  (pl.: *indexes*
   or *indices*)
in·dex·er
in·dex·es  pl.
In·dia
In·di·an
In·di·ana
in·di·cate
in·di·ca·tion
in·dic·a·tive
in·dic·a·tor
in·dic·a·to·ry
in·di·ces  pl.
in·dict  (charge with
   a crime; cf. *indite*)

**109**

in·dict·able
in·dic·tion
in·dict·ment
In·dies
in·dif·fer·ence
in·dif·fer·ent
in·dif·fer·ent·ly
in·di·gence
in·dig·e·nous
(native to)
in·di·gent (poor)
in·di·gest·ibil·i·ty
in·di·gest·ible
in·di·ges·tion
in·dig·nant
in·dig·na·tion
in·dig·ni·ty
in·di·go
in·di·rect
in·di·rec·tion
in·di·rect·ly
in·di·rect·ness
in·dis·cern·ible
in·dis·creet
in·dis·crete
in·dis·cre·tion
in·dis·crim·i·nate
in·dis·crim·i·na·tion
in·dis·pens·able
in·dis·posed
in·dis·po·si·tion
in·dis·put·able
in·dis·sol·u·ble
in·dis·tinct
in·dis·tinct·ly

in·dis·tin·guish·able
in·dite (write;
    cf. *indict*)
in·di·vert·ible
in·di·vid·u·al
in·di·vid·u·al·ism
in·di·vid·u·al·ist
in·di·vid·u·al·i·ty
in·di·vid·u·al·ize
in·di·vid·u·al·ly
in·di·vis·i·ble
In·do·chi·na
In·do—Chi·nese
in·doc·ile
in·doc·tri·nate
in·do·lence
in·do·lent
in·dom·i·ta·ble
in·door
in·doors
in·drawn
in·du·bi·ta·ble
in·duce
in·duce·ment
in·duct
in·duc·tile
in·duc·tion
in·duc·tive
in·duc·tor
in·dulge
in·dul·gence
in·dul·gent
in·du·rate
in·du·ra·tion
in·dus·tri·al

in·dus·tri·al·ism
in·dus·tri·al·ist
in·dus·tri·al·ize
in·dus·tri·ous
in·dus·try
ine·bri·ant
ine·bri·ate
ine·bri·a·tion
in·ebri·ety
in·ed·i·ble
in·ef·fa·ble
in·ef·face·able
in·ef·fec·tive
in·ef·fec·tu·al
in·ef·fi·ca·cious
in·ef·fi·ca·cy
in·ef·fi·cien·cy
in·ef·fi·cient
in·el·e·gance
in·el·e·gant
in·el·i·gi·bil·i·ty
in·el·i·gi·ble
in·el·o·quent
in·eluc·ta·ble
in·ept
in·ep·ti·tude
in·equal·i·ty
in·eq·ui·ta·ble
in·eq·ui·ty
(unfairness;
    cf. *iniquity*)
in·erad·i·ca·ble
in·er·rant
in·ert
in·er·tia
in·es·sen·tial

in·es·ti·ma·ble
in·ev·i·ta·bil·i·ty
in·ev·i·ta·ble
in·ex·act
in·ex·ac·ti·tude
in·ex·cus·able
in·ex·haust·ibil·i·ty
in·ex·haust·ible
in·ex·o·ra·ble
in·ex·pe·di·ent
in·ex·pen·sive
in·ex·pe·ri·ence
in·ex·pert
in·ex·pi·a·ble
in·ex·plain·able
in·ex·pli·ca·ble
in·ex·plic·it
in·ex·press·ible
in·ex·pres·sive
in·ex·pug·na·ble
in·ex·ten·si·ble
in·ex·tin·guish-
   able
in·ex·tri·ca·ble
in·fal·li·bil·i·ty
in·fal·li·ble
in·fa·mous
in·fa·my
in·fan·cy
in·fant
in·fan·ta *fem.*
in·fan·te *mas.*
in·fan·tile
in·fan·try
in·fat·u·ate
in·fat·u·a·tion

in·fect
in·fec·tion
in·fec·tious
in·fec·tive
in·fec·tor
in·fe·lic·i·tous
in·fe·lic·i·ty
in·fer
in·fer·ence
in·fer·en·tial
in·fe·ri·or
in·fe·ri·or·i·ty
in·fer·nal
in·fer·no
in·ferred
in·fer·ring
in·fest
in·fes·ta·tion
in·fi·del
in·fi·del·i·ty
in·field
in·fil·trate
in·fi·nite
in·fin·i·tes·i·mal
in·fin·i·tive
in·fin·i·ty
in·firm
in·fir·ma·ry
in·fir·mi·ty
in·flame
in·flam·ma·ble
in·flam·ma·tion
in·flam·ma·to·ry
in·flate
in·flat·ed
in·fla·tion

in·flect
in·flec·tion
in·flex·i·ble
in·flict
in·flic·tion
in·flow
in·flu·ence
in·flu·en·tial
in·flu·en·za
in·flux
in·form
in·for·mal
in·for·mal·i·ty
in·for·mant
in·for·ma·tion
in·for·ma·tive
in·form·er
in·frac·tion
in·fra·red
in·fra·struc·ture
in·fre·quent
in·fringe
in·fringe·ment
in·fu·ri·ate
in·fuse
in·fu·sion
in·ge·nious (inven-
   tive; cf. *ingenuous*)
in·ge·nue
in·ge·nu·i·ty
in·gen·u·ous (can-
   did; cf. *ingenious*)
in·ges·tion
in·glo·ri·ous
in·got
in·grained

in·grate
in·gra·ti·ate
in·grat·i·tude
in·gre·di·ent
in·gress
in·grown
in·hab·it
in·hab·it·ant
in·hale
in·har·mo·ni·ous
in·here
in·her·ence
in·her·ent
in·her·it
in·her·i·tance
in·hib·it
in·hi·bi·tion
in·hos·pi·ta·ble
in·hu·man
in·hu·man·i·ty
in·hu·ma·tion
in·im·i·cal
in·im·i·ta·ble
in·iq·ui·tous
in·iq·ui·ty
   (wickedness;
   cf. *inequity*)
ini·tial
ini·ti·ate v.
ini·tiate n.
ini·tia·tive
in·ject
in·jec·tion
in·jec·tor
in·ju·di·cious
in·junc·tion

in·jure
in·ju·ries
in·ju·ri·ous
in·ju·ry
in·jus·tice
in·kling
ink·stand
ink·well
in·laid
in·land
in·lay
in·let
in·mate
in·most
in·nate
in·ning
inn·keep·er
in·no·cence
in·no·cent
in·noc·u·ous
in·no·vate
in·no·va·tion
in·nu·en·do
in·nu·mer·a·ble
in·oc·u·late
in·oc·u·la·tion
in·of·fen·sive
in·op·er·a·ble
in·op·por·tune
in·or·di·nate
in·or·gan·ic
in·put
in·quest
in·qui·etude
in·quire
in·qui·ries

in·qui·ry
in·qui·si·tion
in·quis·i·tive
in·quis·i·tor
in·road
in·rush
in·sane
in·san·i·tary
in·san·i·ty
in·sa·tia·ble
in·scribe
in·scrip·tion
in·scru·ta·ble
in·sect
in·sec·ti·cide
in·se·cure
in·se·cu·ri·ty
in·sen·sate
in·sen·si·ble
in·sen·si·tive
in·sep·a·ra·ble
in·sert
in·ser·tion
in·side
in·sid·i·ous
in·sight
   (understanding;
   cf. *incite*)
in·sig·nia
in·sig·nif·i·cance
in·sig·nif·i·cant
in·sin·cere
in·sin·u·ate
in·sin·u·a·tion
in·sip·id
in·sist

in·sis·tence
in·sis·tent
in·sole
in·so·lence
in·so·lent
in·sol·u·ble
in·sol·ven·cy
in·sol·vent
in·som·nia
in·sou·ci·ance
in·sou·ci·ant
in·spect
in·spec·tion
in·spec·tor
in·spi·ra·tion
in·spire
in·sta·bil·i·ty
in·stall
in·stal·la·tion
in·stalled
in·stall·ing
in·stall·ment
in·stance
in·stan·ta·neous
in·stan·ter
in·stant·ly
in·stead
in·step
in·sti·gate
in·sti·ga·tion
in·sti·ga·tor
in·still
in·stilled
in·still·ing
in·stinct
in·stinc·tive

in·sti·tute
in·sti·tu·tion
in·sti·tu·tion·al
in·struct
in·struct·ed
in·struc·tion
in·struc·tion·al
in·struc·tive
in·struc·tor
in·stru·ment
in·stru·men·tal
in·stru·men·tal·i·ty
in·sub·or·di·nate
in·sub·or·di·na·
    tion
in·suf·fer·able
in·suf·fi·cient
in·su·lar
in·su·late
in·su·la·tion
in·su·la·tor
in·sult
in·su·per·a·ble
in·sup·port·able
in·sup·press·ible
in·sur·able
in·sur·ance
in·sure
in·sur·er
in·sur·gent
in·sur·rec·tion
in·tact
in·ta·glio
in·take
in·tan·gi·ble
in·te·ger

in·te·gral
in·te·grate
in·te·gra·tion
in·teg·ri·ty
in·teg·u·ment
in·tel·lect
in·tel·lec·tu·al
in·tel·li·gence
in·tel·li·gent
in·tel·li·gi·ble
in·tem·per·ance
in·tem·per·ate
in·tend
in·ten·dant
in·tense
in·ten·si·fied
in·ten·si·fy
in·ten·si·ty
in·ten·sive
in·tent
in·ten·tion
in·ter
in·ter·ac·tion
in·ter·cede
in·ter·cept
in·ter·ces·sion
in·ter·change·able
in·ter·com
in·ter·com·mu·ni·
    ca·tion
in·ter·course
in·ter·de·nom·i·na·
    tion·al
in·ter·de·pen·dent
in·ter·dict
in·ter·est

in·ter·fere
in·ter·fered
in·ter·fer·ence
in·ter·fer·ing
in·ter·im
in·te·ri·or
in·ter·ject
in·ter·jec·tion
in·ter·leave
in·ter·lin·ear
in·ter·loc·u·tor
in·ter·loc·u·to·ry
in·ter·lope
in·ter·lude
in·ter·mar·riage
in·ter·mar·ry
in·ter·me·di·ary
in·ter·me·di·ate
in·ter·ment
in·ter·mez·zo
in·ter·mi·na·ble
in·ter·min·gle
in·ter·mis·sion
in·ter·mit·tent
in·ter·nal
in·ter·na·tion·al
in·ter·ne·cine
in·ter·nist
in·tern·ment
in·ter·pel·late
(question)
in·ter·po·late (insert)
in·ter·pose
in·ter·pret (trans-
late; cf. *interrupt*)
in·ter·pre·ta·tion

in·ter·pret·er
in·ter·ra·cial
in·terred
in·ter·reg·num
in·ter·re·late
in·ter·ring
in·ter·ro·gate
in·ter·ro·ga·tion
in·ter·rog·a·tive
in·ter·rog·a·to·ry
in·ter·rupt (break
into; cf. *interpret*)
in·ter·rupt·ible
in·ter·rup·tion
in·ter·sect
in·ter·sec·tion
in·ter·sperse
in·ter·state (between
states; cf. *intrastate*)
in·ter·stice
in·ter·sti·tial
in·ter·ur·ban
in·ter·val
in·ter·vene
in·ter·ven·tion
in·ter·view
in·ter·view·er
in·tes·tate
in·tes·ti·nal
in·tes·tine
in·ti·ma·cy
in·ti·mate
in·ti·ma·tion
in·tim·i·date
in·tim·i·da·tion
in·tol·er·a·ble

in·tol·er·ance
in·tol·er·ant
in·to·na·tion
in·tone
in·tox·i·cant
in·tox·i·cate
in·trac·ta·ble
in·tra·mu·ral
in·tran·si·gent
in·tran·si·tive
in·tra·state (within
the state;
cf. *interstate*)
in·trep·id
in·tre·pid·i·ty
in·tri·ca·cy
in·tri·cate
in·trigue
in·trigued
in·tri·gu·ing
in·trin·sic
in·tro·duce
in·tro·duc·tion
in·tro·duc·to·ry
in·troit
in·tro·spec·tion
in·tro·vert
in·trude
in·tru·sion
in·tu·ition
in·tu·itive
in·unc·tion
in·un·date
in·un·da·tion
in·ure
in·vade

in·val·id adj.
in·va·lid n.
in·val·i·date
in·valu·able
in·vari·able
in·va·sion
in·vec·tive
in·veigh
in·vei·gle
in·vent
in·ven·tion
in·ven·tive
in·ven·tor
in·ven·to·ries
in·ven·to·ry
in·verse
in·ver·sion
in·vert
in·vest
in·ves·ti·gate
in·ves·ti·ga·tion
in·ves·ti·ga·tor
in·ves·ti·ture
in·vest·ment
in·ves·tor
in·vet·er·ate
in·vid·i·ous
in·vig·o·rate
in·vin·ci·ble
in·vi·o·la·ble
in·vi·o·late
in·vis·i·ble
in·vi·ta·tion
in·vite
in·vit·ing
in·vo·ca·tion

in·voice
in·voke
in·vol·un·tari·ly
in·vol·un·tary
in·volve
in·vul·ner·a·ble
in·ward
io·dine
ion·iza·tion
ion·ize
ion·o·sphere
io·ta
IOU
Io·wa
ip·e·cac
ip·so fac·to
iras·ci·ble (quick to
    anger; cf. *erasable*)
irate
ir·i·des·cence
ir·i·des·cent
irid·i·um
irk·some
iron·clad
iron gray
iron·i·cal
iron lung
iron·mas·ter
iron·ware
iron·wood
iron·work
iro·ny
ir·ra·di·ate
ir·ra·tio·nal
ir·rec·on·cil·able
ir·re·deem·able

ir·re·duc·ible
ir·re·fra·ga·ble
ir·re·fut·able
ir·reg·u·lar
ir·rel·e·vance
ir·rel·e·vant
ir·re·li·gious
ir·rep·a·ra·ble
ir·re·press·ible
ir·re·proach·able
ir·re·sist·ible
ir·re·sol·u·ble
ir·res·o·lute
ir·res·o·lu·tion
ir·re·spec·tive
ir·re·spon·si·ble
ir·re·triev·able
ir·rev·er·ent
ir·re·vers·ible
ir·re·vo·ca·ble
ir·ri·gate
ir·ri·ga·tion
ir·ri·ta·ble
ir·ri·tant
ir·ri·tate
ir·ri·ta·tion
ir·rupt (break in;
    cf. *erupt*)
ir·rup·tion
is·chi·um
isin·glass
is·land
isle (small island;
    cf. *aisle*)
is·let (small island;
    cf. *eyelet*)

iso·bar
iso·late
iso·la·tion·ism
iso·la·tion·ist
iso·met·rics
isos·ce·les
iso·therm
iso·ther·mal
iso·tope
Is·ra·el
Is·rae·li
Is·ra·el·ite
is·su·able
is·su·ance
is·sue
isth·mus
ital·ic
ital·i·cize
item
item·iza·tion
item·ize
itin·er·ant
itin·er·ary
itin·er·ate
its (possessive)
it's (it is)
it·self
ivo·ry

ja·bot
jack·al

jack·a·napes
jack·ass
jack·boot
jack·et
jack·ham·mer
jack—in—the— box
jack—in—the— pul·pit
jack·knife
jack—of—all— trades
jack—o'—lan·tern
jack·pot
jack·rab·bit
jack·screw
jack·straw
jack—tar
Jac·o·bin
jag·uar
jail·bird
jail·break
ja·lopy
jam (food)
jamb (of a door)
jam·bo·ree
jan·i·tor
jan·i·to·ri·al
Jan·u·ary
ja·pan (varnish)
Jap·a·nese
ja·panned
ja·pan·ning
jar
jar·gon
jarred

jar·ring
jas·mine
jas·per
jaun·dice
jaun·ti·ly
jaun·ty
jav·e·lin
jaw·bone
jaw·break·er
jay·walk
jeal·ous
jeal·ou·sy
Je·ho·vah
je·june
je·ju·num
jel·lied
jel·li·fy
jel·ly·fish
jeop·ar·dize
jeop·ar·dy
jer·e·mi·ad
jerk·i·ly
jer·ky
jest (joke; cf. *gist*)
Je·su·it
jet—pro·pelled
jet·sam
jet stream
jet·ti·son
jet·ty
jeu d'es·prit
jew·el
jew·eled
jew·el·er
jew·el·ry
jibe (agree; cf. *gibe*)

116

jig·gle
jig·saw
jin·go
jin·rik·i·sha
jit·ney
jit·ter·bug
job
job·ber
job·bing
job·less
job lot
job work
jock·ey
jo·cose
joc·u·lar
joc·u·lar·i·ty
jo·cund
jodh·pur
jog
jogged
jog·ging
John·ston R.I.
Johns·town
    N.Y., Pa.
joie de vi·vre
join·der
join·er
joint·ly
join·ture
jok·er
jol·li·ty
jol·ly
jon·quil
josh
jos·tle
jour·nal

jour·nal·ism
jour·nal·ist
jour·nal·is·tic
jour·nal·ize
jour·ney
jour·ney·man
jo·vial
jowl
joy·ful
joy·ous
joy·ride
ju·bi·lant
ju·bi·la·tion
ju·bi·lee
judge·ship
judg·ment
ju·di·ca·to·ry
ju·di·ca·ture
ju·di·cial (of a judge;
    cf. *judicious*)
ju·di·cia·ry
ju·di·cious (of a
    judgment;
    cf. *judicial*)
ju·do
jug·ger·naut
jug·gle
jug·u·lar
juic·i·ly
juic·i·ness
ju·jit·su
juke·box
ju·lep
ju·li·enne
jum·ble
jum·bo

jump·er
jump·i·ness
jump·ing jack
jump seat
junc·tion (joining)
junc·ture (crisis)
jun·gle
ju·nior
ju·ni·per
jun·ket
jun·kie
jun·ta
ju·rid·i·cal
juries
ju·ris·dic·tion
ju·ris·pru·dence
ju·rist
ju·ror
ju·ry
ju·ry·man
jus·tice
jus·ti·fi·able
jus·ti·fi·ca·tion
jus·ti·fied
jus·ti·fi·er
jus·ti·fy
ju·ve·nile
jux·ta·po·si·tion

kaf·fee·klatsch
kai·ser

ka·lei·do·scope
ka·mi·ka·ze
kan·ga·roo
Kan·sas
ka·olin
ka·pok
kar·a·kul
kar·at *or* car·at
  (weight; cf. *caret,*
  *carrot*)
ka·ra·te
kar·ma
ka·ty·did
kay·ak
keel·haul
keel·son
keen·ness
keep·sake
ken·nel
ker·nel (seed;
  cf. *colonel*)
Kear·ney Nebr.
Kear·ny N.J.
Ken·tucky
ker·o·sine
ket·tle·drum
key (to a door;
  cf. *quay*)
key·board
key·hole
Keynes·ian
key·note
key·punch
key·stone
key word
kha·ki

khe·dive
kick·back
kick off n.
kick·off v.
kid·nap
kid·napped
kid·nap·ping
kid·ney
kill (slay; cf. *kiln*)
kill·er
kill·ing
kill·joy
kiln (oven; cf. *kill*)
kilo·cy·cle
ki·lo·gram
ki·lo·hertz
ki·lo·me·ter
ki·lo·volt
kilo·watt
kilo·watt—hour
ki·mo·no
kin·der·gar·ten
kind·heart·ed
kind·li·ness
kin·dling
kind·ness
kin·dred
ki·net·ic
king·bird
king·bolt
king crab
king·dom
king·fish
king·li·ness
king·ly
king·mak·er

king·pin
king·ship
kins·folk
kin·ship
kins·man
ki·osk
kis·met
kitch·en
kitch·en·ette
kitch·en·ware
kit·ten
knap·sack
knave (rogue;
  cf. *nave*)
knav·ery
knead (dough;
  cf. *need*)
knee·cap
knee—deep
knee—high
knew (did know;
  cf. *gnu, new*)
knick·knack
knife
knight (title; cf. *night*)
knight·hood
knit
knit·ted
knit·ting
knives
knock·about
knock down v.
knock·down n., adj.
knock out v.
knock·out n.
knot (tied; cf. *not*)

knot·hole
knot·ted
knot·ting
knot·ty
know·able
know—how n.
knowl·edge
knowl·edge·able
knuck·le
knuck·le·bone
Ko·dak
Koh—i—noor
kohl·ra·bi
kow·tow
ku·dos
ku·lak
küm·mel
kum·quat

la·bel
la·beled
la·bel·ing
la·bi·al
la·bor
lab·o·ra·to·ry
   (science;
   cf. *lavatory*)
la·bor·er

la·bo·ri·ous
la·bor·sav·ing
la·bur·num
lab·y·rinth
lab·y·rin·thine
lac·er·ate
lac·er·a·tion
lach·ry·mal
lach·ry·mose
lack·a·dai·si·cal
la·con·ic
lac·quer
la·crosse
lac·ta·tion
la·cu·na
lad·der
lad·der—back
la·dy·bird
la·dy·bug
la·dy·fin·ger
la·dy·like
la·dy·ship
la·dy's   slip·per
lag·gard
lag·ging
la·goon
lain (rested; cf. *lane*)
la·ity
lam·ben·cy
lam·bent
lam·bre·quin
lamb·skin
lame
la·mé
la·ment
la·men·ta·ble

lam·en·ta·tion
lam·i·nate
lam·i·nat·ed
lamp·black
lam·poon
lam·prey
lan·cet
lan·dau
land·fall
land·grave
land·hold·er
land·ing   craft
land·ing   field
land·ing   gear
land·ing   strip
land·la·dy
land·locked
land·lord
land·lub·ber
land·mark
land·own·er
land—poor
land·scape
land·slide
land·slip
lands·man
land·ward
lane (path; cf. *lain*)
lan·guage
lan·guid
lan·guish
lan·guor·ous
lank·i·ness
lanky
lan·o·lin
lan·tern

lan·yard
lap·dog
la·pel
lap·i·dary
la·pis la·zu·li
lap·ping
lapse (terminate;
   cf. *elapse*)
lar·board
lar·ce·nous
lar·ce·ny
large—scale
lar·ghet·to
lar·i·at
lark·spur
lar·va sing.
lar·vae pl.
lar·yn·gi·tis
lar·ynx
las·civ·i·ous
la·ser
las·si·tude
latch·key
latch·string
late·ness
la·tent
lat·er (afterward;
   cf. *latter*)
lat·er·al
lat·ish
lat·i·tude
lat·ter (subsequent;
   cf. *later*)
lat·tice
lat·tice·work
laud·able

lau·da·num
lau·da·to·ry
laugh·able
laugh·ing·stock
laugh·ter
launch
laun·der
laun·dress
Laun·dro·mat
laun·dry
lau·re·ate
lau·rel
lav·a·to·ry
   (for washing;
   cf. *laboratory*)
lav·en·der
lav·ish
law—abid·ing
law·ful
law·giv·er
law·less
law·mak·er
law·mak·ing
law·suit
law·yer
lax·a·tive
lax·ity
lay·er
lay·man
lay off v.
lay·off n.
lay out v.
lay·out n.
lay over v.
lay·over n.
lay up v.

lay—up n.
la·zi·ly
la·zi·ness
la·zy
la·zy·bones
la·zy Su·san
la·zy tongs
lead (to guide)
lead (a metal; cf. *led*)
lead·en
lead·er
lead·er·ship
lead—in
lead off v.
lead off n., adj.
leads·man
lead time
lead up v.
lead—up n.
lead·work
leaf·let
leaf mold
league
leak·age
leak·proof
lean (thin; cf. *lien*)
lean—to
leap·frog
leap year
lease·back
lease·hold
leath·er
Leath·er·ette
leath·er·neck
leav·en
lec·tern

lec·ture
led (guided; cf. *lead*)
led·ger
lee·ward
lee·way
left—hand·ed
left·over
leg·a·cy
le·gal
le·gal·ism
le·gal·i·ty
le·gal·ize
le·gal·ly
leg·ate
leg·a·tee
le·ga·tion
le·ga·to
leg·end
leg·end·ary
leg·er·de·main
leg·ging
leg·horn
leg·i·bil·i·ty
leg·i·ble
le·gion
leg·is·late
leg·is·la·tion
leg·is·la·tive
leg·is·la·tor
leg·is·la·ture
le·git·i·ma·cy
le·git·i·mate
le·git·i·ma·tize
leg·man
le·gu·mi·nous
lei·sure

lei·sure·li·ness
lei·sure·ly
lem·ming
lem·on·ade
le·mur
length
length·en
length·i·ness
length·wise
lengthy
le·nien·cy
le·nient
Le·nin·ism
len·i·ty
len·tic·u·lar
len·til
leop·ard
le·o·tard
lep·ro·sy
lep·rous
le·sion
les·see
less·en (decrease;
    cf. *lesson*)
less·er
les·son (study;
    cf. *lessen*)
les·sor
le·thal
le·thar·gic
leth·ar·gy
lets (permits)
let's (let us)
let·ter car·ri·er
let·tered
let·ter·head

let·ter—per·fect
let·ter·press
let·tuce
let up v.
let·up n.
lev·ee (embankment;
    cf. *levy*)
lev·el
lev·eled
le·ver·age
le·vi·a·than
lev·i·ta·tion
lev·i·ty
levy (tax; cf. *levee*)
Lew·is·ton
    Idaho, Maine
Lew·is·town
    Mont., Pa.
lex·i·cog·ra·pher
li·a·bil·i·ty
li·a·ble (obligated;
    cf. *libel*)
li·ai·son
li·ar (tells untruths;
    cf. *lyre*)
li·ba·tion
li·bel (defamation;
    cf. *liable*)
li·bel·ant
li·bel·ee
li·bel·ing
li·bel·ous
lib·er·al
lib·er·al·i·ty
lib·er·al·ize
lib·er·al·ly

lib·er·ate
lib·er·a·tion
lib·er·a·tor
lib·er·tine
lib·er·ty
li·bid·i·nous
li·brar·i·an
li·brary
li·bret·tist
li·bret·to
li·cense
li·cen·tious
li·chen
lic·o·rice
lie (untruth; cf. *lye*)
lien (claim; cf. *lean*)
lieu·ten·an·cy
lieu·ten·ant
life belt
life·blood
life·boat
life buoy
life·guard
life·less
life·like
life·line
life·long
life net
life raft
life·sav·er
life·sav·ing
life·time
lig·a·ment
li·ga·tion
lig·a·ture
light·en

light·en·ing
(becoming
light; cf. *lightning*)
ligh·ter·age
light·fast
light—fin·gered
light—head·ed
light·heart·ed
light·house
light—mind·ed
light·ning
(electrical discharge;
cf. *lightening*)
light·proof
light·ship
light·some
light—struck
light·tight
light·weight
light—year
lig·ne·ous
lig·nite
lik·able
like·li·hood
like·ly
like—mind·ed
like·ness
like·wise
li·lac
lil·li·pu·tian
lily—liv·ered
lily—white
limb (branch;
cf. *limn*)
lim·ber
lim·bo

lime·ade
lime·kiln
lime·light
lim·er·ick
lime·stone
lime·wa·ter
lim·i·nal
lim·it
lim·i·ta·tion
lim·it·less
limn (draw; cf. *limb*)
lim·ou·sine
lim·pet
lim·pid
lin·age (number of
lines; cf. *lineage*)
linch·pin
lin·eage (family;
cf. *linage*)
lin·eal (ancestral
line; cf. *linear*)
lin·ea·ment
lin·ear (of lines;
cf. *lineal*)
line·cut
line·man
lin·en
line up v.
line·up n.
lin·ger
lin·ge·rie
lin·go
lin·guist
lin·i·ment
lin·ing
link·age

links (of chain; cf. *lynx*)
li·no·leum
Li·no·type
lin·seed
lin·tel
li·on·ess
li·on·heart·ed
li·po·ma
lip—read v.
lip—read·er n.
lip·read·ing n.
lip·stick
liq·ue·fac·tion
liq·ue·fi·able
liq·ue·fy
li·ques·cence
li·ques·cent
li·queur
liq·uid
liq·ui·date
liq·ui·da·tion
li·quor
lis·ten
list·less
li·ter
lit·er·a·cy
lit·er·al (exact; cf. *littoral*)
lit·er·al·ly
lit·er·ary
lit·er·ate
lit·er·a·tim
lit·er·a·ture
lith·ia
lith·i·um

litho·graph
li·tho·gra·pher
li·thog·ra·phy
lit·i·gant
lit·i·gate
lit·i·ga·tion
li·ti·gious
lit·mus
lit·ter
lit·tle
lit·tle·neck clam
lit·to·ral (shore; cf. *literal*)
li·tur·gi·cal
lit·ur·gy
liv·able
live·li·hood
live·long
liv·ery
liv·ery·man
liv·ing room
liz·ard
lla·ma
load (burden; cf. *lode*)
loan (borrow; cf. *lone*)
loath·some
lob·by·ing
lob·ster
lo·cal (nearby)
lo·cale (locality)
lo·cal·i·ty
lo·cal·ize
lo·cate
lo·ca·tion
lock·jaw
lock·nut

lock·out n.
lock·smith
lock·step
lock·stitch
lock·up n.
lo·co·mo·tion
lo·co·mo·tive
lo·co·mo·tor
lo·cust
lo·cu·tion
lode (ore; cf. *load*)
lode·stone
lodg·ing
lodg·ment
log·a·rithm
log·gia
log·ging
log·i·cal
lo·gi·cian
lo·gis·tics
logo·type
log·roll·ing
loll·ing
lol·li·pop
lone (solitary; cf. *loan*)
lone·li·ness
lone·some
long·boat
long·bow
lon·gev·i·ty
long·hand
long·head·ed
long·horn
lon·gi·tude
lon·gi·tu·di·nal
long·shore·man

long shot
long—suf·fer·ing
long suit
long—wind·ed
look·ing glass
look·out
loop·hole
loose (unattached;
    cf. *lose, loss*)
loose·ly
loose—joint·ed
loos·en
lop
lopped
lop·ping
lop·sid·ed
lo·qua·cious
lo·ran
lord·li·ness
lor·gnette
lose (misplace;
    cf. *loose, loss*)
loss (something lost;
    cf. *loose, lose*)
lo·tion
lot·tery
loud·mouthed
loud·speak·er
Lou·i·si·ana
lou·ver
lov·able
love·less
love·li·ness
love·lorn
love·ly
love·mak·ing

love seat
love·sick
low·born
low·boy
low·bred
low·brow
low—down adj.
low·down n.
low·er·case
low·er·class·man
low·land
low—lev·el adj.
low·li·ness
low—mind·ed
low—necked
low—pres·sure
low—spir·it·ed
low—ten·sion
lox
loy·al·ty
loz·enge
LSD
lu·bri·cant
lu·bri·cate
lu·bri·ca·tion
lu·cid
lu·cid·i·ty
luck·i·er
luck·i·est
luck·i·ly
lucky
lu·cra·tive
lu·cu·bra·tion
lu·di·crous
lug·gage
lu·gu·bri·ous

luke·warm
lul·la·by
lum·ba·go
lum·bar (nerve)
lum·ber (wood)
lum·ber·yard
lu·mi·nary
lu·mi·nous
lu·na·cy
lu·nar
lu·na·tic
lun·cheon
lun·cheon·ette
lunch·room
lu·nette
lurch
lu·rid
lus·cious
lus·ter
lus·ter·ware
lust·ful
lust·i·ly
lus·trous
lusty
Lu·ther·an
lux·u·ri·ant
    (abundant;
    cf. *luxurious*)
lux·u·ri·ate
lux·u·ri·ous (with
    luxury; cf. *luxuriant*)
lux·u·ry
ly·ce·um
lych—gate
lye (chemical; cf. *lie*)
ly·ing

lym·phat·ic
lynch
lynx (animal; cf. *links*)
ly·on·naise
lyre (harp; cf. *liar*)
lyr·ic
lyr·i·cal
lyr·i·cism

ma·ca·bre
mac·ad·am
mac·ad·am·ize
mac·a·ro·ni
mac·a·roon
ma·cé·doine
mac·er·ate
mac·er·a·tion
Ma·chi·a·vel·lian
ma·chic·o·la·tion
ma·chin·able
mach·i·na·tion
ma·chine gun n.
ma·chine—gun v.
ma·chine·like
ma·chine—made
ma·chin·ery
ma·chine—tooled
ma·chin·ist
ma·chree

mack·er·el
mack·in·tosh (rain-
    coat; cf. *McIntosh*)
mac·ro·cosm
mac·ro·eco·nom·
    ics
ma·cron
mad·cap
mad·den·ing
    (enraging)
made (did make;
    cf. *maid*)
made—up adj.
mad·house
mad·ness
mad·ri·gal
mael·strom
mag·a·zine
ma·gen·ta
mag·got
mag·ic
ma·gi·cian
mag·is·te·ri·al
mag·is·tra·cy
mag·is·trate
mag·is·tra·ture
Mag·na Char·ta
mag·na·nim·i·ty
mag·nan·i·mous
mag·nate (rich
    person; cf. *magnet*)
mag·ne·sia
mag·ne·sium
mag·net (attracts
    iron; cf. *magnate*)
mag·net·ic

mag·ne·tism
mag·ne·tite
mag·ne·tize
mag·ne·to
mag·ne·tos
mag·ni·fi·ca·tion
mag·nif·i·cence
mag·nif·i·cent
    (splendid;
    cf. *munificent*)
mag·nif·i·co
mag·ni·fi·er
mag·ni·fy
mag·nil·o·quent
mag·ni·tude
mag·no·lia
mag·num
mag·pie
ma·guey
Mag·yar
ma·ha·ra·ja
ma·hat·ma
ma·hog·a·ny
maid (girl; cf. *made*)
maid·en
maid·en·hair
maid·en·head
maid·en·li·ness
maid·en·ly
maid·ser·vant
mail (letters; cf. *male*)
mail·abil·i·ty
mail·able
mail·bag
mail·box
mail car·ri·er

mail clerk
mail·er
mail·man
mail or·der n.
mail—or·der adj.
main (chief; cf. *mane*)
Maine
main·land
main line n.
main·line v.
main·ly
main·mast
main·sail
main·spring
main·stay
main stem
main·stream
main·tain
main·te·nance
maize (corn;
cf. *maze*)
ma·jes·tic
maj·es·ty
ma·jol·i·ca
ma·jor
ma·jor·do·mo
ma·jor·i·ty
ma·jus·cule
make—be·lieve
make·shift
make up v.
make·up n.
make·weight
mak·ing
mal·a·chite
mal·ad·just·ment

mal·ad·min·is·ter
mal·ad·min·is·tra-
    tion
mal·adroit
mal·a·dy
mal·aise
mal·apert
mal·a·prop·ism
mal·ap·ro·pos
ma·lar·ia
ma·lar·i·al
Ma·lay
mal·con·tent
male (masculine;
    cf. *mail*)
male·dic·tion
male·fac·tion
male·fac·tor
ma·lef·ic
ma·lef·i·cence
ma·lef·i·cent
ma·lev·o·lence
ma·lev·o·lent
mal·fea·sance
mal·for·ma·tion
mal·formed
mal·ice
ma·li·cious (harmful)
ma·lign
ma·lig·nan·cy
ma·lig·nant
ma·lig·ni·ty
ma·lin·ger
ma·lin·ger·er
mal·lard
mal·lea·bil·i·ty

mal·lea·ble
mal·let
mal·nu·tri·tion
mal·odor
mal·odor·ous
mal·po·si·tion
mal·prac·tice
Mal·tese
Mal·thu·sian
malt·ose
mal·treat
malt·ster
mal·ver·sa·tion
mam·mal
mam·mon
mam·moth
man—about—
    town
man·a·cle
man·age
man·age·able
man·age·ment
man·ag·er
man·a·ge·ri·al
man·a·tee
Man·chu
man·ci·ple
man·da·mus
man·da·rin
man·da·tary (agent;
    cf. *mandatory*)
man·date
man·da·to·ry
    (compelling;
    cf. *mandatary*)
man·di·ble

man·do·lin
man·drel (metal)
man·drill (baboon)
mane (hair; cf. *main*)
man—eat·er
man—eat·ing
ma·nege
ma·neu·ver
man·ful
man·ga·nese
man·gel—wur·zel
man·ger
man·gi·ly
man·gle
man·go
man·grove
mangy
man·han·dle
man·hat·tan
man·hole
man·hood
man—hour
man·hunt
ma·nia
ma·ni·ac
ma·ni·a·cal
man·i·cure
man·i·cur·ist
man·i·fest
man·i·fes·ta·tion
man·i·fest·ly
man·i·fes·to
man·i·fold
man·i·kin
ma·nila
ma·nip·u·late

ma·nip·u·la·tion
ma·nip·u·la·tive
ma·nip·u·la·tor
ma·nip·u·la·to·ry
man·i·tou
man·kind
man·like
man·li·ness
man·ly
man—made
man·na
manned
man·ne·quin
man·ner (mode;
    cf. *manor*)
man·ner·ism
man·nish
man·ni·tol
man—of—war
ma·nom·e·ter
man·or (estate;
    cf. *manner*)
ma·no·ri·al
man pow·er
    (1/10 horsepower)
man·pow·er
    (personnel
    available)
man·rope
man·sard
man·ser·vant
man·sion
man·slaugh·ter
man·slay·er
man·sue·tude
man·teau

man·tel (shelf;
    cf. *mantle*)
man·tel·et
man·tel·piece
man·til·la
man·tle (cloak;
    cf. *mantel*)
man·trap
man·u·al
man·u·fac·ture
man·u·fac·tur·er
man·u·mis·sion
ma·nure
manu·script
many
many·fold
many—sid·ed
ma·ple
mapped
map·ping
mar·a·schi·no
mar·a·thon
ma·raud
mar·ble
mar·ble·ize
mar·bling
marc
mar·ca·site
mar·che·sa fem.
mar·che·se mas.
mar·chio·ness fem.
Mar·co·ni
mar·co·ni·gram
Mar·di Gras
mare's nest
mare's tail

mar·ga·rine
mar·ga·rita
mar·gin
mar·gin·al
mar·gi·na·lia
mar·grave
mari·gold
mar·i·jua·na
ma·rine
mar·i·ner
mar·i·o·nette
mar·i·tal
(marriage;
cf. *martial*)
mar·i·time
mark  down v.
mark·down n.
mar·ket
mar·ket·able
mar·ket·ing
mar·ket·place
marks·man
mark  up v.
mark·up n.
mar·line·spike
mar·ma·lade
mar·mo·set
mar·mot
ma·roon
mar·quee (canopy)
mar·que·try
mar·quis mas.
(nobleman)
mar·quise fem.
mar·riage

mar·riage·able
mar·row
mar·row·bone
mar·ry
Mar·seilles
mar·shal (officer;
cf. *martial*)
mar·shal·ed
mar·shal·ing
marsh  gas
marsh·i·ness
marsh·mal·low
marshy
mar·su·pi·al
mar·ten (furbearing
animal; cf. *martin*)
mar·tial (warlike;
cf. *marital, marshal*)
mar·tial·ly
mar·tian
mar·tin (bird;
cf. *marten*)
mar·ti·net
Mar·tin·mas
mar·tyr
mar·tyr·dom
mar·tyr·ol·o·gy
mar·vel
mar·veled
mar·vel·ing
mar·vel·ous
Marx·ian
Mary·land
mas·cot
mas·cu·line
mas·cu·lin·i·ty

mash·er
mash·ie
mask·er
ma·son
Ma·son·ic
ma·son·ry
mas·quer·ade
Mas·sa·chu·setts
mas·sa·cre
mas·sage
mas·seur mas.
mas·seuse fem.
mas·si·cot
mas·sif
mas·sive
massy
mas·ter
mas·ter—at—arms
mas·ter·ful
mas·ter  key
mas·ter·mind
mas·ter·piece
mas·ter  plan
mas·ter's  de·gree
mas·ter  ser·geant
mas·ter·ship
mas·ter·stroke
mas·ter·work
mas·tery
mast·head
mas·ti·cate
mas·ti·ca·tion
mas·tiff
mast·odon
mas·toid
mat·a·dor

match·board
match·book
match·less
match·lock
match·mak·er
match play
match·stick
match·wood
ma·te·ri·al (sub-
    stance; cf. *matériel*)
ma·te·ri·al·ism
ma·te·ri·al·ist
ma·te·ri·al·is·tic
ma·te·ri·al·i·ty
ma·te·ri·al·iza·tion
ma·te·ri·al·ize
ma·te·ri·al·ly
ma·te·ria med·i·ca
ma·té·ri·el
    (equipment;
    cf. *material*)
ma·ter·nal
ma·ter·ni·ty
math·e·mat·i·cal
math·e·ma·ti·cian
math·e·mat·ics
mat·i·nee
ma·tri·arch
ma·tri·ar·chate
ma·tri·ar·chy
ma·tri·cide
ma·tric·u·lant
ma·tric·u·late
ma·tric·u·la·tion
mat·ri·mo·nial
mat·ri·mo·ny

ma·trix
ma·tron
ma·tron·ize
ma·tron·ly
mat·ter
mat·ter—of—fact
mat·ting
mat·tock
mat·tress
mat·u·rate
mat·u·ra·tion
ma·ture
ma·ture·ly
ma·ture·ness
ma·tu·ri·ty
ma·tu·ti·nal
mat·zo
maud·lin
maul·stick
mau·so·le·um
mauve
mav·er·ick
mawk·ish
max·il·la
max·il·lary
max·im
max·i·mal
max·i·mize
max·i·mum
may·be
May Day (May 1)
May·day (a signal)
may·flow·er
may·hem
may·on·naise
may·or

may·or·al·ty
may·pole
maze (puzzle;
    cf. *maize*)
ma·zur·ka
mazy
Mc·In·tosh (apple;
    cf. *mackintosh*)
mead·ow
mead·ow·lark
mea·ger
meal·time
meal·worm
mealy·mouthed
mean (stingy;
    cf. *mien*)
me·an·der
mean·ing·less
mean·ly
mean·ness
mean·time
mean·while
mea·sles
mea·sly
mea·sur·able
mea·sure
mea·sured
mea·sure·less
mea·sure·ment
mea·sur·er
meat (food;
    cf. *meet, mete*)
me·atus
me·chan·ic
me·chan·i·cal
mech·a·ni·cian

me·chan·ics
mech·a·nism
mech·a·nist
med·al (award;
   cf. *meddle*)
med·al·ist
me·dal·lion
med·dle (interfere;
   cf. *medal*)
med·dle·some
me·dia (sing.:
   *medium*)
me·di·al
me·di·an
me·di·ate
me·di·a·tion
me·di·a·tive
me·di·a·tor
me·di·a·to·ry
med·i·ca·ble
med·ic·aid
med·i·cal
me·di·ca·ment
medi·care
med·i·cate
med·i·ca·tion
me·dic·i·na·ble
me·dic·i·nal
med·i·cine
med·i·cine   ball
med·i·cine   man
me·di·eval
me·di·eval·ism
me·di·eval·ist
me·di·o·cre
me·di·oc·ri·ty

med·i·tate
med·i·ta·tion
med·i·ta·tive
Med·i·ter·ra·nean
me·di·um(pl.: *media*)
me·di·um·is·tic
med·lar
med·ley
meer·schaum
meet (encounter;
   cf. *meat, mete*)
meet·ing
meet·ing·house
mega·cy·cle
meg·a·lo·ma·nia
mega·phone
Mei·ster·sing·er
mel·an·cho·lia
mel·an·chol·ic
mel·an·choly
Mel·a·ne·sian
mé·lange
mel·a·nin
mel·a·nism
me·lee
me·lio·rate
me·lio·ra·tion
me·lio·ra·tive
me·lio·ra·tor
me·lio·rism
mel·lif·lu·ous
mel·low
me·lo·de·on
me·lod·ic
me·lo·di·ous
mel·o·dist

mel·o·dize
melo·dra·ma
melo·dra·mat·ic
melo·dra·ma·tist
mel·o·dy
mel·on
melt·able
mem·ber
mem·ber·ship
mem·brane
mem·bra·nous
me·men·to
mem·oir
mem·o·ra·ble
mem·o·ran·dum
   (pl.: *memoranda*
   or *memorandums*)
me·mo·ri·al
me·mo·ri·al·ist
me·mo·ri·al·ize
mem·o·rize
mem·o·ry
men·ace
mé·nage
me·nag·er·ie
men·da·cious
men·dac·i·ty
Men·de·lian
men·di·can·cy
men·di·cant
me·nial
men·in·gi·tis
me·nis·cus
Men·no·nite
meno·pause
men·ses

men·stru·al
men·stru·ate
men·stru·a·tion
men·su·ra·ble
men·su·ral
men·su·ra·tion
men·tal
men·tal·i·ty
men·tal·ly
men·thol
men·tion
men·tion·er
men·tor
menu
Meph·is·toph·e·les
me·phi·tis
mer·can·tile
mer·can·til·ism
mer·ce·nary
mer·cer
mer·cer·ize
mer·chan·dise
mer·chant
mer·chant·able
mer·chant·man
mer·ci·ful
mer·ci·less
mer·cu·ri·al
mer·cu·ric
mer·cu·rous
mer·cu·ry
mer·cy
mere·ly
mer·e·tri·cious
mer·gan·ser
merge

mer·gence
merg·er
me·rid·i·an
me·rid·i·o·nal
me·ringue
me·ri·no
mer·it
mer·i·to·ri·ous
mer·lin
mer·maid
mer·ri·ly
mer·ri·ment
mer·ry
mer·ry—an·drew
mer·ry—go—round
mer·ry·mak·ing
me·sa
mesh·work
me·si·al
mes·mer·ic
mes·mer·ism
mes·mer·ize
me·son
mes·quite
mes·sage
mes·sen·ger
mes·si·ah
mes·si·an·ic
Messrs. (sing.: *Mr.*)
messy
me·tab·o·lism
meta·car·pal
meta·car·pus
met·al (iron;
   cf. *mettle*)
me·tal·lic

met·al·lif·er·ous
met·al·log·ra·phy
met·al·loid
met·al·lur·gi·cal
met·al·lur·gy
met·al·work
meta·mor·phic
meta·mor·phism
meta·mor·phose
meta·mor·pho·ses
   pl.
meta·mor·pho·sis
   sing.
met·a·phor
met·a·phor·i·cal
meta·phys·ic
meta·phy·si·cian
meta·phys·ics
me·tas·ta·sis
meta·tar·sal
meta·tar·sus
mete (measure;
   cf. *meat, meet*)
me·te·or
me·te·or·ic
me·te·or·ite
me·te·or·o·graph
me·te·or·oid
me·te·o·ro·log·i·cal
me·te·o·rol·o·gist
me·te·o·rol·o·gy
me·ter
meth·a·done
me·theg·lin
meth·od
me·thod·i·cal

meth·od·ist
meth·od·ize
meth·od·ol·o·gy
me·tic·u·los·i·ty
me·tic·u·lous
mé·tier
me·ton·y·my
met·ric
met·ri·cal
met·ri·ca·tion
met·ri·fi·ca·tion
me·trol·o·gy
met·ro·nome
me·trop·o·lis
met·ro·pol·i·tan
met·tle (spirit;
  cf. *metal*)
met·tle·some
mews (stables;
  cf. *muse*)
Mex·i·can
mez·za·nine
mez·zo—so·pra·no
mez·zo·tint
mi·as·ma
Mich·ael·mas
Mich·i·gan
mi·crobe
mi·cro·bi·al
mi·cro·bic
mi·cro·cosm
mi·cro·fiche
mi·cro·film
mi·cro·graph
mi·cro·groove
mi·crom·e·ter

mi·cron
mi·cro·or·gan·ism
mi·cro·phone
mi·cro·scope
mi·cro·scop·ic
mi·cro·scop·i·cal-
  ly
mi·cro·sec·ond
mi·cro·wave
mid·air
mid·brain
mid·day
mid·dle
mid·dle—aged
mid·dle·brow
mid·dle class n.
mid·dle—class adj.
mid·dle·man
mid·dle·weight
mid·dling
midg·et
mid·iron
mid·land
mid·most
mid·night
mid·riff
mid·ship·man
mid·sum·mer
mid·term
mid·way
mid·week
mid·west
mid·west·ern·er
mid·wife
mid·win·ter
mid·year

mien (bearing;
  cf. *mean*)
miff
might (strength;
  cf. *mite*)
might·i·ly
might·i·ness
mighty
mi·gnon·ette
mi·graine
mi·grate
mi·gra·tion
mi·gra·to·ry
mi·ka·do
mi·la·dy
milch
mil·dew
mild·ly
mile·age
mile·post
mile·stone
mil·i·tance
mil·i·tan·cy
mil·i·tant
mil·i·ta·rism
mil·i·ta·rist
mil·i·ta·ris·tic
mil·i·ta·rize
mil·i·tary
mil·i·tate
mi·li·tia
mi·li·tia·man
milk choc·o·late
milk·er
milk glass
milk·i·ness

milk leg
milk—liv·ered
milk·maid
milk·man
milk punch
milk shake
milk snake
milk·sop
milk sug·ar
milk toast n.
milk—toast adj.
milk tooth
milk·weed
milky
mill·board
mill·dam
mil·le·nar·i·an
mil·le·na·ry (1,000th anniversary; cf. *millinery*)
mil·len·ni·al
mil·len·ni·um
mill·er
mil·let
mil·li·am·pere
mil·li·gram
mil·li·me·ter
mil·li·ner
mil·li·nery (hats; cf. *millenary*)
mill·ing
mil·lion
mil·lion·aire
mil·lionth
mil·li·volt
mil·li·watt

mill·pond
mill·race
mill·stone
mill·stream
mill wheel
mill·wright
Mil·ton·ic
mim·eo·graph
mi·me·sis
mi·met·ic
mim·ic
mim·icked
mim·ick·ing
mim·ic·ry
mi·mo·sa
min·a·ret
mi·na·to·ry
mince·meat
mince pie
minc·er
minc·ing·ly
mind (brain; cf. *mined*)
mind·er
mind·ful
mind read·er
mined (dug out; cf. *mind*)
min·er (a mine worker; cf. *minor*)
min·er·al
min·er·al·ize
min·er·al·og·i·cal
min·er·al·o·gist
min·er·al·o·gy
Mi·ner·va

min·gle
min·gling
min·ia·ture
min·i·mal
min·i·mi·za·tion
min·i·mize
min·i·mum
min·ing
min·ion
mini·state
min·is·ter (clergyman; cf. *minster*)
min·is·te·ri·al
min·is·trant
min·is·tra·tion
min·is·try
min·i·um
min·i·ver
min·ne·sing·er
Min·ne·so·ta
min·now
mi·nor (underage; cf. *miner*)
mi·nor·i·ty
Mi·no·taur
min·ster (church; cf. *minister*)
min·strel·sy
mint·age
min·u·end
min·u·et
mi·nus
min·ute n. (60 seconds)
mi·nute adj. (small)

**133**

min·ute hand
mi·nute·ly (in detail)
min·ute·man
mi·o·sis (pl.: mi·o·ses)
mir·a·cle
mi·rac·u·lous
mi·rage
mir·ror
mirth·ful
mirth·less
mis·ad·ven·ture
mis·aligned
mis·al·li·ance
mis·an·thrope
mis·an·throp·ic
mis·an·thro·py
mis·ap·pli·ca·tion
mis·ap·pre·hen·sion
mis·ap·pro·pri·ate
mis·be·got·ten
mis·be·have
mis·be·lief
mis·cal·cu·late
mis·car·riage
mis·car·ry
mis·ce·ge·na·tion
mis·cel·la·nea
mis·cel·la·neous
mis·cel·la·ny
mis·chance
mis·chief
mis·chie·vous
mis·con·cep·tion
mis·con·duct
mis·con·struc·tion

mis·con·strue
mis·cre·ant
mis·cue
mis·deal
mis·de·mean·or
mis·di·rect
mi·ser
mis·er·a·ble
mi·se·re·re
mi·ser·li·ness
mi·ser·ly
mis·ery
mis·fea·sance
mis·file
mis·fire
mis·fit
mis·for·tune
mis·giv·ing
mis·gov·ern
mis·guide
mis·hap
mis·in·form
mis·in·ter·pret
mis·in·ter·pre·ta·tion
mis·join·der
mis·judge
mis·lay
mis·lead
mis·man·age
mis·no·mer
mi·sog·a·my
mi·sog·y·nist
mi·sol·o·gy
mis·place
mis·print

mis·pri·sion
mis·pro·nounce
mis·quo·ta·tion
mis·read
mis·reck·on
mis·rep·re·sent
mis·rep·re·sen·ta·tion
mis·rule
mis·sal (book;
    cf. *missile, missive*)
mis·sile (weapon;
    cf. *missal, missive*)
miss·ing
mis·sion
mis·sion·ary
Mis·sis·sip·pi
mis·sive (letter;
    cf. *missal, missive*)
Mis·sou·ri
mis·spell
mis·state
mis·tak·able
mis·take
mis·tak·en
mist·i·ness
mis·tle·toe
mis·took
mis·tral
mis·treat
mis·treat·ment
mis·tress
mis·tri·al
mis·trust
misty
mis·un·der·stand

134

mis·un·der·stand-
ing
mis·us·age
mis·use
mite (something
tiny; cf. *might*)
mi·ter
mit·i·ga·ble
mit·i·gate
mit·i·ga·tion
mit·i·ga·tive
mit·i·ga·tor
mi·tral
mit·ten
mit·ti·mus
mix·er
mix·ture
mix—up
miz·zen·mast
mne·mon·ic adj.
mne·mon·ics n.
Mo·ab·ite
moan (groan;
cf. *mown*)
moat (ditch; cf. *mote*)
mob·cap
mo·bile
mo·bil·i·ty
mo·bi·li·za·tion
mo·bi·lize
mob·oc·ra·cy
mob·ocrat·ic
moc·ca·sin
mo·cha
mock·er
mock·ery

mock·ing·bird
mock·ing·ly
mock—up
mod·al (of a mode;
cf. *model*)
mode (fashion;
cf. *mood*)
mod·el (pattern;
cf. *modal*)
mod·eled
mod·el·ing
mod·er·ate
mod·er·a·tion
mod·er·a·tor
mod·ern
mod·ern·ism
mod·ern·ist
mo·der·ni·ty
mod·ern·ize
mod·est
mod·es·ty
mod·i·cum
mod·i·fi·a·ble
mod·i·fi·ca·tion
mod·i·fi·er
mod·i·fy
mod·ish
mo·diste
mod·u·lar
mod·u·late
mod·u·la·tion
mod·u·la·tor
mod·ule
mod·u·lus
mo·dus vi·ven·di
mo·hair

Mo·ham·med·an
Mo·hawk
moi·ety
moist
moist·en
moist·en·er
mois·ture
mo·lar
mo·las·ses
mold
mold·able
mold·er
mold·i·ness
mold·ing
moldy
mo·lec·u·lar
mol·e·cule
mole·hill
mole·skin
mo·lest
mo·les·ta·tion
mol·li·fi·ca·tion
mol·li·fy
mol·lusk
mol·ly·cod·dle
mol·ten
mo·lyb·de·num
mo·ment
mo·men·tari·ly
mo·men·tary
mo·ment·ly
mo·men·tous
mo·men·tum
mon·arch
mon·ar·chism
mon·ar·chy

mon·as·te·ri·al
mon·as·tery
mo·nas·tic
mo·nas·ti·cism
mon·au·ral
Mon·day
mon·e·tary
mon·e·tize
mon·ey
mon·ey·bags
mon·eyed
mon·ey·lend·er
mon·ey—mak·er
mon·eys
mon·ger
Mon·gol
Mon·go·lian
mon·grel
mon·ies
mo·ni·tion
mon·i·tor
mon·i·tor·ship
mon·i·to·ry
mon·i·tress
monk·ery
mon·key
mon·keys
mon·key·shine
monk·ish
mono·chro·mat·ic
mono·chrome
mon·o·cle
mo·noc·ra·cy
mon·oc·u·lar
mon·o·dy
mo·nog·a·mist

mo·nog·a·mous
mo·nog·a·my
mono·gram
mono·graph
mono·lith
mono·lo·gist
mono·logue
mono·ma·nia
mono·me·tal·lic
mono·met·al·lism
Mo·non·ga·he·la
mono·plane
mo·nop·o·list
mo·nop·o·lis·tic
mo·nop·o·li·za·tion
mo·nop·o·lize
mo·nop·o·ly
mono·rail
mono·syl·lab·ic
mono·syl·la·ble
mono·tone
mo·not·o·nous
mo·not·o·ny
Mono·type
mon·ox·ide
mon·sei·gneur
mon·sieur
mon·si·gnor
mon·soon
mon·ster
mon·strance
mon·stros·i·ty
mon·strous
mon·tage
Mon·tana
month·ly

mon·u·ment
mon·u·men·tal
mood (feeling;
   cf. *mode*)
mood·i·ly
mood·i·ness
moody
moon·beam
moon—blind
moon·fish
moon·light
moon·light·er
moon·lit
moon·rise
moon·shine
moon·shin·er
moon·stone
moon·struck
moor·age
moor·ing
Moor·ish
moose (animal;
   cf. *mouse, mousse*)
mop·board
mop·ping
mop up v.
mop—up n.
mo·raine
mor·al (ethical)
mo·rale (attitude)
mor·al·ism
mor·al·ist
mo·ral·i·ty (virtue;
   cf. *mortality*)
mor·al·iza·tion
mor·al·ize

mo·rass
mor·a·to·ri·um
Mo·ra·vi·an
mor·bid
mor·bid·i·ty
mor·dant (dyeing term)
mor·dent (musical term)
more·over
mo·res
mor·ga·nat·ic
Mor·gan·ton N.C.
Mor·gan·town W.Va.
mor·i·bund
Mor·mon
morn·ing (forenoon; cf. *mourning*)
morn·ing glo·ry
Mo·roc·co (country)
mo·roc·co (leather)
mo·ron
mo·rose
mo·rose·ness
Mor·pheus
mor·phine
mor·ris chair
mor·row
mor·sel
mor·tal
mor·tal·i·ty (death rate; cf. *morality*)
mor·tar
mor·tar·board
mort·gage

mort·gag·ee
mort·gag·or
mor·ti·fi·ca·tion
mor·ti·fy
mor·tise
mor·tu·ary
mo·sa·ic
Mo·ses
mo·sey
Mos·lem
mos·qui·to
moss·back
moss—grown
most·ly
mote (speak; cf. *moat*)
mo·tel
moth·ball
moth—eat·en
moth·er
moth·er·hood
moth·er—in—law
moth·er·land
moth·er·less
moth·er·li·ness
moth·er·ly
moth·er—of—pearl
moth·proof
mo·tif
mo·tion
mo·tion·less
mo·ti·vate
mo·tive
mot·ley
mo·tor

mo·tor·boat
mo·tor bus
mo·tor·cade
mo·tor·car
mo·tor·cy·cle
mo·tor·drome
mo·tor·ist
mo·tor·ize
mo·tor·man
mo·tor·truck
mot·tle
mot·to
mount·able
moun·tain
moun·tain·eer
moun·tain·ous
moun·tain·side
moun·te·bank
Mount·ie
mount·ing
mourn·ful
mourn·ing (griev·ing; cf. *morning*)
mouse (animal; cf. *moose, mousse*)
mouse—ear
mous·er
mouse·trap
mousse (food; cf. *moose, mouse*)
mous·tache
mouth·ful
mouth·piece
mov·abil·i·ty
mov·able
mov·able·ness

move·ment
mov·ie
mov·ies
mov·ing
mow·er
mown (cut down;
   cf. *moan*)
moz·zet·ta
Mr. (pl.: *Messrs.*)
Mrs. (pl.: *Mesdames*)
Ms. (pl.: *Mses.* or *Mss.*)
mu·ci·lage
mu·ci·lag·i·nous
muck·rake n., v.
mu·cous adj.
mu·cus n.
mud·di·ly
mud·di·ness
mud·dle
mud·dy
mud·guard
mud·sling·er
mu·ez·zin
muf·fin
muf·fle
muf·fler
muf·ti
mugged
mug·ger
mug·ging
mug·gi·ness
mug·wump
mu·lat·to
mul·ber·ry
mulct
mu·le·teer

mul·ish
mull·er
mul·lion
mul·ti·far·i·ous
mul·ti·form
Mul·ti·graph
mul·ti·lat·er·al
Mul·ti·lith
mul·ti·me·dia
mul·ti·mil·lion·aire
mul·ti·ped
mul·ti·plex
mul·ti·pli·able
mul·ti·pli·cand
mul·ti·pli·ca·tion
mul·ti·pli·ca·tive
mul·ti·plic·i·ty
mul·ti·pli·er
mul·ti·ply
mul·ti·ra·cial
mul·ti·tude
mul·ti·tu·di·nous
mum·bo jum·bo
mum·mery
mum·mi·fy
mum·my
mun·dane
mu·nic·i·pal
mu·nic·i·pal·i·ty
mu·nic·i·pal·ize
mu·nif·i·cence
mu·nif·i·cent
   (generous;
   cf. *magnificent*)
mu·ni·ment
mu·ni·tion

mu·ral
mur·der
mur·der·er
mur·der·ous
murk·i·ly
murk·i·ness
murky
mur·mur
mur·mur·ing
mur·mur·ous
mus·ca·dine
mus·ca·tel
mus·cle (of body;
   cf. *mussel, muzzle*)
mus·cle—bound
mus·cu·lar
mus·cu·la·ture
muse (meditate;
   cf. *mews*)
mu·se·um
mush·room
mushy
mu·sic
mu·si·cal
mu·si·cale
mu·si·cian
mu·si·col·o·gist
mus·ing
musk deer
mus·ket
mus·ke·teer
mus·ket·ry
musk·mel·on
musk—ox
musk·rat
musky

Mus·lim (religion)
mus·lin (cloth)
mus·sel (shellfish;
   cf. *muscle, muzzle*)
mus·tang
mus·tard (plant;
   cf. *mustered*)
mus·ter
mus·tered (assem-
   bled; cf. *mustard*)
must·i·ness
musty
mu·ta·bil·i·ty
mu·ta·ble
mu·tant
mu·tate
mu·ta·tion
mu·ta·tive
mute·ness
mu·ti·late
mu·ti·la·tion
mu·ti·neer
mu·ti·nous
mu·ti·ny
mut·ism
mut·ter
mut·ton
mut·ton·chops n.
mu·tu·al
mu·tu·al·i·ty
mu·tu·al·ly
muz·zle (mouth;
   cf. *muscle, mussel*)
my·al·gia
my·col·o·gy
my·o·pia

my·o·pic
myr·i·ad
myr·mi·don
myrrh
my·self
mys·te·ri·ous
mys·tery
mys·tic
mys·ti·cal
mys·ti·cism
mys·ti·fi·ca·tion
mys·ti·fy
mys·tique
myth·i·cal
myth·o·log·i·cal
my·thol·o·gy

na·cre
na·cre·ous
na·dir
nain·sook
na·ïve
na·ïve·té
na·ked
nam·by—pam·by
name·able
name·less
name·ly
name·plate

name·sake
nan·keen
nano·sec·ond
na·palm
na·pery
naph·tha
nap·kin
Na·po·le·on·ic
nap·per
nap·ping
nar·cis·sism
nar·cis·sus
nar·co·sis
nar·cot·ic
nar·co·tize
nar·rate
nar·ra·tion
nar·ra·tive
nar·ra·tor
nar·row
nar·row·ly
nar·row—mind·ed
nar·row·ness
na·sal
na·sal·i·ty
na·sal·ize
na·sal·ly
na·scent
nas·ti·ly
nas·ti·ness
nas·tur·tium
nas·ty
na·tal
na·tant
na·ta·tion
na·ta·to·ri·al

na·ta·to·ri·um
na·ta·to·ry
na·tion
na·tion·al
na·tion·al·ism
na·tion·al·i·ty
na·tion·al·ize
na·tion·al·iz·er
na·tion·al·ly
na·tion·wide
na·tive
na·tive·ly
na·tive·ness
na·tiv·ism
na·tiv·i·ty
nat·ty
nat·u·ral
nat·u·ral·ism
nat·u·ral·ist
nat·u·ral·is·tic
nat·u·ral·iza·tion
nat·u·ral·ize
nat·u·ral·ly
nat·u·ral·ness
na·ture
naugh·ti·ly
naugh·ti·ness
naugh·ty
nau·sea
nau·se·ate
nau·seous
nau·ti·cal
nau·ti·lus
na·val (of navy)
nave (of church;
    cf. *knave*)

na·vel (of abdomen)
nav·i·ga·ble
nav·i·gate
nav·i·ga·tion
nav·i·ga·tor
na·vy
na·vy yard
nay (no;
    cf. *née, neigh*)
Naz·a·rene
Ne·an·der·thal
Ne·a·pol·i·tan
near·ly
near·ness
near·sight·ed
neat·ly
neat·ness
Ne·bras·ka
neb·u·la sing.
neb·u·lar
neb·u·las pl.
neb·u·lize
neb·u·los·i·ty
neb·u·lous
nec·es·sar·i·ly
nec·es·sary
ne·ces·si·tate
ne·ces·si·tous
ne·ces·si·ty
neck·er·chief
neck·ing
neck·lace
neck·line
neck·piece
neck·tie
neck·wear

nec·ro·log·i·cal
ne·crol·o·gist
ne·crol·o·gy
nec·ro·man·cy
ne·crop·o·lis
ne·cro·sis
nec·tar
nec·tar·ine
née (born;
    cf. *nay, neigh*)
need (require;
    cf. *knead*)
need·ful
need·i·est
need·i·ness
nee·dle
nee·dle·fish
nee·dle·point
need·less
nee·dle·wom·an
nee·dle·work
needy
ne'er—do—well
ne·far·i·ous
ne·ga·tion
neg·a·tive
ne·glect
ne·glect·ful
neg·li·gee
neg·li·gence
neg·li·gent
neg·li·gi·ble
ne·go·tia·bil·i·ty
ne·go·tia·ble
ne·go·ti·ate
ne·go·ti·a·tion

ne·go·ti·a·tor
Ne·gro
Ne·groes
neigh (of horse;
   cf. *nay, née*)
neigh·bor
neigh·bor·hood
neigh·bor·ing
neigh·bor·ly
nei·ther
nem·a·tode
nem·e·sis
neo·lith·ic
ne·ol·o·gism
ne·ol·o·gist
ne·ol·o·gy
neo·phyte
neo·plasm
ne·o·ter·ic
ne·pen·the
neph·ew
ne·phri·tis
nep·o·tism
Nep·tune
Ne·ro·ni·an
nerve
nerve·less
ner·vous
nervy
ne·science
ne·scient
nest egg
nes·tle
nes·tling v.
nest·ling n.
neth·er·most

net·ting
net·tle
net·work
neu·ral
neu·ral·gia
neur·as·the·nia
neu·ri·tis
neu·rol·o·gist
neu·rol·o·gy
neu·ron
neu·ro·sis
neu·rot·ic
neu·ter
neu·tral
neu·tral·i·ty
neu·tral·iza·tion
neu·tral·ize
neu·tral·ly
Ne·va·da
nev·er
nev·er·the·less
new (recent;
   cf. *gnu, knew*)
New·ark N.J., N.Y.,
   Ohio
new·born
new·com·er
new·el
new·fan·gled
new—fash·ioned
New·found·land
New Hamp·shire
New Jer·sey
new·ly
new·mar·ket
New Mex·i·co

new·ness
news·boy
news·break
news·cast
news·cast·er
news·hound
news·let·ter
news·man
news·mon·ger
news·pa·per
news·pa·per·man
news·print
news·reel
news re·lease
news·stand
news·wor·thy
newsy
New Year
New York
nib·ble
nice·ly
Ni·cene
nice·ness
nice·ty
niche
nick
nick·el
nick·el·if·er·ous
nick·el·ode·on
nick·er
nick·name
nic·o·tine
niece
nig·gard
nig·gard·ly
nig·gling

night (darkness;
   cf. *knight*)
night·cap
night·clothes
night·club
night·dress
night·fall
night·gown
night·hawk
night·in·gale
night  key
night  latch
night  let·ter
night·long
night·ly
night·mare
night  owl
night  rid·er
night—robe
night·shade
night  shift
night·shirt
night·stick
night  ta·ble
night·time
night·walk·er
ni·gres·cent
ni·gri·tude
ni·hil·ism
ni·hil·ist
ni·hil·is·tic
Ni·ke
nim·ble
nim·bus
Nim·rod
nin·com·poop

nine·pin
nine·teen
nine·teenth
nine·ti·eth
nine·ty
nin·ny
ninth
nip·per
nip·ping
nip·ple
Nip·pon·ese
nir·va·na
ni·sei
ni·trate
ni·tric
ni·tride
ni·tri·fi·ca·tion
ni·tri·fy
ni·trite
ni·tro·gen
ni·trog·e·nous
ni·tro·glyc·er·in
ni·trous
ni·zam
No·ah
no·bil·i·ty
no·ble·man
no·ble·wom·an
no·bly
no·body
noct·am·bu·list
noc·tur·nal
noc·turne
nod·ded
nod·ding
nod·u·lar

nod·ule
noise·less
nois·i·ly
noi·some
noisy
no·mad
no·mad·ic
no·mad·ism
nom de guerre
nom de plume
no·men·cla·ture
nom·i·nal
nom·i·nal·ly
nom·i·nate
nom·i·na·tion
nom·i·na·tive
nom·i·na·tor
nom·i·nee
non·bio·de·grad-
  able
non·cha·lance
non·cha·lant
non·com·ba·tant
non·com·mis-
  sioned
non·com·mit·tal
non com·pos
  men·tis
non·con·duc·tor
non·con·form·ist
non·con·for·mi·ty
non·co·op·er·a·tion
non·de·script
non·en·ti·ty
non·ex·is·tent
non·fea·sance

non·in·ter·ven·tion
non·join·der
non·me·tal·lic
non·pa·reil
non·par·ti·san
non·prof·it
non·re·sis·tance
non·re·sis·tant
non·re·stric·tive
non·sched·uled
non·sense
non·sen·si·cal
non se·qui·tur
non·sked
non·skid
non·stop
non·suit
non·sup·port
non·union
non·vi·o·lence
non·vi·o·lent
noo·dle
noon·day
noon·tide
noon·time
nor·mal
nor·mal·i·ty
nor·mal·iza·tion
nor·mal·ize
nor·mal·ly
Norse·man
North Car·o·li·na
North Da·ko·ta
north·east
north·east·er·ly
north·east·ern

north·east·ward
north·er·ly
north·ern
North·ern·er
north·land
north·ward
north·west
north·west·er·ly
north·west·ern
Nor·we·gian
nose·bleed
nose cone
nose dive n.
nose—dive v.
nose drops
nose·gay
nose·piece
nose ring
nose·wheel
no—show
no·sog·ra·phy
no·sol·o·gy
nos·tal·gia
nos·tril
nos·trum
not (negative; cf. *knot*)
no·ta·bil·i·ty
no·ta·ble
no·ta·ble·ness
no·ta·bly
no·tar·i·al
no·ta·ri·za·tion
no·ta·rize
no·ta·ry
no·ta·tion
note·book

not·ed
note·less
note·pa·per
note·tak·er n.
note—tak·ing n.
note·wor·thi·ness
note·wor·thy
noth·ing
noth·ing·ness
no·tice
no·tice·able
no·ti·fi·ca·tion
no·ti·fy
no·tion
no·to·ri·ety
no·to·ri·ous
not·with·stand·ing
nour·ish
nour·ish·ment
no·va·tion
nov·el
nov·el·ette
nov·el·is·tic
nov·el·ist
nov·el·ize
no·vel·la
nov·el·ty
No·vem·ber
no·ve·na
nov·ice
no·vi·tiate
No·vo·cain
now·a·days
no·way
no·ways
no·where

no·wise
nox·ious
noz·zle
nu·ance
nu·cle·ar
nu·cle·ate
nu·cle·ation
nu·cle·us
nu·di·ty
nu·ga·to·ry
nug·get
nui·sance
nul·li·fi·ca·tion
nul·li·fi·er
nul·li·fy
num·ber
num·ber·less
numb·ness
nu·mer·al
nu·mer·ate
nu·mer·a·tion
nu·mer·a·tor
nu·mer·i·cal
nu·mer·ol·o·gy
nu·mer·ous
nu·mis·mat·ic
nu·mis·ma·tist
num·skull
nun·cu·pa·tive
nun·nery
nup·tial
nurse·maid
nurs·ery
nurs·ery·man
nurs·ling
nur·ture

nut·crack·er
nut·meg
nut·pick
nu·tria
nu·tri·ent
nu·tri·ment
nu·tri·tion
nu·tri·tion·al
nu·tri·tion·ist
nu·tri·tious
nu·tri·tious·ly
nu·tri·tious·ness
nu·tri·tive
nut·shell
nut·ti·ness
nut·ty
nuz·zle
nuz·zling
ny·lon
nymph

oa·kum
oar (of a boat;
    cf. *or, ore*)
oar·lock
oars·man
oa·ses pl.
oa·sis sing.
oat·cake

oat·meal
ob·bli·ga·to
ob·du·ra·cy
ob·du·rate
obe·di·ence
obe·di·ent
obei·sance
obe·lisk
obese
obe·si·ty
obey
ob·fus·cate
ob·fus·ca·tion
obi·ter dic·tum
obit·u·ary
ob·ject
ob·jec·tion
ob·jec·tion·able
ob·jec·tive
ob·jec·tive·ly
ob·jec·tive·ness
ob·jec·tiv·i·ty
ob·jet d'art
ob·jur·ga·tion
ob·la·tion
ob·li·gate
ob·li·ga·tion
oblig·a·to·ry
oblige
oblig·ing
oblique
obliq·ui·ty
oblit·er·ate
oblit·er·a·tion
obliv·i·on
obliv·i·ous

ob·long
ob·lo·quy
ob·nox·ious
oboe
obo·ist
ob·scene
ob·scen·i·ty
ob·scur·ant
ob·scu·ra·tion
ob·scure
ob·scure·ness
ob·scu·ri·ty
ob·se·quies
ob·se·qui·ous
ob·se·quy
ob·serv·able
ob·ser·vance
ob·ser·vant
ob·ser·va·tion
ob·ser·va·tion·al
ob·ser·va·to·ry
ob·serve
ob·serv·er
ob·sess
ob·ses·sion
ob·ses·sive
ob·so·lesce
ob·so·les·cence
ob·so·lete
ob·sta·cle
ob·stet·ri·cal
ob·ste·tri·cian
ob·stet·rics
ob·sti·na·cy
ob·sti·nate
ob·strep·er·ous

ob·struct
ob·struc·tion
ob·struc·tion·ist
ob·struc·tive
ob·tain
ob·tain·able
ob·trud·er
ob·tru·sion
ob·tru·sive
ob·tu·rate
ob·tuse
ob·verse
ob·vi·ate
ob·vi·ous
oc·a·ri·na
oc·ca·sion
oc·ca·sion·al
oc·ca·sion·al·ly
Oc·ci·dent
oc·ci·den·tal
Oc·ci·den·tal·ism
Oc·ci·den·tal·ize
oc·cip·i·tal
oc·ci·put
oc·clude
oc·clu·sion
oc·cult
oc·cul·ta·tion
oc·cult·ism
oc·cult·ist
oc·cu·pan·cy
oc·cu·pant
oc·cu·pa·tion·al
oc·cu·py
oc·cur
oc·curred

oc·cur·rence
oc·cur·ring
ocean·go·ing
oce·an·ic
ocean·og·ra·pher
o'clock
oc·ta·gon
oc·tag·o·nal
oc·tan·gu·lar
oc·tave
oc·ta·vo
Oc·to·ber
oc·to·ge·nar·i·an
oc·to·pus
oc·u·lar
oc·u·list
odd·i·ty
odd·ly
odd·ness
ode (poem; cf. *owed*)
odi·ous
odi·um
odor
odor·if·er·ous
odor·less
odor·ous
Odys·seus
od·ys·sey
of·fal
off—bal·ance
   adj., adv.
off·beat
off·cast
off—cen·ter
off—col·or
of·fend

of·fend·er
of·fense
of·fen·sive
of·fer
of·fer·ing
of·fer·to·ry
off·hand
of·fice
of·fice·hold·er
of·fi·cer
of·fi·cial (authorized;
   cf. *officious*)
of·fi·cial·ism
of·fi·cial·ly
of·fi·ci·ary
of·fi·ci·ate
of·fi·ci·a·tion
of·fi·ci·nal·ly
of·fi·cious (meddle-
   some; cf. *official*)
off·ing
off·ish
off—key
off·print
off·scour·ing
off—sea·son
off·set
off·shoot
off·shore
off·side
off·spring
off·stage
off—white
off year
of·ten
of·ten·times

oft·times
Ohio
ohm
ohm·me·ter
oil cake
oil·cloth
oil·er
oil field
oil·i·ness
oil pan
oil·skin
oil slick
oil·stone
oil well
oily
oint·ment
Okla·ho·ma
old age n.
old—age adj.
old·en
old—fash·ioned
old·ish
old—line
Old Nick
old·ster
old—time adj.
old—tim·er n.
old—world adj.
oleo·graph
oleo·mar·ga·rine
ol·fac·tion
ol·fac·to·ry
oli·garch
oli·gar·chy
ol·ive
olym·pi·ad

Olym·pi·an
Olym·pic
Olym·pus
om·elet
om·i·nous
omis·si·ble
omis·sion
omit
omit·ted
omit·ting
om·ni·bus
om·ni·di·rec·tion-
  al
om·nip·o·tence
om·nip·o·tent
om·ni·pres·ent
om·ni·science
om·ni·scient
om·niv·o·rous
once—over n.
one (single thing;
   cf. *won*)
one—horse adj.
one·ness
oner·ous
one·self
one—sid·ed
one—step n.
one·time
one—track adj.
one—up·man·ship
one—way adj.
on·ion
on·ion·skin
on·look·er
on·ly

on·rush
on·set
on·slaught
on·to
on·tog·e·ny
on·to·log·i·cal
on·tol·o·gy
onus
on·ward
on·yx
oozy
opac·i·ty
opal·es·cent
opaque
open
open air n.
open—air adj.
open—and—shut
open—end adj.
open·er
open—eyed
open·hand·ed
open·heart·ed
open—hearth
open house
open·ing
open market n.
open—mar·ket adj.
open—mind·ed
open—mouthed
open·ness
open·work
op·era
op·er·a·ble
op·er·ate
op·er·at·ic

op·er·a·tion·al
op·er·a·tive
op·er·a·tor
op·er·et·ta
op·er·ose
Ophe·lia
oph·thal·mol·o·gy
oph·thal·mo·scope
opi·ate
opine
opin·ion
opin·ion·at·ed
opi·um
op·po·nent
op·por·tune
op·por·tun·ism
op·por·tun·ist
op·por·tu·ni·ty
op·pos·able
op·pose
op·po·site
op·po·si·tion
op·press
op·pres·sion
op·pres·sive
op·pres·sor
op·pro·bri·ous
op·pro·bri·um
op·ta·tive
op·ti·cal
op·ti·cian
op·tics
op·ti·mism
op·ti·mist
op·ti·mis·tic
op·ti·mum

op·tion
op·tion·al
op·tom·e·trist
op·tom·e·try
op·u·lence
op·u·lent
or (conjunction;
   cf. *oar, ore*)
or·a·cle
orac·u·lar
oral (spoken;
   cf. *aural*)
or·ange
or·ange·ade
or·ange·wood
ora·tion
or·a·tor
or·a·tor·i·cal
or·a·to·rio
or·a·to·ry
or·bic·u·lar
or·bit
or·chard
or·ches·tra
or·ches·tral
or·ches·trate
or·ches·tra·tion
or·chid
or·dain
or·deal
or·der
or·der·li·ness
or·der·ly
or·di·nal
or·di·nance (law;
   cf. *ordnance*)

or·di·nari·ly
or·di·nary
or·di·nate
or·di·na·tion
ord·nance
   (munitions;
   cf. *ordinance*)
ore (mineral;
   cf. *oar, or*)
Or·e·gon
or·gan
or·gan·ic
or·gan·ism
or·gan·ist
or·gan·iz·able
or·ga·ni·za·tion
or·ga·nize
or·gy
ori·ent
ori·en·tal
ori·en·tal·ism
ori·en·tal·ize
ori·en·tate
ori·en·ta·tion
or·i·fice
ori·ga·mi
or·i·gin
orig·i·nal
orig·i·nal·i·ty
orig·i·nal·ly
orig·i·nate
orig·i·na·tion
orig·i·na·tive
orig·i·na·tor
ori·ole
Ori·on

or·i·son
or·na·ment
or·na·men·tal
or·na·men·ta·tion
or·nate
or·ni·thol·o·gy
oro·tund
or·phan
or·phan·age
Or·pheus
or·tho·dox
or·tho·graph·ic
or·thog·ra·phy
or·tho·pe·dic
os·cil·late (back and
   forth; cf. *osculate*)
os·cil·la·tion
os·cil·la·tor
os·cu·late (kiss;
   cf. *oscillate*)
os·cu·la·tion
os·cu·la·to·ry
Osi·ris
os·mi·um
os·mo·sis
os·prey
os·si·fi·ca·tion
os·si·fy
os·su·ary
os·ten·si·ble
os·ten·sive
os·ten·sive·ly
os·ten·ta·tion
os·ten·ta·tious
os·teo·path
os·teo·path·ic

os·te·op·a·thy
os·tra·cism
os·tra·cize
os·trich
oth·er
oth·er·wise
Ot·ta·wa
ot·to·man
ought (should;
   cf. *aught*)
our (possessive;
   cf. *hour*)
our·self
our·selves
oust·er
out—and—out
out·bal·ance
out·bid
out·board
out·bound
out·build·ing
out·burst
out·cast
out·class
out·come
out·crop
out·cry
out·curve
out·dat·ed
out·dis·tance
out·do
out·door adj.
out·doors
out·er
out·er—di·rect·ed
out·er·most

out·face
out·field
out·fit
out·fit·ter
out·flank
out·fox
out·gen·er·al
out·go
out·go·ing
out·grow
out·growth
out·guess
out·house
out·ing
out·land·er
out·land·ish
out·last
out·law
out·law·ry
out·lay
out·let
out·line
out·live
out·look
out·ly·ing
out·ma·neu·ver
out·match
out·mod·ed
out·num·ber
out—of—door
out—of—the—way
out·pa·tient
out·play
out·point
out·post

out·pour·ing
out·put
out·rage
out·ra·geous
out·reach
out·rid·er
out·rig·ger
out·right
out·run
out·sell
out·set
out·side
out·sid·er
out·sit
out·skirt
out·smart
out·soar
out·speak
out·spo·ken
out·spread
out·stand·ing
out·stay
out·stretch
out·ward
out·ward·ly
out·wear
out·weigh
out·wit
out·work
oval
oval·ly
ova·ry
ova·tion
ov·en
over
over·abun·dance

over·all
over·arm
over·awe
over·bal·ance
over·bear·ing·ly
over·board
over·build
over·bur·den
over·cap·i·tal·iza·tion
over·cast
over·charge
over·coat
over·come
over·do (too much; cf. *overdue*)
over·draft
over·draw
over·drawn
over·due (past due; cf. *overdo*)
over·em·pha·sis
over·flow
over·grow
over·hand
over·hang
over·haul
over·head
over·hear
over·land
over·look
over·lord
over·ly
over·night
over·pass
over·pow·er

over·pro·duc·tion
over·rat·ed
over·reach
over·ride
over·rule
over·run
over·seas
over·shad·ow
over·shoe
over·sight
over·size
over·sized
over·sleep
over·spread
over·stay
over·step
over·sub·scribe
over·sup·ply
overt
over·take
over—the—count-
   er
over·throw
over·time
overt·ly
over·tone
over·ture
over·turn
over·weigh
over·weight
over·whelm·ing·ly
over·work
owed (did owe;
   cf. *ode*)
owl·et
owl·ish

own·er·ship
ox·al·ic ac·id
ox·bow
ox·eye
ox·ford
ox·heart
ox·i·da·tion
ox·ide
ox·i·dize
ox·tail
ox·tongue
ox·y·gen
ox·y·gen·ate
oys·ter
oys·ter bed
oys·ter·man
ozone

pace·mak·er
pac·er
pachy·derm
pach·ys·an·dra
pa·cif·ic
pac·i·fi·ca·tion
pa·cif·i·ca·tor
pa·cif·i·ca·to·ry
pa·cif·i·cist
pac·i·fi·er

pac·i·fism
pac·i·fy
pack·age
pack·er
pack·et
pack·horse
pack·ing
pack·ing·house
pack·man
pack rat
pack·sack
pack·sad·dle
pack·thread
pad·ding
pad·dle
pad·dler
pad·dock
pad·lock
pa·dre
pa·gan
pa·gan·ism
pa·gan·ize
pag·eant
pag·eant·ry
pag·i·na·tion
pa·go·da
paid
pail (bucket; cf. *pale*)
pain (hurt; cf. *pane*)
pain·ful
pain·less
pains·tak·ing
paint box
paint·brush
paint·er
paint·ing

paint·pot
pair (two;
   cf. *pare, pear*)
pa·ja·mas
pal·ace
pa·lan·quin
pal·at·able
pal·a·tal
pal·a·tal·iza·tion
pal·a·tal·ize
pal·ate (roof of the
   mouth;
   cf. *palette, pallet*)
pa·la·tial
pal·a·tine
pa·la·ver
pale (white; cf. *pail*)
pale·face
pal·ette (for paint;
   cf. *palate, pallet*)
pal·frey
pal·ing
pal·i·sade
Pal·la·di·an
pal·la·di·um
pall·bear·er
pal·let (couch;
   cf. *palate, palette*)
pal·li·ate
pal·li·a·tion
pal·lia·tive
pal·lid
pal·lor
pal·met·to
palm·ist·ry
pal·o·mi·no

pal·pa·ble
pal·pate (examine
   by touch)
pal·pi·tate (throb)
pal·pi·ta·tion
pal·sied
pal·sy
pal·try (trivial;
   cf. *poultry*)
pam·per
pam·phlet
pam·phle·teer
pan·a·cea
Pan—Amer·i·can
pan·a·tela
pan·cake
pan·chro·mat·ic
pan·cre·as
pan·cre·atin
pan·dem·ic
pan·de·mo·ni·um
pan·dow·dy
pane (of glass;
   cf. *pain*)
pan·e·gyr·ic
pan·e·gyr·i·cal
pan·e·gy·rist
pan·el
pan·eled
pan·el·ing
pan·el·ist
pan·han·dle
pan·ic
pan·icked
pan·ic—strick·en
pan·ni·kin

pan·o·ply
pan·ora·ma
pan·oram·ic
pan·sy
pan·ta·loon
pan·the·ism
pan·the·ist
pan·the·is·ti·cal
pan·the·on
pan·ther
pan·to·graph
pan·to·mime
pan·try
pa·pa·cy
pa·pal
pa·pa·ya
pa·per
pa·per·back
pa·per·board
pa·per   chase
pa·per   clip
pa·per   cut·ter
pa·per·hang·er
pa·per   knife
pa·per·weight
pa·per·work
pa·pe·terie
pa·pier—mâ·ché
pa·poose
pa·pri·ka
pa·py·rus
par·a·ble
pa·rab·o·la
par·a·bol·ic
para·chute
pa·rade

par·a·dise
par·a·dox·i·cal
par·af·fin
par·a·gon
para·graph
par·al·lax
par·al·lel
par·al·leled
par·al·lel·ing
par·al·lel·ism
par·al·lel·o·gram
pa·ral·y·sis
par·a·lyt·ic
par·a·lyze
par·a·mount
para·noia
para·noi·ac
para·noid
par·a·pet
par·a·pher·na·lia
para·phrase
para·pro·fes·sion·al
par·a·site
par·a·sit·ic
par·a·sit·i·cide
para·sol
para·troop·er
par·boil
par·cel (bundle;
    cf. *partial*)
par·celed
par·cel·ing
parch·ment
par·don
par·don·able

par·don·er
pare (peel;
    cf. *pair, pear*)
par·e·go·ric
par·ent
par·ent·age
par·en·ter·al
pa·ren·the·ses pl.
pa·ren·the·sis sing.
par·en·thet·i·cal
par·ent·hood
pa·re·sis
par·fait
pa·ri·ah
pa·ri·etal
pari—mu·tu·el
par·ish (church;
    cf. *perish*)
pa·rish·io·ner
Pa·ri·sian
par·i·ty
park·way
par·lance
par·lay (gamble)
par·ley (conference)
par·lia·ment
par·lia·men·tar·i·an
par·lia·men·ta·ry
par·lor
par·lor car
par·lor·maid
par·lous
pa·ro·chi·al
par·o·dy
pa·role

par·ox·ysm
par·ox·ys·mal
par·quet
par·que·try
par·ra·keet
par·ri·cide
par·rot
parse
Par·si·fal
par·si·mo·ni·ous
par·si·mo·ny
pars·ley
pars·nip
par·son
par·son·age
par·take
par·tak·er
part·ed
par·terre
Par·the·non
par·tial (part;
    cf. *parcel*)
par·tial·i·ty
par·tial·ly
par·tic·i·pant
par·tic·i·pate
par·tic·i·pa·tion
par·tic·i·pa·tor
par·ti·cip·i·al
par·ti·ci·ple
par·ti·cle
par·tic·u·lar
par·tic·u·lar·i·ty
par·tic·u·lar·iza·tion
par·tic·u·lar·ize

par·tic·u·lar·ly
par·ti·san
par·ti·san·ship
par·ti·tion
part·ly
part·ner
part·ner·ship
par·tridge
part—time
par·tu·ri·tion
par·ty
par·ve·nu
par·vis
pas·chal
pa·sha
pass·able
pas·sage
pas·sage·way
pass·book
pas·sé
passed (of movement; cf. *past*)
passe·men·terie
pas·sen·ger
passe—par·tout
pass·er·by
pas·si·ble
pass·ing
pas·sion
pas·sion·ate
pas·sion·flow·er
pas·sion·less
pas·sive
pass·key
pass·port
pass·word

past (of time; cf. *passed*)
paste·board
pas·tel
pas·tern
pas·teur·iza·tion
pas·teur·ize
pas·tiche
pas·tille
pas·time
pas·tor
pas·to·ral
pas·to·ral·ism
pas·to·ral·ly
pas·tor·ate
pas·tor·ship
pas·tra·mi
past·ry
pas·tur·age
pas·ture
pas·ty
pa·tchou·li
patch test
patch·work
patchy
pate (head; cf. *pâté*, *patty*)
pâ·té (spiced ground meat; cf. *pate*, *patty*)
pa·tel·la
pat·ent
pat·ent·able
pat·en·tee
pa·ter·fa·mil·i·as
pa·ter·nal
pa·ter·nal·ism

pa·ter·nal·ly
pa·ter·ni·ty
Pat·er·son N.J.
pa·thet·ic
path·find·er
patho·log·ic
patho·log·i·cal
pa·thol·o·gy
pa·thos
path·way
pa·tience
pa·tient
pa·ti·na
pa·tio
pa·tri·arch
pa·tri·ar·chal
pa·tri·arch·ate
pa·tri·ar·chy
pa·tri·cian
pat·ri·cide
pat·ri·mo·ny
pa·tri·ot
pa·tri·ot·ic
pa·tri·o·tism
pa·trol
pa·trolled
pa·trol·ling
pa·trol·man
pa·tron
pa·tron·age
pa·tron·ize
pat·ro·nym·ic
pa·troon
pat·ten
pat·ter
pat·tern

Pat·ter·son N.Y.
pat·ty (little pie;
  cf. *pate, pâté*)
pau·ci·ty
paunch·i·ness
pau·per
pau·per·ism
pau·per·ize
pave·ment
pa·vil·ion
pav·ing
pawn·bro·ker
pawn·bro·king
pawn·er
pawn·shop
pay·able
pay·check
pay·day
pay dirt
pay·ee
pay·er
pay·load
pay·mas·ter
pay·ment
pay off v.
pay·off n.
pay·roll
peace (calm;
  cf. *piece*)
peace·able
peace·ful
peace·mak·er
peace pipe
peace·time
peachy
pea·cock

pea·hen
peak (top;
  cf. *peek, pique*)
peal (loud ringing;
  cf. *peel*)
pea·nut
pear (fruit;
  cf. *pair, pare*)
pearly
pear—shaped
peas·ant·ry
peb·ble
pec·ca·dil·lo
pec·can·cy
pec·cant
pec·to·ral
pec·u·late
pec·u·la·tion
pec·u·la·tor
pe·cu·liar
pe·cu·liar·i·ty
pe·cu·liar·ly
pe·cu·ni·ary
ped·a·gog·ic
ped·a·gog·i·cal
ped·a·gogue
ped·a·go·gy
ped·al (of a bicycle;
  cf. *peddle*)
ped·aled
ped·al·ing
ped·ant
pe·dan·tic
ped·ant·ry
ped·dle (sell;
  cf. *pedal*)

ped·dler
ped·dling
ped·es·tal
pe·des·tri·an
pe·des·tri·an·ism
pe·di·a·tri·cian
pe·di·at·rics
ped·i·cure
ped·i·gree
ped·i·ment
pe·dom·e·ter
peek (look;
  cf. *peak, pique*)
peel (pare; cf. *peal*)
peep·hole
peep show
peep sight
peer (look; cf. *pier*)
peer·age
peer·ess
peer·less
pee·vish
Peg·a·sus
pegged
peg·ging
pe·jo·ra·tive
Pe·la·gian
pel·i·can
pe·lisse
pel·la·gra
pel·let
pell—mell
pel·lu·cid
pelt·ry
pel·vis
pe·nal

| | | |
|---|---|---|
| pe·nal·iza·tion | pen·ni·less | pep·sin |
| pe·nal·ize | Penn·syl·va·nia | per·ad·ven·ture |
| pen·al·ty | Penn·syl·va·nian | per·am·bu·la·tion |
| pen·ance | pen·ny | per·am·bu·la·tor |
| pen·chant | pen·ny·weight | per an·num |
| pen·cil | pen·ny—wise | per·cale |
| pen·ciled | pen·ny·worth | per cap·i·ta |
| pen·cil·ler | pe·no·log·i·cal | per·ceiv·able |
| pen·dant | pe·nol·o·gist | per·ceive |
| pen·den·cy | pe·nol·o·gy | per·cent |
| pen·dent | pen·sile | per·cent·age |
| pend·ing | pen·sion | per·cen·tile |
| pen·drag·on | pen·sion·ary | per·cept |
| pen·du·lous | pen·sion·er | per·cep·ti·ble |
| pen·du·lum | pen·sive | per·cep·tion |
| pen·e·tra·bil·i·ty | pen·stock | per·cep·tive |
| pen·e·tra·ble | pen·ta·gon | per·cep·tu·al |
| pen·e·trate | pen·tag·o·nal | per·chance |
| pen·e·tra·tion | pen·tath·lon | Per·che·ron |
| pen·e·tra·tive | Pen·te·cost | per·cip·i·ence |
| pen·guin | pent·house | per·cip·i·ent |
| pen·hold·er | pe·nult | per·co·late |
| pen·i·cil·lin | pen·ul·ti·mate | per·co·la·tor |
| pen·in·su·la | pe·nu·ri·ous | per·cus·sion |
| pen·in·su·lar | pen·u·ry | per·cus·sive |
| pen·i·tence | pe·on | per di·em |
| pen·i·tent | pe·on·age | per·di·tion |
| pen·i·ten·tial | pe·o·ny | per·e·gri·na·tion |
| pen·i·ten·tia·ry | peo·ple | pe·remp·to·ri·ly |
| pen·i·tent·ly | pep·per | pe·remp·to·ri·ness |
| pen·knife | pep·per—and— | pe·remp·to·ry |
| pen·man | salt adj. | pe·ren·ni·al |
| pen·man·ship | pep·per·box | per·fect |
| pen name | pep·per·corn | per·fect·ible |
| pen·nant | pep·per·mint | per·fec·tion |
| pen·nies | pep·pery | per·fec·tion·ism |

155

per·fect·ly
per·fec·to
per·fid·i·ous
per·fi·dy
per·fo·rate
per·fo·ra·tion
per·fo·ra·tor
per·force
per·form
per·for·mance
per·form·er
per·fume
per·fum·er
per·fum·ery
per·func·to·ry
per·haps
per·il·ous
pe·rim·e·ter
pe·ri·od
pe·ri·od·ic
pe·ri·od·i·cal
pe·riph·er·al
pe·riph·ery
pe·riph·ra·sis
peri·phras·tic
peri·scope
peri·scop·ic
per·ish (die;
   cf. *parish*)
per·ish·able
peri·to·ni·tis
per·i·win·kle
per·jure
per·jur·er
per·ju·ry
per·ma·nence

per·ma·nen·cy
per·ma·nent
per·me·abil·i·ty
per·me·able
per·me·ate
per·me·ation
per·mis·si·ble
per·mis·sion
per·mis·sive
per·mit
per·mit·ted
per·mit·ting
per·mu·ta·tion
per·ni·cious
per·nick·e·ty
per·ora·tion
per·ox·ide
per·pen·dic·u·lar
per·pe·trate
per·pe·tra·tion
per·pe·tra·tor
per·pet·u·al
per·pet·u·al·ly
per·pet·u·ate
per·pet·u·a·tion
per·pet·u·a·tor
per·pe·tu·ity
per·plex
per·plexed
per·plexed·ly
per·plex·i·ty
per·qui·site
per·ry
per·se·cute (harass;
   cf. *prosecute*)
per·se·cu·tion

per·se·cu·tor
Per·seus
per·se·ver·ance
per·se·vere
Per·sian
per·si·flage
per·sim·mon
per·sist
per·sis·tence
per·sis·ten·cy
per·sis·tent
per·son
per·son·able
per·son·age
per·son·al
   (not public;
   cf. *personnel*)
per·son·al·i·ty
   (disposition;
   cf. *personalty*)
per·son·al·ize
per·son·al·ly
per·son·al·ty
   (property;
   cf. *personality*)
per·son·i·fi·ca·tion
per·son·i·fy
per·son·nel
   (employees;
   cf. *personal*)
per·spec·tive
   (appearance to the
   eye; cf. *prospective*)
per·spi·ca·cious
per·spi·cac·i·ty
per·spi·cu·ity

per·spic·u·ous
per·spi·ra·tion
per·spi·ra·to·ry
per·spire
per·suade
per·sua·si·ble
per·sua·sion
per·sua·sive
per·tain
per·ti·na·cious
per·ti·nac·i·ty
per·ti·nence
per·ti·nen·cy
per·ti·nent
per·turb
per·turb·able
per·tur·ba·tion
pe·rus·al
pe·ruse
pe·rus·er
Pe·ru·vi·an
per·vade
per·va·sive
per·verse
per·ver·sion
per·ver·si·ty
per·ver·sive
per·vert
per·vert·ed
per·vert·er
per·vi·ous
pes·si·mism
pes·si·mist
pes·si·mis·tic
pes·ter
pest·hole

pest·house
pes·ti·cide
pes·tif·er·ous
pes·ti·lence
pes·ti·lent
pes·ti·len·tial
pes·tle
pet·al
pet·cock
pet·it (petty)
pe·tite (small)
pe·ti·tion
pe·ti·tion·er
pet·it point
pet·ri·fac·tion
pet·ri·fac·tive
pet·ri·fy
pet·ro·chem·i·cal
pet·rol
pet·ro·la·tum
pe·tro·leum
pet·ro·log·ic
pe·trol·o·gy
pet·ti·coat
pet·ti·fog
pet·ti·fog·gery
pet·ti·ly
pet·ti·ness
pet·ty
pet·u·lance
pet·u·lan·cy
pet·u·lant
pe·tu·nia
pew·ter
pew·ter·er
pha·lan·ges pl.

pha·lanx sing.
phan·tasm
phan·tas·ma·go·
ria
phan·tom
pha·raoh
phar·i·see
phar·ma·ceu·ti·cal
phar·ma·cist
phar·ma·co·poe·ia
phar·ma·cy
pheas·ant
phe·nom·e·na pl.
phe·nom·e·nal
phe·nom·e·nol·o·
gy
phe·nom·e·non sing.
phi·al
phi·lan·der
phi·lan·der·er
phil·an·throp·ic
phil·an·throp·i·cal
phi·lan·thro·pist
phi·lan·thro·py
phil·a·tel·ic
phi·lat·e·ly
Phil·har·mon·ic
phi·lip·pic
Phil·ip·pine
phi·lis·tine
phil·o·log·i·cal
phi·lol·o·gist
phi·lol·o·gy
phi·los·o·pher
philo·soph·ic
philo·soph·i·cal

phi·los·o·phy
phil·ter (drug;
  cf. *filter*)
phlegm
phleg·mat·ic
pho·bia
Phoe·ni·cian
phoe·nix
pho·net·ic
pho·ne·ti·cian
pho·nics
pho·no·graph
phos·phate
phos·pho·resce
phos·pho·res-
  cence
phos·pho·res·cent
phos·pho·ric
phos·pho·rous adj.
phos·pho·rus n.
pho·to·cop·i·er
pho·to·copy
pho·to·elec·tric
pho·to·en·grav·ing
pho·to·ge·nic
pho·to·graph
pho·tog·ra·pher
pho·to·graph·ic
pho·tog·ra·phy
pho·to·gra·vure
pho·to·li·thog·ra-
  phy
pho·to·mu·ral
pho·to·play
pho·to·re·con·nais-
  sance

pho·to·stat
phrase·ol·o·gy
phre·net·ic
phre·nol·o·gist
phre·nol·o·gy
phys·ic (medicine;
  cf. *physique*,
  psychic)
phys·i·cal
  (of the body;
  cf. *fiscal*)
phy·si·cian
phys·i·cist
phys·ics
phys·i·og·no·my
phys·i·og·ra·phy
phys·i·ol·o·gist
phys·i·ol·o·gy
phy·sique
  (of the body;
  cf. *physic, psychic*)
pi·a·nis·si·mo
pi·a·nist
pi·ano n.
pi·anos
pi·as·ter
pi·az·za
pi·ca
pic·a·dor
pi·ca·resque
pic·a·yune
pic·ca·lil·li
pic·co·lo
pic·co·lo·ist
pick·ax
pick·er·el

pick·et
pick·le
pick·lock
pick·pock·et
pick up v.
pick·up n.
pic·nic n., v.
pic·nicked
pic·nick·er
pic·nick·ing
pi·cot
pic·to·graph
pic·tog·ra·phy
pic·to·ri·al
pic·ture
pic·tur·esque
pid·gin (language;
  cf. *pigeon*)
pie·bald
piece (part;cf. *peace*)
piece goods
piece·meal
piece·work
pie chart
pie·plant
pier (dock; cf. *peer*)
pi·ety
pi·geon (bird;
  cf. *pidgin*)
pi·geon·hole
pi·geon—toed
pi·geon·wing
pig·fish
pig·gery
pig·gish
pig·gy·back

pig·head·ed
pig iron
pig·ment
pig·men·tary
pig·men·ta·tion
pigmy
pig·pen
pig·skin
pig·sty
pig·tail
pig·tailed
pig·weed
pike·man
pike perch
pik·er
pike·staff
pi·las·ter
pil·chard
pil·fer
pil·grim
pil·grim·age
pil·ing
pil·lage
pil·lar
pill·box
pil·lion
pil·lo·ry
pil·low
pil·low·case
pi·lot
pi·lot·house
pim·ple
pin·afore
pince—nez
pinch—hit
pin curl

pin·cush·ion
pine·ap·ple
pin·feath·er
pin·fold
Ping—Pong
pin·head
pin·head·ed
pin·hole
pin·ion
pink·eye
pin·na·cle
pi·noch·le
pin·point
pin·prick
pin·stripe
pin·up
pin·wheel
pi·o·neer
pi·ous
pipe clay n.
pipe—clay v.
pipe dream
pipe·line
pip·er
pipe·stone
pipe wrench
pi·quan·cy
pi·quant
pique (provoke;
   cf. *peak, peek*)
pi·ra·cy
pi·ra·nha
pi·rate
pi·rat·i·cal
pir·ou·ette
pis·ca·to·ry

pis·ta·chio
pis·til (of plant)
pis·tol (weapon)
pis·tole (old coin)
pis·tol—whip
pis·ton
pitch—black
pitch—dark
pitch·er
pitch·fork
pitch·man
pitch pipe
pitch·stone
pit·e·ous
pit·fall
pit·head
pith·i·ly
pith·i·ness
pithy
piti·able
piti·ful
piti·less
pit·man
pit saw
pit·tance
pit·ter—pat·ter
Pitts·burg Calif.,
   Kansas
Pitts·burgh Pa.
pi·tu·itary
pity
piv·ot
piv·ot·al
piz·za
piz·ze·ria
piz·zi·ca·to

159

pla·ca·bil·i·ty

pla·ca·ble

plac·ard

pla·cate

pla·ca·to·ry

pla·ce·bo

place·kick

place·ment

plac·id

pla·cid·i·ty

pla·gia·rism

pla·gia·rist

pla·gia·rize

pla·gia·ry

plague

plain (simple;
   cf. *plane*)

plain·clothes·man

plain·ness

plains·man

plain·spo·ken

plain·tiff
   (complainant)

plain·tive (mournful)

plait (fold;
   cf. *plat, plate, pleat*)

plane (airplane;
   cf. *plain*)

plan·et

plan·e·tar·i·um

plan·e·tary

plan·gent

plank·ing

plank·ton

plan·ner

plan·tain

plan·tar (of the sole;
   cf. *planter*)

plan·ta·tion

plant·er (farmer;
   cf. *plantar*)

plaque

plas·ter

plas·ter·board

plas·ter·er

plas·tic

plas·tic·i·ty

plat (map;
   cf. *plait, plate, pleat*)

plate (dish;
   cf. *plait, plat, pleat*)

pla·teau

plate·ful

plate glass

plat·en

plat·er

plat·form

plat·ing

plat·i·num

plat·i·tude

plat·i·tu·di·nous

pla·ton·ic

Pla·to·nism

pla·toon

plat·ter

plau·dit

plau·si·bil·i·ty

plau·si·ble

play back v.

play·back n.

play·bill

play·boy

play·er

play·ful

play·go·er

play·ground

play·house

play·let

play off v.

play—off n.

play·pen

play·room

play school n.

play·suit

play·thing

play·time

play·wright

play yard

pla·za

plea

plead·able

plead·er

plead·ing

pleas·ant

pleas·ant·ry

pleas·ing

plea·sur·able

plea·sure

pleat (arrange in
   pleats; cf. *plait,
   plat, plate*)

ple·be·ian

pleb·i·scite

plec·trum

pledge

pledg·ee

pled·get

ple·na·ry

pleni·po·ten·tia·ry
plen·i·tude
plen·te·ous
plen·ti·ful
plen·ty
ple·num
ple·o·nasm
pleth·o·ra
pleu·ri·sy
pli·abil·i·ty
pli·able
pli·an·cy
pli·ant
pli·ers
plod·ded
plod·der
plod·ding
plot·ted
plot·ter
plot·ting
plow·boy
plow·man
plow·share
plug
plugged
plug·ging
plug—ug·ly
plum (fruit)
plum·age
plumb (weight)
plumb bob
plumb·er
plumb·ing
plumb line
plum·met
plump·ness

plun·der
plun·der·er
plung·er
plu·per·fect
plu·ral
plu·ral·ism
plu·ral·is·tic
plu·ral·i·ty
plu·ral·iza·tion
plu·ral·ize
plu·toc·ra·cy
plu·to·crat
plu·to·crat·ic
plu·to·ni·um
ply·wood
pneu·mat·ic
pneu·mat·ics
pneu·mo·nia
pneu·mon·ic
poach·er
pock·et
pock·et·book
pock·et·ful
pock·et—
   hand·ker·chief
pock·et·knife
pock·mark
po·di·a·try
po·di·um
po·em
po·esy
po·et
po·et·as·ter
po·et·ic
po·et·i·cal
po·et·ry

po·grom
poi·gnan·cy
poi·gnant
poin·set·tia
point—blank
point·ed
point·er
point·less
poi·son
poi·son·ous
poi·son—pen adj.
pok·er
po·lar
po·lar·i·ty
po·lar·iza·tion
po·lar·ize
Po·lar·oid
pole (rod; cf. *poll*)
pole·ax
pole·cat
po·lem·ic
po·lem·i·cal
pole·star
pole vault n.
pole—vault v.
pole—vault·er n.
po·lice·man
poli·clin·ic (dispen-
   sary; cf. *polyclinic*)
pol·i·cy
pol·i·cy·hold·er
pol·ish
Pol·ish
pol·ish·er
po·lit·bu·ro
po·lite

po·lite·ness
pol·i·tic
po·lit·i·cal
po·lit·i·cal·ly
pol·i·ti·cian
pol·i·tics
pol·i·ty
pol·ka
pol·ka dot
poll (vote; cf. *pole*)
pol·len
pol·li·nate
pol·li·wog
poll tax
pol·lut·ant
pol·lute
pol·lu·tion
po·lo·naise
pol·ter·geist
pol·troon
poly·an·dry
poly·an·thus
poly·chro·mat·ic
poly·chrome
poly·clin·ic (hospital; cf. *policlinic*)
po·lyg·a·mist
po·lyg·a·mous
po·lyg·a·my
poly·glot
poly·gon
poly·graph
poly·graph·ic
pol·yp
poly·phon·ic
poly·syl·lab·ic

poly·syl·la·ble
poly·tech·nic
poly·un·sat·u·rat-ed
po·made
pome·gran·ate
pom·mel
pom·pa·dour
pom·pa·no
pom·pos·i·ty
pomp·ous
pon·cho sing.
pon·chos pl.
pon·der
pon·der·a·ble
pon·der·ous
pon·gee
pon·iard
pon·tiff
pon·tif·i·cal
pon·tif·i·cate
pon·toon
po·ny
po·ny·tail
poo·dle
pooh—pooh
pool·room
poor box
poor farm
poor·house
poor·ly
poor—spir·it·ed
pop·corn
pop—eyed
pop·gun
pop·in·jay

pop·lar (tree; cf. *popular*)
pop·lin
pop·over
pop·py
pop·py·cock
pop·u·lace (people; cf. *populous*)
pop·u·lar (widely liked; cf. *poplar*)
pop·u·lar·i·ty
pop·u·lar·i·za·tion
pop·u·lar·ize
pop·u·late
pop·u·la·tion
pop·u·lous (thickly populated; cf. *populace*)
por·ce·lain
por·cu·pine
pore (study; cf. *pour*)
pork·er
pork·pie hat
po·rous
por·phy·ry
por·poise
por·ridge
por·rin·ger
por·ta·bil·i·ty
por·ta·ble
por·tage
por·tal
por·tend
por·tent
por·ten·tous
por·ter

por·ter·house
port·fo·lio
port·hole
por·ti·co
por·tiere
por·tion
port·li·ness
port·ly
port·man·teau
por·trait
por·trai·ture
por·tray
por·tray·al
Por·tu·guese
por·tu·laca
pos·it
po·si·tion
pos·i·tive
pos·i·tron
pos·se
pos·sess
pos·sessed
pos·ses·sion
pos·ses·sive
pos·sess·or
pos·si·bil·i·ty
pos·si·ble
post·age
post·al
post·box
post·boy
post·card
post·clas·si·cal
post·date
post·doc·tor·al
post·er

pos·te·ri·or
pos·ter·i·ty
pos·tern
post·grad·u·ate
post·haste
post·hole
post horn
post—horse
post·hu·mous
post·hyp·not·ic
pos·til·ion
post·lude
post·man
post·mark
post·mas·ter
post·mis·tress
post·mor·tem
post·na·sal
post—obit
post of·fice n.
post—of·fice adj.
post—of·fice box
post·paid
post·pone
post·pone·ment
post·pran·di·al
post·script
pos·tu·lant
pos·tu·late
pos·ture
post·war
po·ta·ble
pot·ash
po·tas·si·um
po·ta·tion
po·ta·to

po·ta·toes
pot·bel·lied
pot·bel·ly
pot·boil·er
pot·boy
pot cheese
po·ten·cy
po·ten·tate
po·ten·tial
po·ten·ti·al·i·ty
po·tent·ly
pot·hole
pot·hook
pot·house
po·tion
pot·latch
pot·luck
pot·pie
pot·pour·ri
pot roast
pot·sherd
pot·shot
pot still
pot·tage
pot·ter
pot·tery
pouch
Pough·keep·sie N.Y.
poul·ter·er
poul·tice
poul·try (fowl;
    cf. *paltry*)
poul·try·man
pound·age
pound cake
pour (rain; cf. *pore*)

pov·er·ty—
  strick·en
pow·der
pow·dery
pow·er·boat
pow·er·ful
pow·er·less
pow·wow
prac·ti·ca·bil·i·ty
prac·ti·ca·ble
  (feasible)
prac·ti·cal (useful)
prac·ti·cal·i·ty
prac·ti·cal·ly
prac·tice
prac·tic·er
prac·ti·tio·ner
prag·mat·ic
prag·mat·i·cal
prag·ma·tism
prag·ma·tist
prai·rie
praise·wor·thi·ness
praise·wor·thy
pra·line
prank·ish
prat·tle
pray (beseech;
  cf. *prey*)
prayer
prayer book
prayer·ful
preach·er
preach·ment
pre·am·ble
pre·can·cel

pre·car·i·ous
pre·cau·tion
pre·cau·tion·ary
pre·cede (go before;
  cf. *proceed*)
pre·ce·dence (pri-
  ority; cf. *precedents*)
pre·ce·den·cy
pre·ce·dent adj.
prec·e·dent n.
prec·e·dents
  (previous acts;
  cf. *precedence*)
pre·ced·ing
pre·cept
pre·cep·tive
pre·cep·tor
pre·cep·to·ry
pre·ces·sion
pre·ces·sion·al
pre·cinct
pre·cious
prec·i·pice
pre·cip·i·tance
pre·cip·i·tan·cy
pre·cip·i·tant
pre·cip·i·tate
pre·cip·i·tate·ly
pre·cip·i·tate·ness
pre·cip·i·ta·tion
pre·cip·i·ta·tor
pre·cip·i·tous
pre·cise
pre·ci·sion
pre·clude
pre·clu·sion

pre·clu·sive
pre·co·cious
pre·coc·i·ty
pre·con·ceive
pre·con·cep·tion
pre·con·cert
pre·cook
pre·cur·sor
pre·cur·so·ry
pred·a·to·ry
pre·de·cease
pre·de·ces·sor
pre·des·ti·nar·i·an
pre·des·ti·na·tion
pre·des·tine
pre·de·ter·mine
pre·dic·a·ment
pred·i·cate
pred·i·ca·tion
pred·i·ca·tive
pre·dict
pre·dict·able
pre·dic·tion
pre·dic·tive
pre·dic·tor
pre·di·lec·tion
pre·dis·pose
pre·dis·po·si·tion
pre·dom·i·nance
pre·dom·i·nant
pre·dom·i·nate
pre·dom·i·na·tion
pre·em·i·nence
pre·em·i·nent
pre·empt
pre·emp·tive

pre·fab
pre·fab·ri·cate
pref·ace
pref·a·to·ry
pre·fect
pre·fec·ture
pre·fer
pref·er·a·ble
pref·er·ence
pref·er·en·tial
pre·ferred
pre·fer·ring
pre·fix
pre·flight
preg·nan·cy
preg·nant
pre·heat
pre·his·tor·ic
pre·judge
prej·u·dice
prej·u·di·cial
prel·a·cy
prel·ate
pre·lim·i·nary
pre·lude
pre·ma·ture
pre·ma·tu·ri·ty
pre·med·i·tate
pre·med·i·ta·tion
pre·mier
pre·miere
prem·ise
prem·is·es (real
  estate; cf. *promises*)
pre·mi·um
pre·mo·ni·tion

pre·mon·i·to·ry
pre·na·tal
pre·oc·cu·pan·cy
pre·oc·cu·pa·tion
pre·oc·cu·pied
pre·oc·cu·py
pre·or·dain
pre·paid
prep·a·ra·tion
pre·par·a·tive
pre·par·a·to·ry
pre·pare
pre·pared
pre·pared·ness
pre·pay
pre·pay·ment
pre·pon·der·ance
pre·pon·der·ant
pre·pon·der·ate
prep·o·si·tion
prep·o·si·tion·al
pre·pos·sess
pre·pos·sess·ing
pre·pos·ses·sion
pre·pos·ter·ous
pre·po·ten·cy
pre·re·cord
pre·req·ui·site
pre·rog·a·tive
pres·age n.
pre·sage v.
Pres·by·te·ri·an
pre·scient
pre·scribe (order as
  a remedy;
  cf. *proscribe*)

pre·scrip·ti·ble
pre·scrip·tion
pre·scrip·tive
pres·ence (of mind;
  cf. *presents*)
pre·sent v.
pres·ent adj., n.
pre·sent·able
pre·sen·ta·tion
pre·sen·ta·tive
pres·ent—day
pre·sen·tee
pre·sen·ti·ment
  (foreboding;
  cf. *presentment*)
pres·ent·ly
pre·sent·ment
  (from grand jury;
  cf. *presentiment*)
pres·ents (gifts;
  cf. *presence*)
pres·serv·able
pres·er·va·tion
pres·er·va·tive
pre·serve
pre·side
pres·i·den·cy
pres·i·dent
pres·i·den·tial
pre·sid·er
press agent n.
press·board
press box
pressed
press·er
press—gang

**165**

press·ing
press·man
press·mark
press·room
press·run
pres·sure
pres·sur·ize
press·work
pres·ti·dig·i·ta·tion
pres·ti·dig·i·ta·tor
pres·tige
pres·ti·gious
pres·tis·si·mo
pre·sum·able
pre·sume
pre·sump·tion
pre·sump·tive
pre·sump·tu·ous
pre·sup·pose
pre·tend
pre·tend·ed
pre·tend·er
pre·tense
pre·ten·sion
pre·ten·tious
pret·er·it
pre·ter·nat·u·ral
pre·text
pret·ti·ly
pret·ti·ness
pret·ty
pret·zel
pre·vail
pre·vail·ing
prev·a·lence
prev·a·lent

pre·var·i·cate
pre·var·i·ca·tion
pre·var·i·ca·tor
pre·vent
pre·vent·able
pre·ven·tion
pre·ven·tive
pre·view
pre·vi·ous
pre·vi·sion
prey (victim; cf. *pray*)
price—cut·ter
price·less
price tag
prick·le
prick·li·ness
prick·ly
priest·ess
priest·hood
priest·ly
pri·ma·cy
pri·ma don·na
pri·ma fa·cie
pri·mar·i·ly
pri·ma·ry
pri·mate
prim·er
pri·me·val
prim·i·tive
pri·mo·gen·i·ture
pri·mor·di·al
prim·rose
prince·ly
prin·cess
prin·ci·pal (chief;
    cf. *principle*)

prin·ci·pal·i·ty
prin·ci·pal·ly
prin·ci·ple (rule;
    cf. *principal*)
print·able
print·er
print·ery
print·ing
pri·or
pri·or·ess
pri·or·i·ty
pri·or·ship
prism
pris·mat·ic
pris·on
pris·on·er
pris·tine
pri·va·cy
pri·vate
pri·va·teer
pri·vate·ly
pri·va·tion
priv·et
priv·i·lege
priv·i·ly
priv·i·ty
privy
prize·fight
prize ring
prob·a·bil·i·ty
prob·a·ble
prob·a·bly
pro·bate
pro·ba·tion
pro·ba·tion·al
pro·ba·tion·ary

pro·ba·tion·er
pro·ba·tive
pro·ba·to·ry
pro·bi·ty
prob·lem
prob·lem·at·ic
prob·lem·at·i·cal
pro·bos·cis
pro·ca·the·dral
pro·ce·dur·al
pro·ce·dure
pro·ceed (move
   forward; cf. *precede*)
pro·ceed·ing
pro·cess
pro·ces·sion
pro·ces·sion·al
pro·ces·sor
pro·claim
proc·la·ma·tion
pro·cliv·i·ty
pro·con·sul
pro·cras·ti·nate
pro·cras·ti·na·tion
pro·cras·ti·na·tor
pro·cre·a·tion
pro·cre·a·tive
pro·crus·te·an
proc·tor
proc·to·ri·al
pro·cur·a·ble
proc·u·ra·tion
proc·u·ra·tor
pro·cure
pro·cure·ment
prod·i·gal

prod·i·gal·i·ty
pro·di·gious
prod·i·gy
pro·duce
pro·duc·er
prod·uct
pro·duc·tion
pro·duc·tive
pro·duc·tiv·i·ty
pro·fa·na·tion
pro·fa·na·to·ry
pro·fane
pro·fan·i·ty
pro·fess
pro·fessed·ly
pro·fes·sion
pro·fes·sion·al
pro·fes·sion·al·ism
pro·fes·sion·al·ly
pro·fes·sor
pro·fes·so·ri·al
pro·fes·sor·ship
prof·fer
prof·fer·ing
pro·fi·cien·cy
pro·fi·cient
pro·file
prof·it (gain;
   cf. *prophet*)
prof·it·able
prof·i·teer
prof·it·less
prof·li·ga·cy
prof·li·gate
pro for·ma
pro·found

pro·fun·di·ty
pro·fuse
pro·fu·sion
pro·gen·i·tor
prog·e·ny
prog·no·sis
prog·nos·tic
prog·nos·ti·cate
prog·nos·ti·ca·tion
pro·gram
pro·grammed
pro·gram·ming
prog·ress n.
pro·gress v.
pro·gres·sive
pro·hib·it
pro·hi·bi·tion·ist
pro·hib·i·tive
pro·hib·i·to·ry
proj·ect n.
pro·ject v.
pro·jec·tile
pro·jec·tion·ist
pro·jec·tive
pro·jec·tor
pro·le·tar·i·an
pro·le·tar·i·at
pro·lif·er·ate
pro·lif·ic
pro·lix
pro·logue
pro·long
pro·lon·gate
prom·e·nade
prom·i·nence
prom·i·nent

pro·mis·cu·ity

pro·mis·cu·ous

prom·ise

prom·is·es (pledges; cf. *premises*)

prom·i·sor

prom·is·so·ry

prom·on·to·ry

pro·mote

pro·mot·er

pro·mo·tion

pro·mo·tion·al

prompt

prompt·book

prompt·er

promp·ti·tude

prompt·ly

prompt·ness

pro·mul·gate

pro·mul·ga·tion

pro·nom·i·nal

pro·noun

pro·nounce

pro·nounce·able

pro·nounced

pro·nounce·ment

pro·nounc·ing

pro·nun·ci·a·men·to

pro·nun·ci·a·tion

proof·read·er

proof·room

prop·a·ga·ble

pro·pa·gan·da

pro·pa·gan·dist

pro·pa·gan·dize

prop·a·gate

prop·a·ga·tion

prop·a·ga·tive

pro·pel

pro·pel·lant

pro·pelled

pro·pel·ler

pro·pel·ling

pro·pense

pro·pen·si·ty

prop·er·ly

prop·er·tied

prop·er·ty

proph·e·cy n. (a prediction; cf. *prophesy*)

proph·e·si·er

proph·e·sy v. (to predict; cf. *prophecy*)

proph·et (predicts future; cf. *profit*)

pro·phet·ic

pro·phet·i·cal

pro·phy·lac·tic

pro·phy·lax·is

pro·pin·qui·ty

pro·pi·ti·ate

pro·pi·ti·a·tion

pro·pi·ti·ator

pro·pi·tia·to·ry

pro·pi·tious

pro·po·nent

pro·por·tion

pro·por·tion·al

pro·por·tion·ate

pro·pos·al

pro·pose (to state; cf. *purpose*)

prop·o·si·tion

pro·pound

pro·pri·etary

pro·pri·etor

pro·pri·ety

pro·pul·sion

pro·pul·sive

pro   ra·ta

pro·rate

pro·sa·ic

pro·sce·ni·um

pro·scribe (outlaw; cf. *prescribe*)

pro·scrip·tion

pro·scrip·tive

prose

pros·e·cute (legal trial; cf. *persecute*)

pros·e·cu·tion

pros·e·cu·tor

pros·e·lyte

pro·sit

pros·pect

pro·spec·tive (expected; cf. *perspective*)

pro·spec·tus

pros·per

pros·per·i·ty

pros·per·ous

pros·tate

pros·the·sis

pros·thet·ics
pros·ti·tute
pros·ti·tu·tion
pros·trate
pros·tra·tion
prosy
pro·tag·o·nist
pro·te·an
pro·tect
pro·tec·tion
pro·tec·tion·ism
pro·tec·tion·ist
pro·tec·tive
pro·tec·tor
pro·tec·tor·ate
pro·té·gé
pro·tein
pro tem
pro·test
prot·es·tant
Prot·es·tant·ism
pro·tes·ta·tion
pro·to·col
pro·to·plasm
pro·to·type
pro·tract
pro·trac·tile
pro·trac·tion
pro·trac·tor
pro·trude
pro·tru·sion
pro·tru·sive
pro·tu·ber·ance
pro·tu·ber·ant
prov·able
proved

prov·en
prov·e·nance
prov·en·der
prov·erb
pro·ver·bi·al
pro·vide
pro·vid·ed
prov·i·dence
prov·i·dent
prov·i·den·tial
pro·vid·er
prov·ince
pro·vin·cial
pro·vin·cial·ism
pro·vi·sion
pro·vi·sion·al
pro·vi·sion·ary
pro·vi·sion·er
pro·vi·so
pro·vi·so·ry
prov·o·ca·tion
pro·voc·a·tive
pro·voke
pro·vok·ing
prow·ess
prox·i·mal
prox·i·mate
prox·im·i·ty
prox·i·mo
proxy
prude
pru·dence
pru·dent
pru·den·tial
prud·ish
pru·ri·ence

pru·ri·ent
pry·ing
psalm
psalm·book
psalm·ist
psalm·o·dy
pseud·onym
pseud·on·y·mous
psit·ta·co·sis
pso·ri·a·sis
Psy·che
psy·chi·at·ric
psy·chi·a·trist
psy·chi·a·try
psy·chic (of the
    mind; cf. *physic,*
    *physique*)
psy·cho·anal·y·sis
psy·cho·an·a·lyst
psy·cho·an·a·lyze
psy·cho·log·i·cal
psy·chol·o·gist
psy·chol·o·gize
psy·chol·o·gy
psy·cho·path
psy·cho·path·ic
psy·cho·sis
psy·cho·so·mat·ic
psy·cho·ther·a·py
pu·ber·ty
pub·lic
pub·li·ca·tion
pub·li·cist
pub·lic·i·ty
pub·li·cize
pub·lic·ly

pub·lic·ness
pub·lic—spir·it·ed
pub·lish
pub·lish·er
puck·ery
pud·ding
pud·dle
pud·dling
pu·den·cy
pudg·i·ness
pueb·lo
pu·er·ile
Puer·to Ri·co
puff·i·ness
puffy
pu·gi·lism
pu·gi·list
pu·gi·lis·tic
pug·na·cious
pug·nac·i·ty
pug nose
pug—nosed
puis·sance
puis·sant
pul·chri·tude
pul·chri·tu·di·nous
pul·let
pul·ley
Pull·man
pull over v.
pull·over adj., n.
pul·mo·nary
pul·mo·tor
pulp·i·ness
pul·pit
pulp·wood

pulpy
pul·sate
pul·sa·tion
pul·ver·ize
pum·ice
pum·mel
pum·meled
pum·mel·ing
pum·per·nick·el
pump·kin
punch·board
punch—drunk
pun·cheon
punc·til·io
punc·til·i·ous
punc·tu·al
punc·tu·al·i·ty
punc·tu·al·ly
punc·tu·ate
punc·tu·a·tion
punc·tu·a·tor
punc·ture
pun·dit
pun·gen·cy
pun·gent
pun·ish
pun·ish·able
pun·ish·er
pun·ish·ment
pu·ni·tive
pun·ster
punt·er
pu·ny
pu·pil
pup·pet
pup·pet·ry

pup·py
pup tent
pur·blind
pur·chas·able
pru·chase
pur·dah
pure·ly
pur·ga·tion
pur·ga·tive
pur·ga·to·ri·al
pur·ga·to·ry
purge
pu·ri·fi·ca·tion
pu·ri·fi·er
pu·ri·fy
pur·ist
pu·ri·tan
pu·ri·tan·i·cal
pu·ri·ty
pur·lieu
pur·loin
pur·ple
pur·plish
pur·port
pur·port·ed·ly
pur·pose (intention;
    cf. *propose*)
pur·pose·ly
pur·po·sive
purr
purse—proud
purs·er
pur·su·ance
pur·su·ant
pur·sue
pur·suit

pu·ru·lent
pur·vey
pur·vey·ance
pur·vey·or
pur·view
push·ball
push broom
push but·ton n.
push—but·ton adj.
push·cart
push·i·ness
push·ing
push·over n.
push·pin
push—pull adj.
push—up n.
pu·sil·la·nim·i·ty
pu·sil·lan·i·mous
pus·tu·lant
pus·tu·lar
pus·tu·late
pus·tu·la·tion
pus·tule
pu·ta·tive
put—on adj., n.
pu·tre·fac·tion
pu·tre·fac·tive
pu·tre·fy
pu·tres·cence
pu·tres·cent
pu·trid
put·ter
put·ty
put up v.
put—up adj.
puz·zle

puz·zle·ment
puz·zler
pyg·my
py·lon
py·lo·rus
py·or·rhea
pyr·a·mid
py·ra·mi·dal
pyre
py·ro·ma·nia
py·ro·ma·ni·ac
py·rox·y·lin
pyr·rhic
py·thon

quack·ery
quad·ran·gle
qua·dran·gu·lar
quad·rant
qua·dran·tal
qua·drat·ic
qua·dren·ni·al
qua·dren·ni·um
quad·ri·lat·er·al
qua·drille
qua·dril·lion
quad·ru·ped
qua·dru·pe·dal

qua·dru·ple
qua·dru·plet
qua·dru·pli·cate
quaff
quag·mire
qual·i·fi·ca·tion
qual·i·fied
qual·i·fy
qual·i·ta·tive
qual·i·ty
qualm
quan·da·ry
quan·ti·ta·tive
quan·ti·ty
quan·tum
quar·an·tine
quark
quar·rel
quar·reled
quar·rel·ing
quar·rel·some
quar·ry
quar·ry·ing
quar·ter
quar·ter·back
quar·ter·deck
quar·ter·ly
quar·ter·mas·ter
quar·tet
quar·to
quarts (measures)
quartz (mineral)
qua·sar
qua·si
qua·si—ju·di·cial
qua·si—pub·lic

171

qua·train
qua·tre·foil
qua·ver·ing·ly
quay (wharf; cf. *key*)
quea·si·ness
quea·sy
queer
quench·less
quer·u·lous
que·ry
ques·tion
ques·tion·able
ques·tion·er
ques·tion·naire
queue (waiting line; cf. *cue*)
quib·ble
quib·bling
quick·en
quick—fire adj.
quick fire n.
quick—freeze n., v.
quick·ie
quick·lime
quick—lunch n.
quick·sand
quick·sil·ver
quick·step
quick—tem·pered
quick—wit·ted
quid·di·ty
quid·nunc
qui·es·cence
qui·es·cent
qui·et (silent; cf. *quit, quite*)

qui·et·ness
qui·etude
qui·etus
qui·nine
quin·tes·sence
quin·tet
quin·tu·plet
quin·tu·pli·cate
quip
quipped
quip·ping
quire (24 sheets; cf. *choir*)
quit (leave; cf. *quiet, quite*)
quit·claim
quite (completely; cf. *quiet, quit*)
quit·tance
quit·ter
quiv·er
qui vive
quix·ot·ic
quiz
quizzed
quiz·zi·cal
quiz·zing
quoin (printing; cf. *coign, coin*)
quoit
quon·dam
quo·rum
quo·ta
quot·able
quo·ta·tion
quote

quo·tid·i·an
quo·tient

rab·bet (groove; cf. *rabbit*)
rab·bi
rab·bit (animal; cf. *rabbet*)
rab·bit·ry
rab·ble
rab·ble—rous·er
ra·bid
ra·bies
rac·coon
race·course
race·horse
rac·er
race·track
race·way
ra·cial
rac·i·ly
rac·i·ness
rac·ing
rac·ism
rac·ist
rack·et
rack·e·teer
ra·con·teur

ra·dar
ra·dar·scope
ra·di·al
ra·di·ance
ra·di·an·cy
ra·di·ant
ra·di·ant·ly
ra·di·ate
ra·di·a·tion
ra·di·a·tor
rad·i·cal
rad·i·cal·ism
rad·i·cal·ly
ra·dii (sing.: *radius*)
ra·dio
ra·dio·ac·tive
ra·dio·gram
ra·dio·graph
ra·di·og·ra·phy
ra·dio·iso·tope
ra·di·om·e·ter
ra·dio·phone
ra·dio·sonde
ra·dio·tele·graph
ra·dio·tele·phone
ra·dio·ther·a·py
rad·ish
ra·di·um
ra·di·us (pl.: *radii*)
raf·fle
raf·ter
rafts·man
rag·a·muf·fin
rag·ged
rag·ing
rag·lan

rag·man
ra·gout
rag·pick·er
rag·time
rag·weed
rail·bird
rail fence
rail·head
rail·ing
rail·lery
rail·road
rail—split·ter
rail·way
rai·ment
rain (water;
    cf. *reign, rein*)
rain·bow
rain check
rain·coat
rain dance
rain·drop
rain·fall
rain gauge
rain·mak·ing
rain·proof
rain·spout
rain·squall
rain·storm
rain·wa·ter
rain·wear
rainy
raise (lift;
    cf. *rays, raze*)
rai·sin
rai·son d'être
ra·ja *or* ra·jah

rake·hell
rake—off
rak·ish
ral·ly
ram·ble
ram·bler
ram·bling
ram·bunc·tious
ram·e·kin
ram·i·fi·ca·tion
ram·i·fy
ram·pant
ram·part
ram·rod
ram·shack·le
ranch·man
ran·cid
ran·cor
ran·cor·ous
ran·dom
rangy
ran·kle
ran·sack
ran·som
ra·pa·cious
ra·pac·i·ty
rap·id
ra·pid·i·ty
rap·id·ly
ra·pi·er
rap·ine
rapped (struck;
    cf. *rapt, wrapped*)
rap·port
rapt (engrossed;
    cf. *rapped, wrapped*)

rap·ture
rap·tur·ous
rare·bit
rar·efac·tion
rar·efied
rar·efy
rare·ly
rare·ness
rar·i·ty
ras·cal
ras·cal·i·ty
rash·ly
rash·ness
rasp·ber·ry
rasp·ing·ly
rat·able
ratch·et
rath·er
raths·kel·ler
rat·i·fi·ca·tion
rat·i·fy
rat·ing
ra·tio
ra·ti·o·ci·na·tion
ra·tion
ra·tio·nal
ra·tio·nale
ra·tio·nal·iza·tion
ra·tio·nal·ize
rat·like
rat·line
rat race
rat·tail
rat·tan
rat·tle
rat·tle·brained

rat·tler
rat·tle·snake
rat·tle·trap
rat·trap  n.
rau·cous
rav·age
rav·el
rav·eled
rav·el·ing
ra·ven
rav·en·ing
rav·en·ous
ra·vine
rav·i·o·li
rav·ish·ing·ly
raw·boned
raw·hide
ray·on
rays  (of light;
    cf. *raise, raze*)
raze  (tear down;
    cf. *raise, rays*)
ra·zor
ra·zor·back
re·act
re·ac·tion
re·ac·tion·ary
re·ac·ti·vate
re·ac·tor
read·able
read·er·ship
read·i·ly
read·i·ness
re·ad·just·ment
ready—made
ready—to—wear

re·af·firm
re·agent
re·al  (true; cf. *reel*)
re·alia
re·al·ism
re·al·ist
re·al·is·tic
re·al·i·ty  (real event;
    cf. *realty*)
re·al·iza·tion
re·al·ize
re·al·ly
realm
Re·al·tor
re·al·ty  (property;
    cf. *reality*)
re·ap·point
re·ap·prais·al
re·ar·range
rear  guard
re·arm
rea·son
rea·son·able
rea·son·ing
re·as·sem·ble
re·as·sur·ance
re·as·sure
reb·el  adj.
re·bel  v.
re·belled
re·bel·ling
re·bel·lion
re·bel·lious
re·birth
re·buff
re·buke

re·bus
re·but·tal
re·cal·ci·tran·cy
re·cal·ci·trant
re·cant
re·ca·pit·u·late
re·ca·pit·u·la·tion
re·cap·ture
re·cede
re·ceipt
re·ceiv·able
re·ceive
re·ceiv·er·ship
re·cent
re·cep·ta·cle
re·cep·tion
re·cep·tive
re·cess
re·ces·sion
re·ces·sion·al
re·ces·sive
re·cid·i·vism
rec·i·pe
re·cip·i·ent
re·cip·ro·cal
re·cip·ro·cate
re·cip·ro·ca·tion
rec·i·proc·i·ty
re·cit·al
rec·i·ta·tion
rec·i·ta·tive
re·cite
reck·less
reck·on
re·claim
rec·la·ma·tion

re·cline
re·cluse
rec·og·ni·tion
rec·og·niz·able
re·cog·ni·zance
rec·og·nize
re·coil
re—col·lect
  (collect again)
rec·ol·lect (recall)
rec·ol·lec·tion
rec·om·mend
rec·om·men·da-
  tion
re·com·mit
rec·om·pense
rec·on·cile
rec·on·cil·i·a·tion
re·con·di·tion
re·con·firm
re·con·fir·ma·tion
re·con·nais·sance
re·con·noi·ter
re·con·sid·er
re·con·struc·tion
re·cord v.
rec·ord n.
re·cord·er
re·course
re·cov·er (regain)
re—cov·er
  (cover again)
re·cov·ery
rec·re·ant
rec·re·a·tion
re·crim·i·na·tion

re·cru·des·cence
re·cruit
rect·an·gle
rect·an·gu·lar
rec·ti·fi·ca·tion
rec·ti·fi·er
rec·ti·fy
rec·ti·lin·ear
rec·ti·tude
rec·to·ry
rec·tum
re·cum·bent
re·cu·per·ate
re·cu·per·a·tion
re·cur
re·curred
re·cur·rence
re·cur·rent
re·cur·ring
red—bait·ing
red·bird
red—blood·ed
red·breast
red·bud
red·cap
red—car·pet adj.
red·coat
Red Cross
re·dec·o·rate
re·deem
re·deem·able
re·deem·er
re·demp·tion
re·de·vel·op·ment
red—hand·ed
  adj., adv.

red·head
red—hot
re·dis·count
re·dis·trib·ute
re·dis·trict
red lead
red—let·ter
red·o·lence
red·o·lent
re·dou·ble
re·doubt·able
re·dound
red—pen·cil v.
re·dress
red·skin
red tape
re·duce
re·duc·tion
re·dun·dan·cy
re·dun·dant
red·wing
red·wood
re·echo
re·ed·u·cate
reek (smell;
   cf. *wreak, wreck*)
reel (spool; cf. *real*)
re·elect
re·em·pha·size
re·em·ploy
re·en·act
re·en·grave
re·en·list
re·en·trance
re·en·try
re·es·tab·lish

re·ex·am·i·na·tion
re·ex·am·ine
re·fer
ref·er·ee
ref·er·ence
ref·er·en·dum
re·ferred
re·fer·ring
re·fine
re·fined
re·fine·ment
re·fin·er
re·fin·ery
re·flect
re·flec·tion
re·flec·tive
re·flec·tor
re·flex
re·flex·ive
re·for·es·ta·tion
re·form
ref·or·ma·tion
re·for·ma·to·ry
re·formed
re·frac·tion
re·frac·to·ry
re·frain
re·fresh
re·fresh·ment
re·frig·er·ant
re·frig·er·ate
re·frig·er·a·tion
re·frig·er·a·tor
ref·uge
ref·u·gee
re·ful·gent

re·fur·bish
re·fus·al
re·fuse (reject)
ref·use (garbage)
re·fut·able
ref·u·ta·tion
re·fute
re·gain
re·gal
re·gale
re·ga·lia
re·gard
re·gard·ful
re·gard·less
re·gat·ta
re·gen·cy
re·gen·er·ate
re·gen·er·a·tive
re·gent
reg·i·cide
re·gime
reg·i·men
reg·i·ment
reg·i·men·tal
reg·i·men·ta·tion
re·gion
re·gion·al
re·gis·seur
reg·is·ter (to enroll;
   cf. *registrar*)
reg·is·tered
reg·is·trar (record
   keeper; cf. *register*)
reg·is·tra·tion
reg·is·try
reg·nant

re·gress
re·gres·sion
re·gres·sive
re·gret
re·gret·ful
re·gret·ta·ble
re·gret·ted
re·gret·ting
reg·u·lar
reg·u·lar·i·ty
reg·u·lar·ize
reg·u·late
reg·u·la·tion
reg·u·la·to·ry
re·gur·gi·tate
re·ha·bil·i·tate
re·hash
re·hear·ing
re·hears·al
re·hearse
reign (sovereignty;
    cf. *rain, rein*)
re·im·burs·able
re·im·burse
rein (of a horse;
    cf. *rain, reign*)
re·in·car·na·tion
rein·deer
re·in·force
re·in·force·ment
re·in·sert
re·in·state
re·in·sur·ance
re·in·sure
re·in·vest
re·in·vig·o·rate

re·it·er·ate
re·it·er·a·tion
re·ject
re·jec·tion
re·joice
re·join
re·join·der
re·ju·ve·nate
re·kin·dle
re·lapse
re·late
re·la·tion·ship
rel·a·tive
rel·a·tiv·i·ty
re·lax
re·lax·ation
re·laxed
re·lay
re·lease
rel·e·gate
re·lent
re·lent·less
rel·e·vance
rel·e·vant
re·li·able
re·li·ance
re·li·ant
rel·ic
rel·ict
re·lief
re·lieve
re·li·gion
re·li·gious
re·lin·quish
rel·i·quary
rel·ish

re·luc·tance
re·luc·tant
re·ly
re·main
re·main·der
re·mand
re·mark
re·mark·able
re·mar·riage
re·me·di·a·ble
re·me·di·al
rem·e·dy
re·mem·ber
re·mem·brance
re·mind
re·mind·er
rem·i·nisce
rem·i·nis·cence
rem·i·nis·cent
re·mis·sion
re·mit·tance
re·mit·tent
rem·nant
re·mon·e·tize
re·mon·strance
re·mon·strate
re·mon·stra·tion
re·morse
re·morse·less
re·mote
re·mov·able
re·mov·al
re·move
re·mu·ner·ate
re·mu·ner·a·tion
re·mu·ner·a·tive

**177**

re·nais·sance
ren·der
ren·dez·vous
ren·di·tion
ren·e·gade
re·nege
re·ne·go·tia·ble
re·ne·go·ti·ate
re·new
re·new·able
re·new·al
ren·net
re·nom·i·nate
re·nounce
ren·o·vate
ren·o·va·tion
re·nown
rent·al
re·nun·ci·a·tion
re·open
re·or·der
re·or·ga·ni·za·tion
re·pair
re·pair·man
rep·a·ra·tion
rep·ar·tee
re·past
re·pa·tri·ate
re·pa·tri·a·tion
re·pay
re·peal
re·peat
re·peat·er
re·pel
re·pelled
re·pel·lent

re·pel·ling
re·pent
re·pen·tance
re·pen·tant
re·per·cus·sion
rep·er·toire
rep·er·to·ry
rep·e·ti·tion
rep·e·ti·tious
re·pet·i·tive
re·pine
re·place
re·place·able
re·place·ment
re·plen·ish·ment
re·plete
re·plev·in
rep·li·ca
rep·li·cate
re·ply
re·port
re·port·er
re·pose
re·pos·i·to·ry
re·pos·sess
re·pous·sé
rep·re·hend
rep·re·hen·si·ble
re·pre·sent
rep·re·sen·ta·tion
rep·re·sen·ta·tive
re·press
re·pressed
re·pres·sion
re·pres·sive
re·prieve

rep·ri·mand
re·print
re·pri·sal
re·proach
re·proach·ful
rep·ro·bate
re·pro·duce
re·pro·duc·tion
re·pro·duc·tive
re·proof
re·prove
rep·tile
rep·til·ian
re·pub·lic
re·pub·li·can
re·pu·di·ate
re·pu·di·a·tion
re·pug·nance
re·pug·nant
re·pulse
re·pul·sion
re·pul·sive
re·pur·chase
rep·u·ta·ble
rep·u·ta·tion
re·pute
re·quest
re·qui·em
re·quire
re·quire·ment
req·ui·site
req·ui·si·tion
re·quit·al
re·quite
rere·dos
re·run

re·sal·able
re·scind
re·scis·sion
re·script
res·cue
re·search
re·sem·blance
re·sem·ble
re·sent
re·sent·ful
re·sent·ment
res·er·va·tion
re·serve
re·served
res·er·voir
re·shuf·fle
re·side
res·i·dence (home;
    cf. *residents*)
res·i·dent
res·i·den·tial
res·i·dents
    (those who
    reside; cf. *residence*)
re·sid·u·al
re·sid·u·ary
re·si·due
re·sid·u·um
re·sign
res·ig·na·tion
re·sil·ience
re·sil·ient
res·in
res·in·ous
re·sist
re·sis·tance

re·sis·tant
re·sis·tiv·i·ty
re·sis·tor
res·o·lute
res·o·lu·tion
re·solve
res·o·nance
res·o·nant
res·o·na·tor
re·sort
re·sound
re·source
re·source·ful
re·spect
re·spect·abil·i·ty
re·spect·able
re·spect·ful
re·spect·ful·ly (with
    deference;
    cf. *respectively*)
re·spec·tive
re·spec·tive·ly
    (in that order;
    cf. *respectfully*)
res·pi·ra·tion
res·pi·ra·tor
re·spi·ra·to·ry
re·spite
re·splen·dent
re·spond
re·spon·dent
re·sponse
re·spon·si·bil·i·ty
re·spon·si·ble
re·spon·sive
rest (repose; cf. *wrest*)

res·tau·rant
res·tau·ra·teur
rest home
rest house
res·ti·tu·tion
res·tive
rest·less
res·to·ra·tion
re·stor·ative
re·store
re·strain
re·straint
re·strict
re·stric·tion
re·stric·tive
re·sult
re·sul·tant
re·sume v.
ré·su·mé n.
re·sump·tion
re·sur·gence
res·ur·rect
res·ur·rec·tion
re·sus·ci·tate
re·sus·ci·ta·tion
re·tail
re·tain
re·tain·er
re·tal·i·ate
re·tal·i·a·tion
re·tal·ia·to·ry
re·tard
re·tar·da·tion
re·ten·tion
re·ten·tive
re·ten·tiv·i·ty

ret·i·cence
ret·i·cent
ret·i·cule
ret·i·na
ret·i·nene
re·tire
re·tire·ment
re·tool
re·tort
re·touch
re·trace
re·tract
re·trac·tile
re·trac·tion
re·treat
re·trench
ret·ri·bu·tion
re·triev·able
re·trieve
re·triev·er
ret·ro·ac·tive
ret·ro·ces·sion
ret·ro·grade
ret·ro·gres·sion
ret·ro—rock·et
ret·ro·spect
ret·ro·spec·tive
re·trous·sé
re·turn
re·turn·able
re·union
re·unite
re·us·able
re·use
re·val·ue
re·vamp

re·veal
rev·eil·le
rev·el
rev·e·la·tion
rev·eled
rev·el·ing
re·venge
rev·e·nue
re·ver·ber·ate
re·ver·ber·a·tion
re·ver·ber·a·to·ry
re·vere
rev·er·ence
rev·er·end
rev·er·ent
rev·er·en·tial
rev·er·ie
re·ver·sal
re·verse
re·vers·ible
re·ver·sion
re·ver·sion·ary
re·vert
re·vert·ed
re·vet·ment
re·vict·ual
re·view (restudy;
    cf. *revue*)
re·view·er
re·vile
re·vise
re·vi·sion
re·vi·tal·ize
re·viv·al
re·vive
re·viv·i·fy

re·vo·ca·ble
re·vo·ca·tion
re·voke
re·volt
rev·o·lu·tion
rev·o·lu·tion·ary
rev·o·lu·tion·ist
rev·o·lu·tion·ize
re·volve
re·volv·er
re·vue (theatrical per-
    formance; cf. *review*)
re·vul·sion
re·ward
re·wind
re·word
re·work
re·write
rhap·sod·ic
rhap·so·dist
rhap·so·dize
rhap·so·dy
rheo·stat
rhe·sus
rhet·o·ric
rhe·tor·i·cal
rheum (watery dis-
    charge; cf. *room*)
rheu·mat·ic
rheu·ma·tism
rhine·stone
rhi·ni·tis
rhi·noc·er·os
Rhode Is·land
rhom·boid
rhu·barb

rhyme (verse;
  cf. *rime*)
rhythm
rhyth·mic
rib·ald
rib·ald·ry
rib·bon
ric·er
rick·ets
rick·ety
ric·o·chet
rid·dle
rid·er·less
ridge·pole
rid·i·cule
ri·dic·u·lous
rif·fle (shuffle; cf. *rifle*)
riff·raff
ri·fle (gun; cf. *riffle*)
ri·fle·man
ri·fle·scope
ri·fling
right (correct;
  cf. *rite, write*)
righ·teous·ness
right·ful
right hand n.
right—hand adj.
right—hand·ed
right—of—way
right wing n.
right—wing·er n.
rig·id
ri·gid·i·ty
rig·or·ous
rime (frost; cf. *rhyme*)

ring (a bell; cf. *wring*)
ring·bolt
ring·bone
ring·dove
ring·lead·er
ring·mas·ter
ring·side
ring·worm
rinse
ri·ot·ous
ri·par·i·an
rip·en
ri·poste
rip·ple
rip·rap
rip—roar·ing
rip·saw
rip·snort·er
rip·tide
ris·i·bil·i·ty
risk·i·ness
ris·qué
rite (ceremony;
  cf. *right, write*)
rit·u·al
ri·val
ri·valed
ri·val·ing
ri·val·ry
riv·er·bed
riv·er·boat
riv·er·side
riv·et
riv·u·let
road (highway;
  cf. *rode, rowed*)

road·bed
road·block
road hog
road·house
road·stead
road·ster
road test
road·way
road·work
robbed
rob·bery
rob·bing
rob·in
ro·bot
ro·bust
ro·bus·tious
rock bot·tom n.
rock·bound
rock·et
rock·et·ry
rock 'n' roll
rock—ribbed
rock salt
rock·slide
rock snake
rock wool
rock·work
ro·co·co
rode (did ride;
  cf. *road, rowed*)
ro·dent
ro·deo
rod·man
roe (fish eggs; cf. *row*)
roent·gen
rogue

rogu·ish
role (part)
roll (turn over)
roll back v.
roll·back n.
roll call
roll·er coast·er
ro·maine
ro·mance
ro·man·tic
ro·man·ti·cism
rood (crucifix;
  cf. *rude, rued*)
roof·less
roof·top
rook·ery
rook·ie
room (of a house;
  cf. *rheum*)
room·er (lodger;
  cf. *rumor*)
room·ette
room·ful
room·i·ness
room·mate
roost·er
root (of a tree;
  cf. *rout, route*)
root beer
root·less
root·let
rope·danc·er
rope·walk
Ror·schach
ro·sa·ry
ro·se·ate

rose·bud
rose·bush
rose—col·ored
rose·mary
ro·se·o·la
ro·sette
rose wa·ter n.
rose·wa·ter adj.
rose·wood
ros·in
ros·ter
ros·trum
ro·ta·ry
ro·tate
ro·ta·tion
rote (memory;
  cf. *wrote*)
ro·tis·ser·ie
ro·to·gra·vure
rot·ten·stone
ro·tund
ro·tun·da
ro·tun·di·ty
rouge
rough (rude; cf. *ruff*)
rough·age
rough—and—
  ready
rough—and—
  tum·ble
rough·cast
rough—dry
rough·en
rough—hew
rough·house
rough·neck

rough·rid·er
rough·shod
rou·lade
rou·leau
rou·lette
round·about
roun·de·lay
round·house
round—shoul-
  dered
rounds·man
round up v.
round·up n.
roust·about
rout (disperse;
  cf. *root, route*)
route (highway;
  cf. *root, rout*)
route·man
rou·tine
rou·tin·ize
row (a boat; cf. *roe*)
row·boat
row·di·ness
row·dy
rowed (did row;
  cf. *road, rode*)
row·el
row house
row·lock
roy·al
roy·al·ist
roy·al·ty
ru·ba·to
rubbed
rub·ber

rub·ber·ize
rub·ber·neck
rub·ber  stamp  n.
rub·ber—stamp  v.
rub·bing
rub·bish
rub·ble
rub·ble·work
rub  down  v.
rub·down  n.
Ru·bi·con
ru·bi·cund
ru·bric
ruck·sack
ruck·us
rud·der
rud·dy
rude  (rough;
    cf. *rood, rued*)
ru·di·ment
ru·di·men·ta·ry
rued  (regretted;
    cf. *rood, rude*)
rue·ful
ruff  (collar; cf. *rough*)
ruf·fi·an
ruf·fle
rug·ged
rug·ged·iza·tion
ru·in·ous
rum·ba
rum·ble
ru·mi·nant
ru·mi·nate
ru·mi·na·tion
rum·mage

ru·mor  (gossip;
    cf. *roomer*)
ru·mor·mon·ger
rum·ple
rum·pus
rum·run·ner
run·about
run·around  n.
run  away  v.
run·away  adj., n.
run  down  v.
run—down  adj.
run·down  n.
rung  (a bell;
    cf. *wrung*)
run  in  v.
run—in  n.
run·ner
run·ner—up
run  off  v.
run·off  n.
run—of—the—
    mill
run—of—the—
    mine
run  on  v.
run—on  adj., n.
run  over  v.
run—over  adj.
run·over  n.
run·proof
run  through  v.
run—through  n.
run·way
ru·pee
rup·ture

ru·ral
ru·ral·ly
rus·set
rus·tic
rus·ti·cate
rus·tle
rust·proof  adj.
rust—proof  v.
ru·ta·ba·ga
ruth·less
rye  (grain; cf. *wry*)

Sab·bath
sab·bat·i·cal
sa·ber
sa·ble
sab·o·tage
sab·o·teur
sa·bra
sac  (pouch in
    animal; cf. *sack*)
sac·cha·rin  n.
sac·cha·rine  adj.
sac·er·do·tal
sa·chem
sack  (bag; cf. *sac*)
sack·cloth
sack  coat

sack·ful
sack race
sac·ra·ment
sac·ra·men·tal
sa·cred
sac·ri·fice
sac·ri·fi·cial
sac·ri·lege
sac·ri·le·gious
sac·ris·tan
sac·ris·ty
sac·ro·sanct
sa·crum
sad·den
sad·der
sad·dest
sad·dle
sad·dle·bag
sad·dle·bow
sad·dle·cloth
sad·dler
sad·iron
sa·dism
sa·dist
sa·dis·tic
sad·ness
safe—con·duct
safe·crack·er
safe—de·pos·it
safe·guard
safe·keep·ing
safe·ty
saf·fron
sa·ga
sa·ga·cious
sa·gac·i·ty

sag·a·more
sage·brush
sa·hib
sail (of a ship;
    cf. *sale*)
sail·boat
sail·cloth
sail·fish
sail·or
saint·li·ness
saint·ly
sa·laam
sal·abil·i·ty
sal·able
sa·la·cious
sal·ad
sal·a·man·der
sa·la·mi
sal·a·ried
sal·a·ry
sale (selling; cf. *sail*)
sal·era·tus
sales
sales check
sales·clerk
sales·man
sales·man·ship
sales·room
sales·wom·an
sal·i·cyl·ic
sa·lience
sa·lient
sa·line
sa·li·va
sal·i·vary
sal·low

sal·ma·gun·di
salm·on
sa·lon (shop)
sa·loon (tavern)
sal·ta·to·ry
salt·box
salt·cel·lar
sal·tine
salt·i·ness
salt marsh
salt·pe·ter
salt·shak·er
salt wa·ter n.
salt·wa·ter adj.
salt·works
salty
sa·lu·bri·ous
sal·u·tary
sal·u·ta·tion
sa·lu·ta·to·ri·an
sa·lute
sal·vage
sal·va·tion
Sa·mar·i·tan
same·ness
sa·mite
sam·o·var
sam·pan
sam·ple
sam·pler
sam·pling
sam·u·rai
san·a·to·ri·um
san·a·to·ry (healing;
    cf. *sanitary*)
sanc·ti·fi·ca·tion

sanc·ti·fy
sanc·ti·mo·nious
sanc·tion
sanc·ti·ty
sanc·tu·ary
sanc·tum
san·dal
san·dal·wood
sand·bag
sand·bank
sand·bar
sand·blast
sand·box
sand·bur
sand·er
sand·glass
sand·hog
sand·lot
sand·man
sand·pa·per
sand·pile
sand·pip·er
sand·soap
sand·stone
sand·storm
sand ta·ble
sand trap
sand·wich
sand·worm
sang·froid
san·gui·nary
san·guine
san·i·tary (hygienic;
  cf. *sanatory*)
san·i·ta·tion
san·i·ty

sans·cu·lotte
sap·ling
sa·pon·i·fy
sap·phire
sap·suck·er
sap·wood
sar·a·band
sar·casm
sar·cas·tic
sar·co·ma
sar·coph·a·gi pl.
sar·coph·a·gus sing.
sar·dine
sar·don·ic
sard·onyx
sar·gas·so
sa·rong
sar·sa·pa·ril·la
sar·to·ri·al
sas·sa·fras
sa·tan·ic
satch·el
sa·teen
sat·el·lite
sa·tia·ble
sa·ti·ate
sa·ti·ety
sat·in
sat·in·wood
sat·ire
sa·tir·ic
sa·tir·i·cal
sat·i·rize
sat·is·fac·tion
sat·is·fac·to·ri·ly
sat·is·fac·to·ry

sat·is·fy
sa·trap
sat·u·rate
sat·u·rat·ed
sat·u·ra·tion
Sat·ur·day
sat·ur·nine
sa·tyr
sauce·pan
sau·cer
sau·er·bra·ten
sau·er·kraut
Sault Sainte
  Ma·rie
sau·na
saun·ter
sau·sage
sau·té
sau·terne
sav·age
sav·age·ry
sa·van·na
sa·vant
sav·ior
sa·vory
saw·dust
sawed—off
saw·horse
saw·mill
saw—toothed
saw·yer
sax·o·phone
scab·bard
scaf·fold
scaf·fold·ing
scal·a·wag

scal·lion
scal·lop
scal·pel
scam·per
scan·dal
scan·dal·ize
scan·dal·ous
Scan·di·na·vian
scan·ner
scan·ning
scan·sion
scant·i·ly
scant·ling
scanty
scape·goat
scap·u·la
scap·u·lar
scar·ab
scarce·ly
scar·ci·ty
scare·crow
scar·i·fy
scar·la·ti·na
scar·let
scath·ing
scat·ter
scat·ter·brain
scav·en·ger
sce·nar·io
scen·ery
scene·shift·er
sce·nic
scent (odor;
   cf. *cent, sent*)
scep·ter
sched·ule

sche·mat·ic
scheme
scher·zo
schism
schist
schmaltz
schnook
schol·ar
schol·ar·ly
schol·ar·ship
scho·las·tic
scho·las·ti·cism
school·bag
school board
school·boy
school bus
school·child
school·girl
school·house
school·man
school·mas·ter
school·mate
school·room
school·teach·er
school·work
schoo·ner
sci·at·ic
sci·at·i·ca
sci·ence
sci·en·tif·ic
sci·en·tist
scim·i·tar
scin·til·la
scin·til·late
sci·on
scis·sors

scle·ro·sis
scoff·law
scor·bu·tic
score·board
score·card
score·keep·er
scorn·ful
scor·pi·on
scot—free
scoun·drel
scourge
scout·mas·ter
scrap·book
scrap·per
scrap·ple
scratch
scratch·i·ness
scratchy
screech
screed
screen
screen·play
screw·ball
screw·driv·er
scrib·ble
scrim·mage
scrim·shaw
scrip (paper money)
script (manuscript)
scrip·tur·al
scrip·ture
scriv·en·er
scrof·u·la
scroll·work
scrubbed
scrub·bing

scrump·tious
scru·ple
scru·pu·lous
scru·ti·nize
scru·ti·ny
scuf·fle
scuf·fling
scull (boat; cf. *skull*)
scul·lery
scul·lion
sculp·tor
sculp·tur·al
sculp·ture
scur·ril·i·ty
scur·ri·lous
scur·vy
scut·tle
scut·tle·butt
scut·tling
scythe
sea (ocean; cf. *see*)
sea·bag
sea bass
sea·beach
sea·bird
sea·board
sea·boot
sea·borne
sea breeze
sea chest
sea·coast
sea dog
sea·drome
sea·far·er
sea·far·ing
sea fight

sea·food
sea·fowl
sea·front
sea·girt
sea·go·ing
sea green
sea gull
sea horse
sea—lane
sea legs
seal ring
seal·skin
seam (of a dress;
    cf. *seem*)
sea·man
sea·man·like
sea·man·ship
seam·ster mas.
seam·stress fem.
sé·ance
sea·plane
sea·port
sear (burn; cf. *seer*)
search·light
sea room
sea·scape
sea scout
sea·shell
sea·shore
sea·sick
sea·side
sea·son
sea·son·able
sea·son·al
sea·wall
sea·ward

sea·wa·ter
sea·way
sea·weed
sea·wor·thi·ness
sea·wor·thy
se·ba·ceous
se·cant
se·cede
se·ces·sion
se·clude
se·clu·sion
sec·ond
sec·ond·ari·ly
sec·ond·ary
sec·ond class n.
sec·ond—class adj.
sec·ond—guess v.
sec·ond·hand adj.
sec·ond—rate adj.
se·cre·cy
se·cret
sec·re·tari·al
sec·re·tary
se·crete
se·cre·tion
se·cre·tive
se·cre·to·ry
sec·tar·i·an
sec·ta·ry
sec·tion
sec·tion·al·ly
sec·tor
sec·u·lar
sec·u·lar·ism
se·cure
se·cu·ri·ty

se·dan
se·date
se·da·tion
sed·a·tive
sed·en·tary
sed·i·ment
sed·i·men·ta·ry
se·di·tion
se·di·tious
se·duce
se·duc·er
se·duc·tion
se·duc·tive
sed·u·lous
see (perceive; cf. *sea*)
seed (of a plant;
   cf. *cede*)
seed·i·ness
seed·ling
seed·pod
seedy
seem (appear;
   cf. *seam*)
seem·li·ness
seem·ly
seep·age
seer (prophet; cf. *sear*)
seer·suck·er
see·saw
seg·ment
seg·re·gate
seg·re·gat·ed
seg·re·ga·tion
seg·re·ga·tion·ist
seis·mic
seis·mo·graph

seis·mo·log·i·cal
seis·mom·e·ter
seize
seiz·ing
sei·zure
sel·dom
se·lect
se·lec·tion
se·lec·tive
se·lect·man
Se·lect·ric
se·le·ni·um
self—abase·ment
self—ad·dressed
self—ag·gran·dize·
   ment
self—as·sured
self—cen·tered
self—com·posed
self—con·fi·dence
self—con·scious
self—con·tained
self—con·trol
self—de·fense
self—de·struc·tion
self—de·ter·mi·na·
   tion
self—dis·ci·pline
self—ed·u·cat·ed
self—ef·face·ment
self—em·ployed
self—es·teem
self—ex·e·cut·ing
self—ex·pres·sion
self—glo·ri·fi·ca·
   tion

self—gov·ern·ment
self—im·por·tance
self—im·posed
self—im·prove·
   ment
self—in·crim·i·na·
   tion
self—in·dul·gence
self—in·sured
self—in·ter·est
self·ish
self·less
self—liq·ui·dat·
   ing
self—made
self—pity
self—pos·sessed
self—pos·ses·sion
self—pres·er·va·
   tion
self—pro·tec·tion
self—re·gard
self—re·li·ance
self—re·spect
self—ris·ing
self—sac·ri·fice
self·same
self—start·er
self—suf·fi·cien·cy
self—suf·fi·cient
self—willed
self—wind·ing
sell·er (one who
   sells; cf. *cellar*)
selt·zer
sel·vage

se·man·tic
sema·phore
sem·blance
se·mes·ter
semi·an·nu·al
semi·ar·id
semi·au·to·mat·ic
semi·au·ton·o·
   mous
semi·cir·cle
semi·civ·i·lized
semi·clas·si·cal
semi·co·lon
semi·con·duc·tor
semi·con·scious
semi·crys·tal·line
semi·dark·ness
semi·de·tached
semi·fi·nal
semi·fin·ished
semi—in·de·pen·
   dent
semi—in·di·rect
semi·month·ly
sem·i·nar
sem·i·nary
semi·per·ma·nent
semi·pre·cious
semi·pri·vate
semi·pro
semi·pro·fes·
   sion·al
semi·pub·lic
semi·skilled
semi·trans·lu·cent
semi·trans·par·ent

semi·vow·el
semi·week·ly
sem·pi·ter·nal
sen·ate
sen·a·tor
sen·a·to·ri·al
send—off n.
se·nes·cent
se·nile
se·nil·i·ty
se·nior
se·nior·i·ty
sen·sa·tion
sen·sa·tion·al
sens·es (sensations;
   cf. *census*)
sense·less
sen·si·bil·i·ty
sen·si·ble
sen·si·tive
sen·si·tiv·i·ty
sen·si·tize
sen·so·ry
sen·su·al
sen·su·ous
sent (dispatched;
   cf. *cent, scent*)
sen·tence
sen·ten·tious
sen·tient
sen·ti·ment
sen·ti·men·tal
sen·ti·men·tal·ism
sen·ti·men·tal·i·ty
sen·ti·nel
sen·try

sep·a·ra·ble
sep·a·rate
sep·a·ra·tion
sep·a·rat·ist
sep·a·ra·tor
se·pia
Sep·tem·ber
sep·tet
sep·tic
sep·ti·ce·mia
sep·tu·a·ge·nar·
   i·an
sep·ul·cher
se·pul·chral
sep·ul·ture
se·quel
se·quence
se·quen·tial
se·ques·ter
se·ques·trate
se·quin
se·quoia
se·ra·glio
ser·aph
se·raph·ic
ser·e·nade
ser·en·dip·i·ty
se·rene
se·ren·i·ty
serf (peasant; cf. *surf*)
serge (cloth; cf. *surge*)
ser·geant
se·ri·al (series;
   cf. *cereal*)
se·ri·al·iza·tion
se·ri·al·ize

se·ri·a·tim
se·ries (related group;
  cf. *serious, serous*)
ser·if
seri·graph
se·rio·com·ic
se·ri·ous (grave;
  cf. *series, serous*)
se·ri·ous—mind-
  ed adj.
ser·mon
ser·mon·ize
se·rous (like serum;
  cf. *series, serous*)
ser·pent
ser·pen·tine
ser·ra·tion
se·rum
ser·vant
ser·vice
ser·vice·able
ser·vile
ser·vil·i·ty
ser·vi·tor
ser·vi·tude
ser·vo·mech·a·
  nism
ser·vo·mo·tor
ses·a·me
ses·qui·cen·ten·
  ni·al
ses·qui·pe·da·lian
ses·sion (a meeting;
  cf. *cession*)
set·back n.
set off v.

set·off n.
set out v.
set·out n.
set piece
set·screw
set·tee
set·ter
set·tle·ment
set·tling
set to v.
set—to n.
set up v.
set·up n.
sev·en·teenth
sev·en—up
sev·er
sev·er·al
sev·er·al·fold
sev·er·al·ty
sev·er·ance
se·vere
se·ver·i·ty
sew (stitch; cf. *so, sow*)
sew·age
sew·er
sew·er·age
sex·tant
sex·tet
sex·ton
shab·bi·ness
shab·by
shack·le
shad·ow
shad·ow box n.
shad·ow·box v.
shad·owy

shag·bark
shag·gi·ness
sha·green
shake·down adj., n.
shake·out n.
shake up v.
shake—up n.
shak·i·ly
shal·lop
shal·lot
shal·low
sham
sham·ble
shame
shame·faced
shame·ful
shame·less
sham·ing
sham·poo
sham·rock
shang·hai
shan·ty
shan·ty·town
shape·less
shape·li·ness
shape·ly
shape—up n.
share·crop·per
share·hold·er
shark·skin
sharp·en·er
sharp·er
sharp—eyed
sharp·shoot·er
sharp—sight·ed
sharp—tongued

sharp—wit·ted
shat·ter·proof
shave·tail
shawl
sheaf
shear (cut; cf. *sheer*)
sheath n.
sheathe v.
sheath·ing
sheath  knife
sheen
sheep—dip
sheep  dog
sheep·fold
sheep·herd·er
sheep·ish
sheep·skin
sheer (thin; cf. *shear*)
sheet  met·al
Sheet·rock
shel·lac
shel·lacked
shel·lack·ing
shell·back
shell·fire
shell·fish
shell  game
shell·proof
shell  shock n.
shel·ter
she·nan·i·gan
shep·herd
sher·bet
sher·iff
sher·ry
shib·bo·leth

shield
shift·i·ly
shift·i·ness
shift·less
shifty
shil·ling
shimmed
shim·mer
shim·my
shin·gle
ship·board
ship·fit·ter
ship·mas·ter
ship·mate
ship·ment
ship·pa·ble
shipped
ship·per
ship·ping
ship·shape
ship·wreck
ship·wright
ship·yard
shirr·ing
shirt·ing
shirt·mak·er
shirt·tail
shirt·waist
shish  ke·bab
shiv·er
shock·proof
shod
shod·di·ly
shod·di·ness
shod·dy
shoe

shoed
shoe·horn
shoe·ing
shoe·lace
shoe·mak·er
shoe·string
shoe  tree
sho·gun
shone (gave light;
   cf. *shown*)
shoot (to fire;
   cf. *chute*)
shop·keep·er
shop·lift·er
shop·lift·ing
shop·per
shop·talk
shop·worn
short·age
short·bread
short·cake
short·change
short  cir·cuit n.
short—cir·cuit v.
short·com·ing
short·cut n., adj.
short—cut v.
short·en·ing
short·hand
short·hand·ed
short  haul n.
short—haul adj.
short·horn
short—lived
short—range adj.
short  ribs

**191**

short·sight·ed
short—spo·ken
short·stop
short—tem·pered
short—term
short·wave
short weight n.
short—weight v.
short—wind·ed
shot·gun
shot put
shot—put·ter
shoul·der
shov·el
shov·eled
shov·el·ful
shov·el·ing
show·boat
show·case
show·down
show·er
show·i·er
show·i·est
show·i·ly
show·i·ness
show·man
shown (displayed;
   cf. shone)
show off v.
show—off n.
show·piece
show·place
show·room
showy
shrap·nel
shred

shred·der
shred·ding
shrewd
shrew·ish
shriek
shrimp
shrink·age
shriv·el
shriv·eled
shriv·el·ing
shrub·bery
shud·der
shuf·fle
shuf·fle·board
shut·down
shut—eye
shut—in adj., n.
shut·off
shut out v.
shut·out n.
shut·ter
shut·ter·bug
shut·tle·cock
shy·ster
sib·i·lant
sib·ling
sib·yl
sib·yl·line
sick bay
sick·bed
sick call
sick·en·ing
sick·ish
sick·le
sick leave
sick·li·ness

sick·ness
sick·room
side·band
side·board
side·burns
side·car
side·light
side·line
side·long
si·de·re·al
side·sad·dle
side·show
side·slip
side·spin
side·split·ting
side step n.
side·step v.
side·swipe
side·track
side·walk
side·wall
side·ways
side·wise
si·dle
siege
si·en·na
si·es·ta
sieve
sigh
sight (vision;
   cf. cite, site)
sight·less
sight·li·ness
sight·ly
sight—read v.
sight—see·ing

sig·moid
sig·nal
sig·naled
sig·nal·ing
sig·nal·ize
sig·nal·man
sig·na·to·ry
sig·na·ture
sign·board
sig·net
sig·nif·i·cance
sig·nif·i·cant
sig·ni·fi·ca·tion
sig·ni·fy
sign·post
si·lage
si·lence
si·lenc·er
si·lent
si·le·sia
si·lex
sil·hou·ette
sil·i·ca
sil·i·cate
sil·i·con (element)
sil·i·cone (compound)
sil·i·co·sis
silk·en
silk·i·ness
silk—stock·ing adj.
silk·weed
silk·worm
silky
sil·ly
si·lo

si·los
sil·ver
sil·ver·smith
sil·ver—tongued
sil·ver·ware
sil·very
sim·i·an
sim·i·lar
sim·i·lar·i·ty
sim·i·le
si·mil·i·tude
sim·mer
si·mon—pure
sim·per
sim·ple
sim·ple·mind·ed
sim·ple·ton
sim·plex
sim·plic·i·ty
sim·pli·fi·ca·tion
sim·pli·fy
sim·ply
sim·u·la·crum
sim·u·late
sim·u·la·tion
si·mul·ta·neous
sin·cere
sin·cer·i·ty
si·ne·cure
sin·ew
sin·ewy
sin·ful
singe
singed
singe·ing
sin·gle

sin·gle—breast·ed
sin·gle—hand·ed
sin·gle—mind·ed
sin·gle·ness
sin·gle—space v.
sin·gle·ton
sin·gle—track adj.
sin·gly
sing·song
sin·gu·lar
sin·gu·lar·i·ty
sin·is·ter
sink·age
sink·er
sink·hole
sin·u·os·i·ty
sin·u·ous
si·nus
Sioux City Iowa
si·phon
si·ren
sir·loin
si·roc·co
sis·ter—in—law
sit—down n.
site (place;
  cf. *cite, sight*)
sit—in n.
sit·u·at·ed
sit·u·a·tion
six—pack
sixth
six·ti·eth
siz·able
siz·zle
siz·zling

193

skat·er
skein
skel·e·ton
skep·tic
skep·ti·cal
skep·ti·cism
sketch
sketch·book
sketch·i·ly
sketchy
skew·er
ski
ski·ing
skid
skid·ded
skid·ding
skid row
ski jump
ski lift
skilled
skil·let
skill·ful
skimpy
skin
skin·flint
skinned
skin·ning
skin·tight
skip
skipped
skip·per
skip·ping
skir·mish
skit·tish
skiv·er
skulk

skull (bone of head;
   cf. *scull*)
skull·cap
skunk
sky blue n.
sky—blue adj.
sky·cap
sky·coach
sky div·er
sky—high
sky·lark
sky·light
sky·line
sky·rock·et
sky·scrap·er
sky·ward
sky wave
sky·way
sky·writ·er
sky·writ·ing
slack·en
sla·lom
slam
slammed
slam·ming
slan·der
slan·der·ous
slap·dash
slap·hap·py
slap·jack
slapped
slap·ping
slap·stick
slat·tern
slat·tern·li·ness
slaugh·ter

slaugh·ter·house
slav·ery
slav·ish
slay (kill; cf. *sleigh*)
slea·zi·ness
slea·zy
sledge
sledge·ham·mer
sleep·er
sleep·i·ness
sleep·less
sleep·walk·er
sleepy
sleeve·less
sleigh (winter
   vehicle; cf. *slay*)
sleigh bell
slen·der
sleuth
sleuth·hound
slide rule
slight
slime
sling·shot
slip
slip·case
slip·cov·er
slip·knot
slip noose
slip—on n.
slip·over n.
slip·page
slipped
slip·per
slip·peri·ness
slip·pery

slip·ping
slip sheet n.
slip—sheet v.
slip·shod
slip up v.
slip·up n.
slith·er
sliv·er
sloe (fruit; cf. *slow*)
sloe—eyed
slo·gan
sloop
slope
slop·pi·ness
slop·py
sloth·ful
slouch
slouch·i·ness
slouchy
slo·ven·li·ness
slov·en·ly
slow (not fast; cf. *sloe*)
slow·down n.
slow·poke
slow—wit·ted
sloyd
sludge
slug·gard
slug·gish
sluice
sluice·way
slum·ber
slum·lord
slush
small·pox
smart·en

smash·up n.
smat·ter·ing
smi·lax
smith·er·eens
smoke·house
smoke·jack
smoke·less
smok·er
smoke·stack
smok·ing
    room n.
smok·ing—room
    adj.
smoky
smol·der
smooth
smooth·bore
smooth—tongued
smor·gas·bord
smoth·er
smudge
smug·gle
smut·ty
snaf·fle
sna·fu
snag
snagged
snag·ging
snail—paced
snake pit
snake·root
snake·skin
snaky
snap·drag·on
snap·shot
snare drum

sneak·er
sneak thief
sneer
sneeze
snick·er
snip
snipped
snip·pety
snip·pi·ness
snip·ping
snip·py
sniv·el
sniv·eled
sniv·el·ing
snob
snob·bery
snob·bish
snor·kel
snow·ball
snow·bank
snow—blind
snow·blow·er
snow·bound
snow·capped
snow·drift
snow·drop
snow·fall
snow·flake
snow line
snow·man
snow·mo·bile
snow·plow
snow·shed
snow·shoe
snow·storm
snow·suit

snow tire
snow—white adj.
snowy
snub
snubbed
snub·bing
snub—nosed
snuff·box
snuff·er
snuf·fle
so (thus; cf. *sew*, *sow*)
soap·box
soap·i·ness
soap·stone
soap·suds
soapy
soar (rise aloft;
    cf. *sore*)
soared (did soar;
    cf. *sward*, *sword*)
so·ber
so·ber·sides
so·bri·e·ty
so·bri·quet
so—called
soc·cer
so·cia·bil·i·ty
so·cia·ble
so·cial
so·cial·ism
so·cial·ist
so·cial·ite
so·cial·ize
so·cial·ly
so·cial—mind·ed
so·ci·e·tal

so·ci·e·ty
so·cio·eco·nom·ic
so·cio·log·i·cal
so·ci·ol·o·gy
so·cio·po·lit·i·cal
sock·et
so·da
so·dal·i·ty
sod·den
so·di·um
soft·ball
soft—boiled
soft·en
soft·head·ed
soft·heart·ed
soft—shoe
soft soap n.
soft—soap v.
soft—spo·ken
soft·ware
soft·wood
sog·gi·ness
sog·gy
soi—di·sant
so·journ
so·lace
so·lar
sol·der
sol·dier
sole (only; cf. *soul*)
so·le·cism
sole·ly
sol·emn
so·lem·ni·ty
sol·em·ni·za·tion
sol·em·nize

so·le·noid
sol·feg·gio
so·lic·it
so·lic·i·ta·tion
so·lic·i·tor
so·lic·i·tous
so·lic·i·tude
sol·id
sol·i·dar·i·ty
so·lid·i·fi·ca·tion
so·lid·i·fy
so·lid·i·ty
sol·id—state
so·lil·o·quies
so·lil·o·quize
so·lil·o·quy
sol·i·taire
sol·i·tary
sol·i·tude
so·lo
sol·stice
sol·u·bil·i·ty
sol·u·ble
so·lu·tion
solv·able
sol·ven·cy
sol·vent
som·ber
som·bre·ro
some (part; cf. *sum*)
some·body
some·day adv.
some·how
some·one
some·place adv.
som·er·sault

some·thing
some·time adv.
some·times
some·what
some·where
som·me·lier
som·nam·bu·lism
som·no·lent
son (child; cf. *sun*)
so·na·ta
song·bird
song·book
song·fest
song·writ·er
son—in—law
son·net
son·ne·teer
so·nor·i·ty
so·no·rous
soothe
sooth·ing·ly
sooth·say·er
soot·i·ness
sooty
soph·ism
so·phis·ti·cate
so·phis·ti·cat·ed
so·phis·ti·ca·tion
soph·ist·ry
soph·o·more
so·po·rif·ic
so·pra·no
sor·cer·er
sor·cery
sor·did
sore (painful; cf. *soar*)

sore·head
sor·ghum
so·ror·i·ty
sor·rel
sor·ri·ly
sor·row
sor·row·ful
sor·ry
sou·brette
souf·flé
soul (spirit; cf. *sole*)
soul·ful
soul·less
soul mate
sound·proof adj., v.
soup·con
sour·dough
sour grapes
South Car·o·li·na
South Da·ko·ta
south·east
south·er·ly
south·ern
South·ern·er
south·land
south·paw
south pole
south·west
sou·ve·nir
sov·er·eign
sov·er·eign·ty
so·vi·et
sow (plant;
   cf. *sew, so*)
soy
soya

soy·bean
space·craft
space·flight
space·man
space·ship
space suit
spa·cious
spade·work
spa·ghet·ti
spal·peen
span·drel
span·gle
span·iel
span·ner
spare·ribs
spar·kle
spark plug
spar·row
spas·mod·ic
spas·tic
spa·tial
spat·ter
spat·u·la
spav·ined
speak·easy
speak·er
spear·fish
spear·head
spear·mint
spe·cial
spe·cial·ist
spe·cial·ize
spe·cial·ty
spe·cie (coin)
spe·cies (variety)
spe·cif·ic

spec·i·fi·ca·tion
spec·i·fy
spec·i·men
spe·cious
spec·ta·cle
spec·tac·u·lar
spec·ta·tor
spec·ter
spec·tral
spec·tro·scope
spec·trum
spec·u·late
spec·u·la·tion
spec·u·la·tive
spec·u·lum
speech
speech·less
speed·boat
speed·i·ly
speed·om·e·ter
speed·up n.
speed·way
spe·le·ol·o·gy
spell·bind·er
spell·bound
spe·lunk·er
spend·thrift
sphag·num
spher·i·cal
sphinx
spick—and—span
  adj.
spic·ule
spicy
spi·der
spig·ot

spike·nard
spill·way
spin·ach
spi·nal
spin·dle
spine·less
spin·et
spin·ster
spi·ral
spi·raled
spi·ral·ing
spi·ral·ly
spi·rea
spir·it·ed
spir·it·less
spir·i·tu·al
spir·i·tu·al·ism
spir·i·tu·al·i·ty
spir·i·tu·ous
spit·ball
spit curl
spite·ful
spit·fire
spit·toon
splash·board
splash·down
splash guard
splen·did
splen·dor
sple·net·ic
splin·ter
split—lev·el adj., n.
splotch
splurge
spoil·age
spoils·man

spoil·sport
spo·ken
spoke·shave
spokes·man
spo·li·a·tion
spon·dee
sponge
spongy
spon·sor
spon·ta·ne·ity
spon·ta·ne·ous
spoon—feed v.
spoon·ful
spo·rad·ic
sport·ive
sports·cast
sport shirt
sports·man
sports·man·ship
sports·wear
sports·writ·er
spot check n.
spot—check v.
spot·less
spot·light n., v.
spot·ted
spot·ter
sprawl
spread ea·gle n.
spread—ea·gle
  adj., v.
spree
spright·li·ness
spright·ly
spring·board
spring·bok

spring—clean-
   ing n.
spring·house
spring·i·ness
spring·time
sprin·kle
sprin·kler
sprin·kling
sprock·et
sprout
spruce
spu·mo·ni *or*
   spu·mo·ne
spur
spu·ri·ous
spurn
spurred
spur·ring
spurt
spur track
sput·nik
sput·ter
spu·tum
spy·glass
squab
squab·ble
squad·ron
squad room
squal·id
squall
squa·lor
squan·der
square dance
square deal
square knot
square—rigged

square root
squash
squat·ter
squaw
squawk
squeak
squea·mish
squee·gee
squir·rel
squirt
sta·bil·i·ty
sta·bi·li·za·tion
sta·bi·lize
sta·bi·liz·er
sta·ble
stac·ca·to
sta·di·um
staff·er
stage·coach
stage·craft
stage fright
stage·hand
stage·struck
stag·ger
stag·nant
stag·nate
stag·na·tion
staid (sedate;
   cf. *stayed*)
stain·less
stair (steps; cf. *stare*)
stair·case
stair·way
stake (marker;
   cf. *steak*)
stake·hold·er

sta·lac·tite
   (hangs down)
sta·lag·mite
   (stands up)
stale·mate
stalk·ing—horse n.
stal·lion
stal·wart
sta·men
stam·i·na
stam·mer
stam·pede
stamp·er
stanch
stan·chion
stan·dard
stan·dard—
   bear·er n.
stan·dard·bred n.
stan·dard·iza·tion
stan·dard·ize
stand by v.
stand·by n.
stand·ee
stand in v.
stand—in n.
stand off v.
stand·off adj., n.
stand·off·ish
stand out v.
stand·out n.
stand·pat·ter
stand·pipe
stand·point
stand·still
stand up v.

stand—up adj.
stan·za
sta·ple
star·board
star—cham·ber adj.
starch·i·ness
starchy
star—crossed
star·dom
star·dust
stare (look; cf. *stair*)
star·fish
star·gaz·er
star·let
star·light
star·ling
star·lit
star·ry—eyed
star shell
star—span·gled
star·tle
star·tling
star·va·tion
starve
state·craft
state·hood
state·house
state·less
state·li·ness
state·ly
state·ment
state·room
states·man
states' right·er
stat·ic
sta·tion

sta·tion·ary (fixed; cf. *stationery*)
sta·tio·ner
sta·tio·nery (paper; cf. *stationary*)
stat·ism
sta·tis·ti·cal
stat·is·ti·cian
sta·tis·tics
stat·u·ary
stat·ue (sculpture; cf. *stature, statute*)
stat·u·esque
stat·u·ette
stat·ure (height; cf. *statue, statute*)
sta·tus
stat·ute (law; cf. *statue, stature*)
stat·u·to·ry
stay—at—home adj., n.
stayed (remained; cf. *staid*)
stay·sail
stead·fast
steadi·ly
steak (meat; cf. *stake*)
steal (rob; cf. *steel*)
stealth
steam·boat
steam·er
steam fit·ter
steam—heat·ed
steam·roll·er
steam·ship

steam ta·ble
steel (metal; cf. *steal*)
steel wool
steel·work
steel·yard
stee·ple
stee·ple·chase
stee·ple·jack
steer·age
steer·age·way
steers·man
stem
stemmed
stem·ware
stem—wind·er
sten·cil
sten·ciled
sten·cil·ing
ste·nog·ra·pher
steno·graph·ic
ste·nog·ra·phy
sten·to·ri·an
step (walk; cf. *steppe*)
step·child
step·daugh·ter
step down v.
step—down n.
step·fa·ther
step in v.
step—in n.
step·lad·der
step·moth·er
step·par·ent
steppe (plain; cf. *step*)
step·ping—off place

step·ping—stone
step·sis·ter
step·son
step stool
step up v.
step—up adj., n.
ste·reo
ste·reo·phon·ic
ste·reo·op·ti·con
ste·reo·scope
ste·reo·type
ster·ile
ste·ril·i·ty
ster·il·ize
ster·ling
ster·num
ster·nu·ta·tion
ster·to·rous
stetho·scope
ste·ve·dore
stew·ard
stew·pan
stick·ful
stick·i·ness
stick·ler
stick·pin
stick—to—it·ive-
 ness
stick up v.
stick·up n.
stiff·en
stiff—necked
sti·fle
stig·ma sing.
stig·ma·ta pl.
stig·ma·tize

stile (fence; cf. *style*)
sti·let·to
still·birth
still·born
still hunt n.
still—hunt v.
still life
stilt·ed
stim·u·lant
stim·u·late
stim·u·la·tion
stim·u·li pl.
stim·u·lus sing.
stin·gi·ness
stin·gy
stink·er
stink·weed
sti·pend
sti·pen·di·ary
stip·ple
stip·u·late
stip·u·la·tion
stir
stirred
stir·ring
stir·rup
stock·ade
stock·bro·ker
stock car
stock clerk
stock·hold·er
stock·ing
stock—in—
 trade n.
stock·job·ber
stock·man

stock·pile n., v.
stock·pot
stock·proof
stock·room
stock·yard
stodg·i·ness
stodgy
sto·ic
stoke·hold
stok·er
stol·id
stom·ach
stom·ach·ache
stone—blind
stone—broke
stone·cut·ter
stone—deaf
stone·ma·son
stone·ware
stone·work
ston·i·ly
stony·heart·ed
stor·able
stor·age
store·front n., adj.
store·house
store·keep·er
store·room
store·wide
storm·bound
storm cloud
storm door
stormy
sto·ry
sto·ry·book
sto·ry·tell·er

stout·heart·ed
stove·pipe
stow·age
stow away v.
stow·away n.
stra·bis·mus
strad·dle
strad·dling
strag·gle
strag·gly
straight (direct;
  cf. *strait*)
straight·away
straight·edge
straight·for·ward
straight—line adj.
straight man
strait (narrow;
  cf. *straight*)
strait·jack·et
strait·laced *or*
  straight·laced
strang·er
stran·gle·hold
stran·gu·late
strap·hang·er
strap·less
strapped
strap·ping
strat·a·gem
stra·te·gic
strat·e·gist
strat·e·gy
strat·i·fy
strato·sphere
stra·tum

straw·ber·ry
straw·board
straw man
stream
stream·lined
street·car
strength
strength·en
stren·u·ous
strep·to·coc·ci pl.
strep·to·coc·cus
  sing.
stress·ful
stretch·er—bear·er
stretch—out n.
stri·a·tion
stric·ture
stri·dent
strike·bound
strike·break·er
strike out v.
strike·out n.
strike over v.
strike·over n.
strin·gent
string·i·ness
strip·ling
stro·bo·scope
strong—arm adj., v.
strong·hold
strong—mind·ed
strong room
strong suit
stron·tium
stro·phe
struc·tur·al

struc·ture
strug·gle
strug·gling
strych·nine
stub
stubbed
stub·bing
stub·born
stub·by
stuc·co
stuc·co·work
stuck—up adj.
stud·book
stu·dent
stud·ied
stu·dio
stu·dios
stu·di·ous
study
stuff
stuff·i·ness
stuff·ing
stuffy
stul·ti·fy
stum·ble·bum
stu·pe·fy
stu·pen·dous
stu·pid
stu·pid·i·ty
stu·por
stur·dy
stur·geon
stut·ter
sty·gian
style (fashion; cf. *stile*)
style·book

styl·ish
styl·ist
styl·i·za·tion
styl·ize
sty·lo·graph·ic
sty·lus
sty·mie
styp·tic
sua·sion
suave
sua·vi·ty
sub·al·tern
sub·av·er·age
sub·base·ment
sub·com·mit·tee
sub·con·scious
sub·con·ti·nent
sub·con·tract
sub·con·trac·tor
sub·cul·ture
sub·cu·ta·ne·ous
sub·deb
sub·deb·u·tante
sub·di·vide
sub·di·vi·sion
sub·due
sub·ed·i·tor
sub·head
sub·ject
sub·jec·tion
sub·jec·tive
sub·ju·gate
sub·junc·tive
sub·lease
sub·li·mate
sub·li·ma·tion

sub·lime
sub·lim·i·nal
sub·lim·i·ty
sub·ma·rine
sub·merge
sub·merg·ible
sub·mers·ible
sub·mer·sion
sub·mis·sion
sub·mis·sive
sub·mit
sub·nor·mal
sub·or·di·nate
sub·or·di·na·tion
sub·orn
sub·poe·na
sub·scribe
sub·scrip·tion
sub·se·quent
sub·ser·vi·ent
sub·side
sub·si·dence
sub·sid·iary
sub·si·dize
sub·si·dy
sub·sist
sub·sis·tence
sub·son·ic
sub·stance
sub·stan·dard
sub·stan·tial
sub·stan·ti·ate
sub·stan·tive
sub·sti·tute
sub·ter·fuge
sub·ter·ra·nean

sub·tle
sub·tle·ty
sub·tly
sub·tract
sub·trac·tion
sub·tra·hend
sub·trea·sury
sub·trop·i·cal
sub·urb
sub·ur·ban·ite
sub·ur·bia
sub·ven·tion
sub·ver·sion
sub·ver·sive
sub·vert
sub·way
suc·ceed
suc·cess
suc·cess·ful
suc·ces·sion
suc·ces·sive
suc·ces·sor
suc·cinct
suc·cor (help;
   cf. *sucker*)
suc·co·tash
suc·cu·lent
suc·cumb
suck·er (fish;
   cf. *succor*)
suc·tion
sud·den
su·do·rif·ic
sue
sued
suede

su·et
suf·fer
suf·fer·ance
suf·fer·ing
suf·fice
suf·fi·cien·cy
suf·fi·cient
suf·fix
suf·fo·cate
suf·fo·ca·tion
suf·fra·gan
suf·frage
suf·frag·ette
suf·frag·ist
suf·fuse
suf·fu·sion
sug·ar
sug·ar beet
sug·ar·cane
sug·ar·coat
sug·ar·loaf
sug·ar·plum
sug·gest
sug·ges·tion
sug·ges·tive
sui·cid·al
sui·cide
su·ing
suit (garment;
　cf. *suite, sweet*)
suit·able
suit·case
suite (a group;
　cf. *suit, sweet*)
suit·or
sul·fur

sulk·i·ness
sulky
sul·len
sul·tan
sul·ta·na
sul·try
sum (total; cf. *some*)
su·mac
sum·ma·ri·ly
sum·ma·rize
sum·ma·ry (brief
　account;
　cf. *summery*)
sum·ma·tion
sum·mer·house
sum·mer·time
sum·mery (like sum-
　mer; cf. *summary*)
sum·mit
sum·mons
sump pump
sump·tu·ary
sump·tu·ous
sun (in the sky;
　cf. *son*)
sun·baked
sun·bath n.
sun·bathe v.
sun·beam
sun·bon·net
sun·burn
sun·burst
sun·dae
Sun·day
sun deck
sun·di·al

sun·down
sun·dries
sun·dry
sun·fast
sun·fish
sun·flow·er
sun·glass·es
sun·glow
sun—god
sunk·en
sun·lamp
sun·light
sun·lit
sun·ni·ly
sun·ny
sun par·lor
sun porch
sun·rise
sun—room
sun·set
sun·shade
sun·shine
sun·shiny
sun·spot
sun·stroke
sun·suit
sun·tan
sun·up
su·per·abun·dant
su·per·an·nu·ate
su·perb
su·per·cal·en·der
su·per·car·go
su·per·cil·ious
su·per·cool
su·per·ego

su·per·er·o·ga·tion
su·per·erog·a·to·ry
su·per·fi·cial
su·per·fi·ci·al·i·ty
su·per·flu·ity
su·per·flu·ous
su·per·heat
su·per·hu·man
su·per·im·pose
su·per·in·duce
su·per·in·tend
su·per·in·ten·dent
su·pe·ri·or
su·pe·ri·or·i·ty
su·per·la·tive
su·per·man
su·per·nal
su·per·nat·u·ral
su·per·nu·mer·ary
su·per·scrip·tion
su·per·sede
su·per·son·ic
su·per·sti·tion
su·per·sti·tious
su·per·struc·ture
su·per·tank·er
su·per·vene
su·per·vise
su·per·vi·sion
su·per·vi·sor
su·pi·nate
su·pine
sup·per
sup·plant
sup·ple
sup·ple·ment

sup·ple·men·tal
sup·ple·men·ta·ry
sup·pli·ance
sup·pli·ant
sup·pli·cant
sup·pli·cate
sup·pli·ca·tion
sup·pli·er
sup·ply
sup·port
sup·port·er
sup·pose
sup·po·si·tion
sup·pos·i·ti·tious
sup·press
sup·pres·sion
sup·pu·ra·tion
su·pra
su·pra·re·nal
su·prem·a·cist
su·prem·a·cy
su·preme
su·preme·ly
sur·base
sur·cease
sur·charge
sur·cin·gle
sure·fire
sure·foot·ed
sure·ly
sure·ty
surf (waves; cf. *serf*)
sur·face
surf·board
sur·feit
surf·er

surf—rid·ing n.
surge (wave; cf. *serge*)
sur·geon
sur·gery
sur·gi·cal
sur·li·ness
sur·ly
sur·mise
sur·mount
sur·name
sur·pass
sur·plice (garment)
sur·plus (excess)
sur·plus·age
sur·prise
sur·re·al·ism
sur·re·but·tal
sur·ren·der
sur·rep·ti·tious
sur·ro·gate
sur·round
sur·tax
sur·veil·lance
sur·vey
sur·vey·or
sur·viv·al
sur·vive
sur·vi·vor
sus·cep·ti·bil·i·ty
sus·cep·ti·ble
sus·pect
sus·pend
sus·pense
sus·pen·sion
sus·pi·cion
sus·pi·cious

sus·tain
sus·te·nance
sut·ler
sut·tee
su·ture
su·zer·ain
svelte
swad·dle
swag·ger
swal·low
swamp
swamp·i·ness
swamp·land
swans·down
swan song
sward (grass;
   cf. *soared, sword*)
swar·thi·ness
swar·thy
swash·buck·ler
swas·ti·ka
swatch
swear·word
sweat·band
sweat·box
sweat·er
sweat gland
sweat·i·ly
sweat·i·ness
sweat pants
sweat shirt
sweat·shop
sweaty
sweep·stakes
sweet (not sour;
   cf. *suit, suite*)

sweet·bread
sweet·bri·er
sweet corn
sweet·en
sweet fern
sweet flag
sweet·heart
sweet·meat
sweet pea
sweet·shop
sweet tooth
sweet wil·liam
swelled—head·ed
   adj.
swelled—head-
   ed·ness n.
swel·ter
swel·ter·ing
swerve
swim·ming·ly
swim·suit
swin·dle
swin·dler
swin·dling
swine·herd
swin·ish
switch·back
switch·blade
  knife
switch·board
switch·er·oo
switch knife
switch·man
switch·yard
swiv·el
swoon

swoop
sword (weapon;
   cf. *soared, sward*)
sword·fish
sword grass
sword knot
sword·play
swords·man
syc·a·more
sy·co·phant
syl·lab·ic
syl·lab·i·cate
syl·la·ble
syl·la·bus
syl·lo·gism
sylph
syl·van
sym·bi·o·sis
sym·bol (emblem;
   cf. *cymbal*)
sym·bol·ic
sym·bol·ism
sym·bol·ize
sym·met·ri·cal
sym·me·try
sym·pa·thet·ic
sym·pa·thize
sym·pa·thiz·er
sym·pa·thy
sym·phon·ic
sym·pho·ny
sym·po·sium
symp·tom
syn·a·gogue
syn·chro·mesh
syn·chro·ni·za·tion

syn·chro·nize
syn·chro·nous
syn·co·pate
syn·co·pa·tion
sny·co·pe
syn·dic
syn·di·cal·ism
syn·di·cate
syn·drome
syn·ec·do·che
syn·er·gism
syn·er·gis·tic
syn·od
syn·onym
syn·on·y·mous
syn·op·sis
syn·tax
syn·the·sis
syn·the·size
syn·thet·ic
sy·ringe
syr·up
sys·tem·at·ic
sys·tem·atize
sys·tol·ic

# T

tab·ard
Ta·bas·co

tab·er·na·cle
ta·ble
tab·leau sing.
tab·leaux pl.
ta·ble·cloth
ta·ble d'hôte
ta·ble—hop
ta·ble·land
ta·ble·spoon·ful
tab·let
ta·ble·ware
tab·loid
ta·boo
ta·bor
tab·o·ret
tab·u·lar
tab·u·late
tab·u·la·tor
ta·chis·to·scope
ta·chom·e·ter
ta·chyg·ra·phy
tac·it
tac·i·turn
tack·le
tac·o·nite
tact·ful
tac·ti·cal
tac·ti·cian
tac·tics
tac·tile
tact·less
tad·pole
taf·fe·ta
taff·rail
tag·board
tag day

tag end
tagged
tag·ging
tag line
tail (end; cf. tale)
tail·board
tail·coat
tail·gate n., v.
tail·light
tai·lored
tai·lor—made
tail·piece
tail pipe
tail·race
tail·spin
tail·stock
tail wind
take down v.
take·down adj.
take—home pay
take off v.
take·off n.
take over v.
take·over n.
take up v.
take—up n.
talc
tale (story; cf. tail)
tale·bear·er
tal·ent
tales·man
    (chosen for jury)
tal·is·man
    (a charm object)
talk·ative
talk·ing—to

Tal·la·has·see Fla.
tal·low
Tal·mud
tal·on
ta·ma·le
tam·a·rack
tam·a·rind
tam·bou·rine
tam·per
tam·pon
tan·a·ger
tan·bark
tan·dem
tan·gent
tan·ger·ine
tan·gi·ble
tan·gle
tan·go
tan·kard
tan·nery
tan·nic
tan·ta·lize
tan·ta·lus
tan·ta·mount
tap dance n.
tap—dance v.
tape·line
ta·per (diminish;
    cf. *tapir*)
tape—re·cord v.
tape re·cord·er n.
tap·es·try
tape·worm
tap·i·o·ca
ta·pir (animal;
    cf. *taper*)

tap·room
tap·root
tar·an·tel·la
ta·ran·tu·la
tar·di·ness
tar·dy
tare (weight; cf. *tear*)
tar·get
tar·iff
tar·la·tan
tar·nish
tar·pau·lin
tar·pon
tar·ra·gon
tar·tan
tar·tar
tar·tar·ic
Tar·ta·rus
task force
task·mas·ter
tas·sel
taste·ful
taste·less
tast·i·ly
tasty
tat·ter·de·ma·lion
tat·ter·sall
tat·ting
tat·too
taught (instructed;
    cf. *taut*)
taunt
taut (tight; cf. *taught*)
tau·tol·o·gy
tav·ern
taw·dri·ness

taw·dry
taw·ny
tax·able
tax·a·tion
tax—ex·empt
taxi
taxi·cab
taxi danc·er
taxi·der·mist
taxi·der·my
tax·ied
taxi·ing
taxi·man
taxi·me·ter
tax·pay·er
T—bone
tea (a drink; cf. *tee*)
tea bag
tea ball
teach·able
teach·er
tea·cup
tea dance
tea gown
tea·house
tea·ket·tle
teak·wood
team (in sports;
    cf. *teem*)
team·mate
team·ster
team·work
tea·pot
tear (rip; cf. *tare*)
tear (weep; cf. *tier*)
tear·drop

tear·ful
tear gas
tea·room
tear sheet
tear·stain
tea·spoon·ful
tea·time
tea tray
tea wag·on
tech·ni·cal
tech·ni·cal·i·ty
tech·ni·cian
Tech·ni·col·or
tech·nique
tech·noc·ra·cy
tech·no·log·i·cal
tech·nol·o·gy
te·dious
te·di·um
tee (in golf; cf. *tea*)
teem (abound with; cf. *team*)
teen·age
teen·ag·er
teens
tee·ter
tee·to·tal·er
Tel·Au·to·graph
tele·cast
tele·gram
tele·graph
te·leg·ra·pher
tele·graph·ic
te·leg·ra·phy
tele·me·ter
tele·path·ic

te·lep·a·thy
tele·phone
tele·phon·ic
te·le·pho·ny
tele·pho·to
Tele·Promp·Ter
tele·scope
tele·scop·ic
Tele·type
Tele·type·set·ter
tele·type·writ·er
tele·vi·sion
tell·tale
tel·pher
tem·blor
te·mer·i·ty
tem·per
tem·per·a·ment
tem·per·ance
tem·per·ate
tem·per·a·ture
tem·pered
tem·pest
tem·pes·tu·ous
tem·plate
tem·ple
tem·po
tem·po·ral
tem·po·rar·i·ly
tem·po·rary
tem·po·rize
tempt
temp·ta·tion
tempt·ress
ten·a·ble
te·na·cious

te·nac·i·ty
ten·an·cy
ten·ant
ten·ant·able
ten—cent store
ten·den·cy
ten·den·tious
ten·der adj., v.
tend·er n.
ten·der·foot
ten·der·heart·ed
ten·der·iz·er
ten·der·loin
ten·don
ten·dril
ten·e·ment
Ten·nes·see
ten·nis
ten·on
ten·or
ten·pin
ten·sile
ten·sion
ten—strike
ten·ta·cle
ten·ta·tive
ten·ter·hook
tenth—rate
tent·mak·er
te·nu·ity
ten·u·ous
ten·ure
te·pee
tep·id
te·qui·la
ter·cen·te·na·ry

ter·gi·ver·sate
ter·ma·gant
ter·mi·na·ble
ter·mi·nal
ter·mi·nate
ter·mi·na·tion
ter·mi·ni pl.
ter·mi·nol·o·gy
ter·mi·nus sing.
ter·mite
tern (bird; cf. *turn*)
terp·si·cho·re·an
ter·race
ter·ra—cot·ta
ter·ra fir·ma
ter·rain
ter·ra·pin
ter·rar·i·um
ter·raz·zo
Ter·re Haute Ind.
ter·res·tri·al
ter·ri·ble
ter·ri·er
ter·rif·ic
ter·ri·fy
ter·ri·to·ri·al
ter·ri·to·ri·al·i·ty
ter·ri·to·ry
ter·ror
ter·ror·ism
ter·ror·ist
ter·ror·ize
terse
ter·tia·ry
tes·sel·la·tion
tes·ta·ment

tes·ta·men·ta·ry
tes·ta·tor
tes·ti·fy
tes·ti·mo·ni·al
tes·ti·mo·ny
test tube n.
test—tube adj.
tet·a·nus
tête—à—tête
teth·er·ball
te·tral·o·gy
Teu·ton·ic
Tex·as
text·book
tex·tile
tex·tu·al
tex·ture
thank·ful
thank·less
thanks·giv·ing
the·ater
the·at·ri·cal
their (possessive;
    cf. *there, they're*)
the·ism
thence·forth
the·od·o·lite
theo·lo·gian
theo·log·i·cal
the·ol·o·gy
the·o·rem
the·o·ret·i·cal
the·o·rize
the·o·ry
the·os·o·phy
ther·a·peu·tics

ther·a·pist
ther·a·py
there (that place;
    cf. *their, they're*)
there·af·ter
there·by
there·for (for it)
there·fore
    (consequently)
there·in·af·ter
there·in·to
there·of
there·on
there·to·fore
there·up·on
there·with
ther·mal
ther·mo·dy·
    nam·ics
ther·mo·elec·tric
ther·mom·e·ter
ther·mo·nu·cle·ar
ther·mo·plas·tic
ther·mo·stat
the·sau·rus
the·sis
they're (they are;
    cf. *their, there*)
thick·et
thick·set
thick—skinned
thief
thieves
thiev·ish
thim·ble·ful
thin

thin·ner
thin—skinned
third class n.
third—class adj.
third—rate adj.
thirst·i·ly
thirsty
this·tle·down
thith·er
tho·rac·ic
tho·rax
tho·ri·um
thorn·i·ness
thorny
thor·ough (complete;
   cf. *threw, through*)
thor·ough·bred
thor·ough·fare
thor·ough·go·ing
thought·ful
thou·sand
thou·sand—leg·ger
thrall·dom
thra·son·i·cal
thread·bare
thread·worm
threat·en·ing·ly
three·fold
three—ply
three·score
three·some
thren·o·dy
thresh·old
threw (past tense of
   *throw*; cf. *thorough*,
   *through*)

thrift·i·ly
thrift·less
thrifty
thrive
throat·i·ness
throaty
throe (effort; cf. *throw*)
throm·bo·sis
throne (royal chair;
   cf. *thrown*)
throng
throt·tle·hold
through
   (by means of;
   cf. *thorough, threw*)
through·out
through·way
throw (hurl; cf. *throe*)
throw·away
throw back v.
throw·back n.
thrown (hurled;
   cf. *throne*)
thrum
thrummed
thrum·ming
thru·way
thumb·nail
thumb·print
thumb·screw
thumb·tack
thun·der·bolt
thun·der·clap
thun·der·cloud
thun·der·head
thun·der·ous

thun·der·show·er
thun·der·storm
Thurs·day
thwart
thyme (spice; cf. *time*)
thy·mus
thy·roid
tib·ia
tic (twitching)
tick (of a clock)
tick·er
tick·et
tick·le
tick·ler
tid·al
tide (ocean; cf. *tied*)
tide·land
tide·mark
tide·wa·ter
ti·di·ly
ti·dy
tied (fastened; cf. *tide*)
tie—in n.
tie·pin
tier (row; cf. *tear*)
tie up v.
tie—up n.
ti·ger
tight·fist·ed
tight—lipped
tight—mouthed
tight·rope
tight·wad
til·bury
tilt·yard
tim·bale

tim·ber (wood;
    cf. *timbre*)
tim·ber·land
tim·ber·line
tim·ber·man
tim·ber·work
tim·bre (of the voice;
    cf. *timber*)
time (duration;
    cf. *thyme*)
time    card
time    clock
time—con·sum·ing
time    draft
time—hon·ored
time·keep·er
time·less
time·li·ness
time    lock
time·ly
time·piece
time—sav·er
time·sav·ing
time·ta·ble
time·worn
time    zone
tim·id
ti·mid·i·ty
tim·o·rous
tim·o·thy
tim·pa·ni
tinc·ture
tin·der·box
tin·foil
tin·gle
tin·ker

tin·plate n.
tin—plate v.
tin·sel
tin·seled
tin·smith
tin·type
tin·ware
tin·work
ti·ny
tip
tipped
tip·ping
tip·ple
tip·staff
tip·ster
tip·sy
tip·toe
tip—top
ti·rade
tire·some
tis·sue
ti·tan
ti·tan·ic
tit·bit
tithe
tith·ing
tit·il·late
tit·i·vate
ti·tle
ti·tle·hold·er
tit·mouse
ti·trate
ti·tra·tion
tit·u·lar
to (preposition;
    cf. *too, two*)

toad·stool
toast·mas·ter
to·bac·co
to·bac·co·nist
to·bog·gan
toc·ca·ta
toc·sin
to·day
tod·dy
toe (of foot; cf. *tow*)
toe    cap
toed
toe    dance n.
toe—dance v.
toe·hold
toe·ing
toe·nail
tof·fee
to·ga
to·geth·er
tog·gle
toi·let
toil·some
toil·worn
to·ken
tol·er·a·ble
tol·er·ance
tol·er·ant
tol·er·ate
tol·er·a·tion
toll·booth
toll    bridge
toll    call
toll·gate
toll·house
toll    road

tom·a·hawk
to·ma·to
tom·boy
tomb·stone
tom·cat
tom·fool·ery
to·mor·row
tom—tom
ton·al
to·nal·i·ty
tone
tone arm
tone—deaf adj.
tongue
tongue—lash v.
tongue—
  lash·ing n.
tongue—tied
ton·ic
to·night
ton·nage
ton·neau
ton·sil
ton·sil·lec·to·my
ton·sil·li·tis
ton·so·ri·al
ton·sure
ton·tine
too (also; cf. to, two)
tool·box
tool·hold·er
tool·house
tool·mak·er
tool·room
tooth·ache
tooth·brush

tooth·pick
tooth·some
to·paz
top boot
top·coat
top flight
top hat
top—heavy adj.
to·pi·ary
top·ic
top·i·cal
top·knot
top·mast
top·most
top·notch n.
top—notch adj.
to·pog·ra·pher
to·pog·ra·phy
  (of geography;
  cf. typography)
top·ping
top·sail
top·side
top·soil
top·sy—tur·vi·ness
top·sy—tur·vy
  adj., adv.
toque
torch·bear·er
torch·light
to·re·ador
tor·ment
tor·men·tor
tor·na·do
tor·pe·do
tor·pid

tor·por
torque
tor·rent
tor·ren·tial
tor·rid
tor·sion
tor·so
tor·ti·lla
tor·toise·shell
tor·to·ni
tor·tu·ous (winding;
  cf. torturous)
tor·ture
tor·tur·ous (painful;
  cf. tortuous)
toss·pot
toss—up n.
to·tal
to·taled
to·tal·ing
to·tal·i·tar·i·an
to·tal·i·ty
to·tal·ize
to·tal·ly
to·tem
touch down v.
touch·down n.
tou·ché
touch·i·ly
touch·i·ness
touch·stone
tough·en
tough—mind·ed
tou·pee
tour de force
tour·ism

tour·ist
tour·ma·line
tour·na·ment
tour·ney
tour·ni·quet
tow (pull; cf. *toe*)
tow·age
to·ward
to·wards
tow·boat
tow·el
tow·el·ing
tow·er
tow·head
tow·line
towns·folk
town·ship
towns·man
towns·peo·ple
tow·path
tow·rope
tox·emia
tox·ic
tox·i·col·o·gy
tox·oph·i·ly
trace·able
trac·ery
tra·chea
tra·cho·ma
trac·ing
track (path; cf. *tract*)
track·age
track·less
track·walk·er
tract (treatise;
    area; cf. *track*)

trac·ta·ble
trac·tion
trac·tor
trade—in n.
trade—last
trade·mark
trade name
trade school
trades·man
trade wind
tra·di·tion
tra·duce
traf·fic
trag·a·canth
tra·ge·di·an
tra·ge·di·enne
trag·e·dy
trag·ic
trail·blaz·er
trail·er
train·bear·er
train·load
train·man
train·sick
trait
trai·tor
trai·tor·ous
trai·tress
tra·jec·to·ry
tram·car
tram·mel
tram·ple
tram·po·line
tram·way
tran·quil
tran·quil·iz·er

tran·quil·li·ty
trans·act
trans·ac·tion
trans·at·lan·tic
tran·scend
tran·scen·dent
tran·scen·den·tal
tran·scen·den·tal-
    ism
trans·con·ti·nen·tal
tran·scribe
tran·script
tran·scrip·tion
trans·duc·er
tran·sept
trans·fer
trans·fer·able
trans·fer·ence
trans·fig·u·ra·tion
trans·fig·ure
trans·fix
trans·form
trans·for·ma·tion
trans·form·er
trans·fuse
trans·gress
trans·gres·sion
trans·gres·sor
tran·sient
tran·sis·tor
tran·sit
tran·si·tion
tran·si·tive
tran·si·to·ry
trans·late
trans·la·tion

trans·la·tor
trans·lit·er·ate
trans·lu·cent
trans·mi·grate
trans·mis·si·ble
trans·mis·sion
trans·mit
trans·mit·tal
trans·mit·ter
trans·mu·ta·tion
trans·mute
trans·oce·an·ic
tran·som
trans·par·en·cy
trans·par·ent
tran·spire
trans·plant
trans·port
trans·por·ta·tion
trans·pose
trans·po·si·tion
trans·ship
tran·sub·stan·ti·a-
    tion
trans·verse
trap·door
tra·peze
trap·nest
trap·per
trap·ping
Trap·pist
trashy
trau·ma
tra·vail (toil)
trav·el (journey)
trav·eled

trav·el·er
trav·el·ing
tra·verse
trav·er·tine
trav·es·ty
treach·er·ous
treach·ery
trea·cle
trea·dle
tread·mill
trea·son
trea·sure
trea·sur·er
trea·sury
treat
trea·tise
treat·ment
trea·ty
tre·ble
tree  fern
tree·nail
tree·top
tre·foil
trel·lis
trem·ble
tre·men·dous
trem·o·lo
trem·or
trem·u·lous
trench
tren·chan·cy
tren·chant
tren·cher
tre·pan
tre·phine
trep·i·da·tion

tres·pass
tres·pass·er
tres·tle
tres·tle·work
tri·ad
tri·al
tri·an·gle
tri·an·gu·lar
tri·an·gu·la·tion
tri·bal
tribe
tribes·man
trib·u·la·tion
tri·bu·nal
tri·bune
trib·u·tary
trib·ute
trick·ery
trick·i·ly
trick·i·ness
trick·le
trick·ster
tri·col·or
tri·cy·cle
tri·dent
tri·en·ni·al
tri·fle
tri·fo·cal
trig·ger
trig·ger—hap·py
trig·o·nom·e·try
tril·lion
tril·li·um
tril·o·gy
Trin·i·ty
trin·ket

tri·par·tite
trip—ham·mer
triph·thong
tri·ple
tri·ple—space v.
trip·let
tri·plex
trip·li·cate
trip·li·ca·tion
tri·pod
trip·tych
tri·reme
tri·sect
trit·u·rate
tri·umph
tri·um·phal
tri·um·phant
tri·um·vi·rate
triv·et
triv·ia
triv·i·al
triv·i·al·i·ty
tro·che (lozenge)
tro·chee
(poetic term)
trog·lo·dyte
trol·ley
trom·bone
troop (of soldiers;
cf. *troupe*)
troop·ship
trope
tro·phy
trop·ic
trot
trot·ted

trot·ting
trou·ba·dour
trou·ble·mak·er
trou·ble·shoot·er
trou·ble·some
trou·blous
troupe (of actors;
cf. *troop*)
trou·sers
trous·seau
tro·ver
trow·el
tru·an·cy
tru·ant
truck·le
truck·load
truck·man
tru·cu·lence
tru·cu·lent
true—blue adj.
true·born
true·heart·ed
true—life adj.
truf·fle
tru·ism
tru·ly
trum·pery
trum·pet
trum·pet·er
trun·cate
trun·cheon
trun·dle
trunk line
trun·nion
trust·bust·er
trust·ee

trust·ee·ship
trust·ful
trust fund
trust·wor·thi·
ness
trust·wor·thy
truth·ful
try·out n.
try square
tryst
tset·se
T—shirt
T square
tu·ba
tu·ber
tu·ber·cu·lar
tu·ber·cu·lin
tu·ber·cu·lo·sis
tu·ber·cu·lous
tube·rose
tu·bu·lar
Tu·dor
Tues·day
tug·boat
tug—of—war
tu·ition
tu·la·re·mia
tu·lip
tu·lip·wood
tulle
tum·ble
tum·bler
tum·ble·weed
tum·brel
tu·mor
tu·mult

tu·mul·tu·ous
tune·ful
tune·less
tune—up n.
tung·sten
tu·nic
tun·nel
tun·neled
tun·nel·ing
tur·ban (headdress;
   cf. *turbine*)
tur·bid
tur·bine (engine;
   cf. *turban*)
tur·bo·jet
tur·bot
tur·bu·lence
tur·bu·lent
tur·gid
tur·key
tur·key—cock
tur·mer·ic
tur·moil
turn (rotate; cf. *tern*)
turn·about
turn·buck·le
turn·coat
turn down v.
turn·down adj., n.
turn in v.
turn—in n.
tur·nip
turn·key
turn off v.
turn·off n.
turn out v.

turn·out n.
turn over v.
turn·over adj., n.
turn·pike
turn·spit
turn·stile
turn·ta·ble
turn up v.
turn·up adj., n.
turn·ver·ein
tur·pen·tine
tur·pi·tude
tur·quoise
tur·ret
tur·tle·dove
tur·tle·neck
tus·sle
tu·te·lage
tu·te·lar
tu·te·lary
tu·tor
tut·ti—frut·ti
twi·light
twitch
two (one and one;
   cf. *to, too*)
two—ply
two—sid·ed
two·some
two—step n.
two—way
ty·coon
ty·ing
tym·pa·num
type·cast
type·face

type·found·er
type·script
type·set·ter
type·write
type·writ·er
type·writ·ing
ty·phoid
ty·phoon
ty·phus
typ·i·cal
typ·i·fy
typ·ist
ty·pog·ra·pher
ty·po·graph·i·cal
ty·pog·ra·phy
   (of printing;
   cf. *topography*)
ty·poth·e·tae
ty·ran·ni·cal
ty·ran·ni·cide
tyr·an·nize
tyr·an·nous
tyr·an·ny
ty·rant
ty·ro

ubiq·ui·tous
ubiq·ui·ty

ud·der
ug·li·ness
ug·ly
uh·lan
ukase
uku·le·le
ul·cer
ul·cer·ation
ul·cer·ative
ul·cer·ous
ul·ster
ul·te·ri·or
ul·ti·mate
ul·ti·ma·tum
ul·ti·mo
ul·tra·con·ser·va·tive
ul·tra·fash·ion·able
ul·tra·ma·rine
ul·tra·mod·ern
ul·tra·na·tion·al·ism
ul·tra·vi·o·let
ulu·la·tion
Ulys·ses
um·bil·i·cal
um·bi·li·cus
um·brage
um·bra·geous
um·brel·la
um·laut
um·pire
un·abashed
un·abat·ed
un·able
un·ac·com·pa·nied

un·ac·count·able
un·ac·cus·tomed
un·adorned
un·adul·ter·at·ed
un·af·fect·ed
un·aligned
un·al·loyed
un·al·ter·able
un—Amer·i·can
una·nim·i·ty
unan·i·mous
un·as·sum·ing
un·avoid·able
un·aware
un·bal·anced
un·be·com·ing
un·be·lief
un·be·liev·er
un·bend
un·bi·ased
un·bid·den
un·bo·som
un·bound·ed
un·but·ton
un·called—for
un·cer·tain
un·char·i·ta·ble
un·civ·i·lized
un·cle
un·clean
un·com·fort·able
un·com·mit·ted
un·com·mu·ni·ca·tive
un·com·pli·men·ta·ry

un·com·pro·mis·ing
un·con·cerned
un·con·di·tion·al
un·con·quer·able
un·con·scio·na·ble
un·con·scious
un·couth
unc·tion
unc·tu·ous
un·de·ni·able
un·der·age
un·der·arm
un·der·brush
un·der·class·man
un·der·clothes
un·der·cov·er
un·der·cur·rent
un·der·de·vel·oped
un·der·dog
un·der·glaze
un·der·go
un·der·grad·u·ate
un·der·ground
un·der·hand·ed
un·der·line
un·der·mine
un·der·neath
un·der·pass
un·der·priv·i·leged
un·der·rate
un·der·score
un·der·sell
un·der·shirt
un·der·sized
un·der·slung

un·der·stand
un·der·stood
un·der·study
un·der·tak·er
un·der·tone
un·der·tow
un·der·val·ue
un·der·wa·ter
un·der·wear
un·der·weight
un·der·world
un·der·write
un·do (unfasten;
  cf. *undue*)
un·doubt·ed·ly
un·due (excessive;
  cf. *undo*)
un·du·la·tion
un·du·ly
un·earned
un·earth·ly
un·easy
un·em·ployed
un·equal
un·equiv·o·cal
un·err·ing
un·ex·cep·tion-
  able
un·ex·pect·ed
un·fa·mil·iar
un·fa·vor·able
un·for·get·ta·ble
un·for·tu·nate
un·furl
un·gain·ly
un·god·ly

un·guent
uni·cam·er·al
uni·fi·ca·tion
uni·form
uni·for·mi·ty
uni·fy
uni·lat·er·al
un·im·proved
un·in·hib·it·ed
un·in·tel·li·gent
un·in·tel·li·gi·ble
un·in·ter·est·ed
union
union·ize
unique
uni·son
unit
unite
uni·ty
uni·ver·sal
uni·ver·sal·i·ty
uni·verse
uni·ver·si·ty
un·kempt
un·law·ful
un·leash
un·less
un·let·tered
un·like·ly
un·lim·it·ed
un·man·ly
un·mind·ful
un·mit·i·gat·ed
un·nat·u·ral
un·nec·es·sary
un·nerve

un·oc·cu·pied
un·par·al·leled
un·pleas·ant
un·prec·e·dent·ed
un·prej·u·diced
un·prin·ci·pled
un·qual·i·fied
un·ques·tion·able
un·rav·el
un·re·al
un·rea·son·able
un·re·con·struct·ed
un·re·gen·er·ate
un·re·mit·ting
un·right·eous
un·rul·i·ness
un·ruly
un·sa·vory
un·scathed
un·schooled
un·scru·pu·lous
un·seem·ly
un·skill·ful
un·so·cia·ble
un·so·phis·ti·cat-
  ed
un·speak·able
un·sprung
un·think·able
un·ti·dy
un·tie
un·til
un·time·li·ness
un·time·ly
un·told
un·touch·able

un·to·ward
un·truth·ful
un·tu·tored
un·usu·al
un·var·nished
un·want·ed
 (undesired;
 cf. *unwonted*)
un·wary
un·well
un·whole·some
un·wield·i·ness
un·wieldy
un·wont·ed
 (unaccustomed;
 cf. *unwanted*)
un·wor·thi·ness
un·wor·thy
un·writ·ten
up·beat adj., n.
up·braid
up·bring·ing
up—coun·try
up·date
up·draft
up·grade
up·heav·al
up·hill adj., adv., n.
up·hold
up·hol·ster
up·hol·ster·er
up·hol·stery
up·keep
up·land
up·lift
up·on

up·per
up·per—class adj.
up·per·class·man
up·per·cut
up·per·most
up·right
up·ris·ing
up·roar·i·ous
up·root
up·set
up·shot
up·stage
up·stairs
up·start
up·state adj., n.
up·stream
up·stroke
up·swept
up—to—date
up·town
up·turn
up·ward
ura·ni·um
ur·ban (of city)
ur·bane (suave)
ur·ban·i·ty
ur·ban·iza·tion
ur·chin
ur·gen·cy
ur·gent
uric
urn (vase; cf. *earn*)
Ur·su·line
ur·ti·car·ia
us·able
us·age

use·ful
use·ful·ness
use·less
ush·er
usu·al
usu·fruct
usu·rer
usu·ri·ous
usurp
usur·pa·tion
usurp·er
usu·ry
Utah
uten·sil
uter·ine
util·i·tar·i·an
util·i·ty
uti·liz·able
uti·lize
ut·most
uto·pi·an·ism
ut·ter
ut·ter·ance
ux·o·ri·ous

va·can·cy
va·cant
va·cate

va·ca·tion
va·ca·tion·ist
vac·ci·nate
vac·ci·na·tion
vac·cine
vac·il·late
vac·il·la·tion
va·cu·ity
vac·u·ous
vac·u·um
va·de me·cum
vag·a·bond
va·ga·ry
va·gran·cy
va·grant
vague
vain (conceited;
   cf. *vane, vein*)
vain·glo·ri·ous
vain·glo·ry
va·lance (drapery;
   cf. *valence*)
vale (valley; cf. *veil*)
vale·dic·to·ri·an
vale·dic·to·ry
va·lence (combining
   power; cf. *valance*)
val·en·tine
va·let
val·e·tu·di·nar·i·an
Val·hal·la
val·iant
val·id
val·i·date
val·i·da·tion
va·lid·i·ty

va·lise
val·ley
val·or
val·o·ri·za·tion
val·or·ous
valu·able
val·u·a·tion
val·ue
val·ue·less
val·vu·lar
vam·pire
van·dal·ism
vane (weather;
   cf. *vain, vein*)
van·guard
va·nil·la
van·ish
van·i·ty
van·quish
van·tage
va·pid
va·por
va·por·iza·tion
va·por·ize
va·por·iz·er
va·por·ous
va·que·ro
vari·able
vari·ance
vari·ant
vari·a·tion
vari·col·ored
var·i·cose
var·ied
var·ie·gate
var·ie·ga·tion

va·ri·ety
var·i·o·rum
var·i·ous
var·nish
vary (diversify;
   cf. *very*)
vas·cu·lar
va·sec·to·my
Vas·e·line
vas·sal
Vat·i·can
vaude·ville
vaude·vil·lian
veg·e·ta·ble
veg·e·tar·i·an
veg·e·tar·i·an·ism
veg·e·tate
veg·e·ta·tion
veg·e·ta·tive
ve·he·mence
ve·he·ment
ve·hi·cle
ve·hic·u·lar
veil (garment;
   cf. *vale*)
vein (blood vessel;
   cf. *vain, vane*)
vel·lum
ve·loc·i·pede
ve·loc·i·ty
ve·lour
vel·vet
vel·ve·teen
ve·nal (mercenary;
   cf. *venial*)
vend·ee

ven·det·ta
ven·dor
ve·neer
ven·er·a·ble
ven·er·ate
ven·er·a·tion
Ve·ne·tian
ven·geance
venge·ful
ve·nial (forgivable; cf. *venal*)
ve·ni·re·man
ven·i·son
ven·om·ous
ve·nous
ven·ti·late
ven·ti·la·tion
ven·ti·la·tor
ven·tral
ven·tri·cle
ven·tril·o·quism
ven·tril·o·quist
ven·ture·some
ven·tur·ous
ven·ue
ve·ra·cious (truthful; cf. *voracious*)
ve·rac·i·ty
ve·ran·da
ver·bal
ver·bal·ism
ver·bal·iza·tion
ver·bal·ly
ver·ba·tim
ver·be·na
ver·biage

ver·bose
ver·dant
ver·dict
ver·di·gris
ver·dure
ver·i·fi·ca·tion
ver·i·fy
ver·i·ly
veri·si·mil·i·tude
ver·i·ty
ver·meil
ver·mi·cel·li
ver·mi·cide
ver·mic·u·late
ver·mi·form
ver·mi·fuge
ver·mil·ion *or* ver·mil·lion
ver·min
ver·min·ous
Ver·mont
ver·nac·u·lar
ver·nal
ver·ni·er
ver·sa·tile
ver·sa·til·i·ty
ver·si·fi·ca·tion
ver·si·fy
ver·sion
ver·sus
ver·te·bra sing.
ver·te·brae pl.
ver·te·bral
ver·te·brate
ver·tex
ver·ti·cal

ver·ti·cal·ly
ver·tig·i·nous
very (extremely; cf. *vary*)
ves·i·cle
ves·pers
ves·sel
ves·tal
ves·ti·bule
ves·tige
ves·ti·gial
vest·ment
vest—pock·et adj.
ves·try
ves·try·man
vet·er·an
vet·er·i·nary
ve·to
ve·toed
ve·toes
vex·a·tion
vex·a·tious
vi·a·ble
via·duct
vi·al (bottle; cf. *vile*, *viol*)
vi·and
vi·brant
vi·bra·phone
vi·brate
vi·bra·tion
vi·bra·to
vi·bra·tor
vi·bra·to·ry
vic·ar
vic·ar·age

vi·car·i·ous
vice (sin; cf. *vise*)
vice ad·mi·ral
vice—chan·cel·lor
vice—con·sul
vice·ge·rent
vice—pres·i·dent
vice·re·gal
vice·roy
vice ver·sa
vi·chys·soise
vic·i·nage
vi·cin·i·ty
vi·cious
vi·cis·si·tude
vic·tim
vic·tim·ize
vic·tor
vic·to·ria
Vic·to·ri·an
vic·to·ri·ous
vic·to·ry
vict·ual
vi·cu·ña
vid·eo
vid·eo·tape
vig·il
vig·i·lance
vig·i·lant
vig·i·lan·te
vi·gnette
vig·or·ous
vile (odious;
    cf. *vial, viol*)
vil·i·fy
vil·lage

vil·lain
vil·lain·ous
vil·lainy
vin·ai·grette
vin·cu·lum
vin·di·cate
vin·di·ca·tion
vin·dic·a·tive
    (justifying)
vin·dic·tive
    (vengeful)
vin·e·gar
vin·e·gary
vine·yard
vin·tage
vint·ner
vi·nyl
vi·ol (instrument;
    cf. *vial, vile*)
vi·o·la
vi·o·late
vi·o·lence
vi·o·lent
vi·o·let
vi·o·lin·ist
VIP
vi·per
vi·ra·go
vir·eo
vir·gin
Vir·gin·ia
vir·ile
vi·ril·i·ty
vir·tu·al
vir·tue
vir·tu·os·i·ty

vir·tu·o·so
vir·tu·ous
vir·u·lence
vir·u·lent
vi·rus
vis·age
vis—à—vis
vis·cer·al
vis·cid
vis·cos·i·ty
vis·count
vis·cous
vise (tool; cf. *vice*)
vis·i·bil·i·ty
vis·i·ble
vi·sion
vi·sion·ary
vis·it
vis·i·ta·tion
vis·i·tor
vi·sor
vis·ta
vi·su·al
vi·su·al·ize
vi·tal
vi·tal·i·ty
vi·tal·ize
vi·ta·min
vi·ti·ate
vit·re·ous
vit·ri·fy
vit·ri·ol
vi·tu·per·a·tion
vi·tu·per·a·tive
vi·va·cious
vi·vac·i·ty

viv·id
vi·vip·a·rous
vivi·sec·tion
vix·en
vi·zier
vo·cab·u·lary
vo·cal
vo·cal·ist
vo·cal·ize
vo·ca·tion (career;
   cf. *avocation*)
vo·ca·tion·al
voc·a·tive
vo·cif·er·ous
vo·der
vod·ka
voice·less
void·able
voir  dire
vol·a·tile
vol·a·til·i·ty
vol·ca·nic
vol·ca·no
vo·li·tion
vol·ley
vol·ley·ball
volt·age
vol·u·bil·i·ty
vol·u·ble
vol·ume
vol·u·met·ric
vo·lu·mi·nous
vol·un·tari·ly
vol·un·tary
vol·un·teer
vo·lup·tu·ary

vo·lup·tuous
vom·it
voo·doo
vo·ra·cious (greedy;
   cf. *veracious*)
vo·rac·i·ty
vor·tex
vo·ta·ry
vo·tive
vouch
vouch·er
vouch·safe
vow·el
voy·age
vul·ca·ni·za·tion
vul·ca·nize
vul·gar
vul·gar·ism
vul·gar·i·ty
vul·gar·iza·tion
vul·ner·a·bil·i·ty
vul·ner·a·ble
vul·ture
vul·tur·ous
vy·ing

wad
wad·ded
wad·ding

wade (in water;
   cf. *weighed*)
wa·fer
waf·fle
wa·ger
Wag·ne·ri·an
wag·on
wain·scot
waist (blouse;
   cf. *waste*)
waist·band
waist·coat
waist·line
wait (delay; cf.
   *weight*)
wait·ress
waive (abandon;
   cf. *wave*)
waiv·er (abandon-
   ment; cf. *waver*)
walk·away
walk·ie—talk·ie
walk  in v.
walk—in adj., n.
walk—on n.
walk  out v.
walk·out n.
walk·over n.
walk—up n.
wal·let
wall·eyed
wall·flow·er
wal·low
wall·pa·per n., v.
wal·nut
wal·rus

wam·pum
wan·der
wan·der·lust
want (desire;
    cf. *wont, won't*)
wan·ton
war·bler
war cry
war dance
war·den
ward·robe
ward·room
ware (goods;
    cf. *wear, where*)
ware·house·man
ware·room
war·fare
war·head
war—horse
war·i·ly
war·i·ness
war·like
war·lord
warm—blood·ed
warmed—over
warm·heart·ed
war·mon·ger
warmth
warm up v.
warm—up n.
warp
war·path
war·plane
war·rant·able
war·ran·tee
war·ran·tor

war·ran·ty
war·ren
war·rior
War·saw Ind.
war·ship
wart·hog
war·time
war whoop
wary
war zone
wash·able
wash and
    wear adj.
wash·ba·sin
wash·board
wash·bowl
wash·cloth
washed—out
washed—up
wash·er
wash·house
Wash·ing·ton
wash out v.
wash·out n.
wash·room
wash·stand
wash·tub
was·sail
wast·age
waste (needless
    destruction;
    cf. *waist*)
waste·bas·ket
waste·ful
waste·land
waste·pa·per

wast·rel
watch·band
watch·case
watch·dog
watch fire
watch·ful
watch·mak·er
watch·man
watch out v.
watch·out n.
watch·tow·er
watch·word
wa·ter
wa·ter·borne
wa·ter·col·or
wa·ter·course
wa·ter·craft
wa·ter·cress
wa·ter·fall
wa·ter·fowl
wa·ter·front
wa·ter·line
wa·ter·logged
wa·ter·man
wa·ter·mark
wa·ter·mel·on
wa·ter pipe
wa·ter po·lo
wa·ter·pow·er
wa·ter·proof
wa·ter—re·pel-
    lent
wa·ter—re·sis·tant
wa·ter·shed
wa·ter·side
wa·ter·spout

wa·ter·tight
wa·ter  tow·er
wa·ter·way
wa·ter·wheel
wa·ter·works
wa·tery
watt·age
Wau·sau Wis.
wave (beckon;
   cf. *waive*)
wave  band
wave·length
wa·ver (hesitate;
   cf. *waiver*)
wavy
wax·en
wax·work
way (direction;
   cf. *weigh*)
way·bill
way·far·er
way·lay
way·side
way·ward
weak adj. (feeble;
   cf. *week*)
weak·fish
weak·heart·ed
weak—kneed
weak·ling
weak—mind·ed
weak·ness
weal (state; welt;
   cf. *we'll, wheal,*
   *wheel*)
wealth

wealth·i·ness
wealthy
weap·on
wear (clothes;
   cf. *ware, where*)
wear·able
wea·ri·less
wea·ri·ly
wea·ri·ness
wea·ri·some
wea·ry
wea·sand
wea·sel
weath·er
   (atmospheric condi-
   tions; cf. *whether*)
weath·er—beat·en
weath·er·proof
weav·er
web·foot n.
web—foot·ed adj.
wed
we'd (we would)
wed·ding
Wedg·wood
wed·lock
Wednes·day
week n. (7 days;
   cf. *weak*)
week·day
week·end
wee·vil
weigh (ponder;
   cf. *way*)
weighed (pondered;
   cf. *wade*)

weight (poundage;
   cf. *wait*)
weight·i·ly
weight·i·ness
weight·less
weight·less·ness
weighty
weird
wel·come
wel·fare
wel·far·ism
wel·kin
well
we'll (we will;
   cf. *weal, wheal,*
   *wheel*)
well—ad·vised
well—be·ing
well—be·loved
well·born
well—bred
well—
   con·di·tioned
well—dis·posed
well—done
well—fa·vored
well—fixed
well—found·ed
well—groomed
well—ground·ed
well—han·dled
well·head
well—heeled
well—knit
well—known
well—mean·ing

well—nigh
well—off
well—or·dered
well—read
well—spo·ken
well·spring
well—thought—of
well—timed
well—to—do
well—turned
well—wish·er
well—worn
wel·ter
we're (we are)
weren't (were not)
were·wolf
West   Ches·ter Pa.
West·ches·ter N.Y.
west·er·ly
west·ern
West·ern·er
West   Vir·gin·ia
west·ward
wet (moist; cf. *whet*)
wet·back
wet   blan·ket n.
wet—blan·ket v.
wet·land
wet   nurse n.
wet—nurse v.
wet   wash
we've (we have)
whale·back
whale·boat
whale·bone
wham·my

wharf
wharf·age
wharf·in·ger
wharves
what·ev·er
what·not
what·so·ev·er
wheal (welt;
    cf. *weal, we'll,*
    *wheel*)
wheat   germ
whee·dle
wheel (turn;
    cf. *weal, we'll,*
    *wheal*)
wheel·bar·row
wheel·base
wheel·chair
wheel·horse
wheel·house
wheel·wright
whence
when·ev·er
when·so·ev·er
where (in what
    place; cf. *ware,*
    *wear*)
where·abouts
where·as
where·at
where·by
where·fore
where·in
where·of
where·so·ev·er
wher·ev·er

where·with
where·with·al
wher·ry
whet (sharpen;
    cf. *wet*)
wheth·er (if;
    cf. *weather*)
whet·stone
whey
which (pronoun;
    cf. *witch*)
which·ev·er
which·so·ev·er
while (during;
    cf. *wile*)
whi·lom
whim·per
whim·si·cal
whine (cry; cf. *wine*)
whip·cord
whip   hand
whip·lash
whip·per·snap·per
whip·pet
whip·ping
whip·poor·will
whip·stitch
whirl·i·gig
whirl·pool
whirl·wind
whisk   broom
whis·ker
whis·key
whis·per
whist
whis·tle

227

whis·tle—stop n., v.
white·bait
white·beard
white book
white·cap
white—col·lar
white·fish
white flag
white—head·ed
white—hot
white lead
white—liv·ered
whit·en
white·wash
white·wood
whith·er (where;
 cf. *wither*)
whit·low
whit·tle
who·dun·it
who·ev·er
whole (entire;
 cf. *hole*)
whole·heart·ed
whole·sale
whole·some
whole—souled
whol·ly (entirely;
 cf. *holey, holly,
 hole*)
whoop
who's (who is)
whose (possessive
 of *who*)
whose·so·ev·er
wick·ed·ness

wick·er·work
wick·et
wide—an·gle adj.
wide—awake adj.
wide—eyed
wide·mouthed
wide·spread
wid·ow
wid·ow·er
wid·ow·hood
wield
wife·like
wig·wag
wig·wam
wild·cat
wild·cat·ter
wil·der·ness
wild—eyed
wild·fire
wild·fowl
wild—goose
 chase
wild·life
wild·wood
wile (trick; cf. *while*)
will·ful
will—o'—the—
 wisp
wil·low·ware
will·pow·er
wind·age
wind·bag
wind·blown
wind·break
wind·burn
wind·fall

wind·jam·mer
wind·lass
wind·mill
win·dow
win·dow·pane
win·dow—shop v.
win·dow—shop-
 per n.
win·dow·sill
wind·pipe
wind·proof
wind·shield
wind·storm
wind·swept
wind up v.
wind·up adj., n.
wind·ward
wine (drink;
 cf. *whine*)
wine·glass
wine·grow·er
wine·press
wine·shop
wine·skin
wing chair
wing—foot·ed
wing nut
wing·span
wing·spread
win·ner
win·now
win·some
Win·ston—Sa·lem
 N.C.
win·ter
win·ter·green

win·ter·ize
win·ter—kill v.
win·ter·kill n.
wire·haired
wire·less
wire—pull·er n.
wire—pull·ing n.
wire·tap
wire·tap·per
Wis·con·sin
wis·dom
wise·acre
wise·crack
wise·ly
wish·bone
wish·ful
wishy—washy adj.
wis·te·ria
wist·ful
witch (hag; cf. *which*)
witch·craft
witch·ery
witch—hunt
with·al
with·draw
with·draw·al
with·er (shrivel;
  cf. *whither*)
with·hold
with·in
with·out
with·stand
wit·ness
wit·ti·cism
wit·ti·ly
wit·ting·ly

wit·ty
wiz·ened
woe·be·gone
wolf·hound
wol·ver·ine
wom·an
wom·an·hood
wom·an·ish
wom·an·kind
wom·an·like
wom·an·li·ness
wom·an·ly
wom·en·folk
won (did win; cf. *one*)
won·der·ful
won·der·land
won·der·ment
won·der·work
won·drous
wont (custom;
  cf. *want, won't*)
won't (will not;
  cf. *want, wont*)
wood (lumber;
  cf. *would*)
wood·bin
wood·bine
wood—bor·ing adj.
wood—carv·er n.
wood carv·ing n.
wood·chop·per
wood·chuck
wood·craft
wood·cut
wood·cut·ter
wood·ed

wood·en
wood·en·head
wood·en·ware
wood·land
wood·lot
wood·man
wood·peck·er
wood·pile
wood pulp
wood·shed
woods·man
wood·turn·er n.
wood turn·ing n.
wood·wind
wood·work
wood·work·ing
wood·yard
wool·en
wool—gath·er v.
wool·gath·er·ing n.
wool·li·ness
wool·ly
wool·sack
Woos·ter Ohio
Worces·ter Mass.
word·age
word·book
word for word
  adv.
word—for—word
  adj.
word·i·ly
word·i·ness
word·ing
word—of—mouth
  adj.

word·smith
word square
wordy
work·able
work·a·day
work·bag
work·bas·ket
work·bench
work·book
work·box
work camp
work·day
worked
work force
work·horse
work·house
work·ing
work·ing·man
work load
work·man
work·man·like
work·man·ship
work out v.
work·out n.
work·room
work·shop
work·ta·ble
work·week
world—beat·er n.
world·li·ness
world·ly
world·ly—
   mind·ed adj.
world·ly—wise
world—shak·ing
   adj.

world—
   wea·ri·ness
world·wide
worm—eat·en
worm gear
worm·hole
worm·wood
worn—out
wor·ri·ment
wor·ri·some
wor·ry·wart
wor·ship
wor·ship·ful
wor·sted
wor·thi·ly
worth·less
worth·while adj.
worth·while—
   ness n.
wor·thy
would (auxiliary
   verb; cf. wood)
wound
wraith
wran·gle
wrap·around
wrapped (enveloped;
   cf. rapped, rapt)
wrap·per
wrap up v.
wrap—up n.
wrath·ful
wreak (inflict;
   cf. reek, wreck)
wreath n.
wreathe v.

wreck (ruin;
   cf. reek, wreak)
wreck·age
wreck·er
wren
wrench
wrest (pull away;
   cf. rest)
wres·tle
wres·tler
wres·tling
wretch·ed
wrig·gle
wrig·gly
wring (twist; cf. ring)
wring·er
wrin·kle
wrin·kling
wrist·band
wrist·let
wrist·lock
wrist pin
wrist·watch
writ
write (compose;
   cf. right, rite)
write down v.
write—down n.
write in v.
write—in adj., n.
write off v.
write—off n.
write out v.
writ·er
write up v.
write—up n.

writhe
writ·ing
writ·ten
wrong
wrong·do·er
wrong·do·ing
wrong·ful
wrong·head·ed
wrote (did write;
  cf. *rote*)
wrought
wrung (twisted;
  cf. *rung*)
wry (distorted;
  cf. *rye*)
wun·der·kind sing.
wun·der·kin·der pl.
Wy·o·ming

Xan·thip·pe
xe·bec
xe·non
xe·no·pho·bia
xe·rog·ra·phy
Xe·rox
X ray n.
X—ray adj., v.
X—ray tube
xy·lo·phone

yacht
yachts·man
yak
yam
Yan·kee
yard·age
yard·arm
yard·bird
yard goods
yard·man
yard·mas·ter
yard·stick
yar·row
yaw
yawl
yawn
year·book
year·ling
year·ly
yearn
yeast
yel·low
yeo·man·ry
ye·shi·va *or*
  ye·shi·vah
yes—man
yes·ter·day
yes·ter·year
yew (tree;
  cf. *ewe, you*)

Yid·dish
yield
yo·del
yo·ga
yo·gurt
yoke (harness;
  cf. *yolk*)
yo·kel
yolk (of egg;
  cf. *yoke*)
Yom Kip·pur
yon·der
yore (past time)
you (pronoun;
  cf. *ewe, yew*)
young
young·ster
your (possessive of
  *you*)
you're (you are)
your·self
your·selves
youth·ful
yt·ter·bi·um
yt·tri·um
yule
yule·tide

za·min·dar
za·ny

zar·zue·la
zeal
zeal·ot
zeal·ot·ry
zeal·ous
ze·bra
ze·bu
ze·na·na
ze·nith
zeph·yr
zep·pe·lin
ze·ro
zest
zig·gu·rat

zig·zag
zig·zagged
zig·zag·ging
zinc
zin·nia
Zi·on·ism
zip
ZIP Code
zipped
zip·per
zip·pered
zip·ping
zir·con
zir·co·ni·um

zith·er
zo·di·ac
zo·di·a·cal
zon·al
zoo·log·i·cal
zo·ol·o·gy
Zou·ave
zoy·sia
zuc·chet·to
zuc·chi·ni
Zu·ni
zwie·back
zy·mase
zy·mot·ic

# REFERENCE SECTION

Writing numbers properly and using punctuation marks correctly are frequently troublesome aspects of writing and typing. Secretaries, editors, proofreaders—in fact, everyone who deals with the written word—will find this Reference Section useful in solving the most common problems that arise in these areas. For a thorough reference on the principles of grammar, usage, and style, see *The Gregg Reference Manual*, Fifth Edition, by William A. Sabin (McGraw-Hill Book Company, 1977).

## BASIC NUMBER RULES

Two sets of basic rules are commonly used for writing numbers—the *word style* and the *figure style*. In high-level executive correspondence and in formal writing, the *word style* is used: numbers from 1 through 100 are spelled out. In addition, all round numbers above 100 are spelled out if they can be expressed in one or two words (hyphenated compounds like *sixty-two* or *ninety-nine* are considered *one* word). All figures are used for other numbers.

> More than *twelve million* people will be affected by the new law.
> The Hall Company announced *twenty-three* new promotions.
> Over *three hundred* invitations were mailed this week.
> BUT: Over *350* invitations were mailed this week.
> (Figures are used when more than two words are required.)

In general business correspondence, numbers represent significant statistics that require emphasis for quick comprehension. Thus in most memos, letters, and reports, the *figure style* is preferred: only numbers from 1 through 10 are spelled out; figures are used for all numbers above 10.

> This morning we interviewed *four* applicants.
> We asked *seven* or *eight* people to review our new product.

Last week we reserved *ten* rooms for our group.
Mr. Pepe invited *11* guests to the dinner.
Our smaller conference room seats only *25* to *30* people, but our larger conference room seats *75* people.
She has received *40*-odd replies to Monday's ad.

In the figure style, even the numbers from 1 through 10 can be expressed in figures (as in this sentence, for example) if the numbers have technical significance or need special emphasis. Thus numbers from 1 through 10 are expressed in figures in tables, in statistical matter, and in expressions of dates, money, ages, time, and percentages.

June 7     $9     3 p.m.     8 percent

In the figure style, numbers from 1 through 10 are also expressed in figures when they are used with abbreviations and symbols, with numbers expressed as numbers, and with measurements.

6 mm     4″     the number 5     9 degrees

Since the figure style is preferred for most business correspondence, the rest of this section on numbers offers special rules for applying the figure style to specific situations.

**Number at Beginning of Sentence.** A number at the beginning of a sentence should always be spelled out.

*Two hundred eighteen* new technicians were hired last year.

However, it is often better to recast such sentences, especially if some numbers are spelled out while others are expressed in figures.

Last year *218* new technicians were hired.

**Indefinite Numbers.** Spell out indefinite numbers.

several hundred dollars     thousands of pages     millions of voters

**Ordinal Numbers.** Use figures for ordinal numbers in certain expressions of dates, in numbered street names above 10, and for special emphasis.

the 17th of May (BUT: May 17) 12th Street (BUT: Tenth Street)
Edward Q. Robles 3d (OR: Edward Q. Robles III)
It's our *50th* Anniversary Sale! (For emphasis.)

In all other cases, spell out ordinal numbers.

**Numbers Referring to Same Subject.** When a sentence has two or more numbers, express them similarly, even if one is above 10 and one is below 10.

We could find only 6 of the 38 references required.

**Large Numbers.** In sentences, numbers in the millions or billions are usually easier to read when they are partly spelled out and partly written in figures:

for example, *7.5 billion* OR *7¹/₂ billion* (instead of 7,500,000,000)

However, express related numbers in the same way:

between $750,000 and $1,000,000 (NOT: between $750,000 and $1 million)

Also, repeat the word *million* or *billion* with each number to avoid confusion.

from $3 million to $4 million (NOT: from $3 to $4 million)

**Fractions.** Spell out most fractions that stand alone (that is, that are not preceded by a whole number), but use figures if the spelled-out form is long, if the fraction is used with a unit of measurement, or if the fraction is used in a technical sense.

one-half the population                half an hour ago
two-thirds of our personnel            three-fourths of our stores
¹/₂ inch (about 1¹/₄ centimeters)      multiply by ³/₅

**Mixed Numbers.** A mixed number—a whole number plus a fraction—is written in figures.

The cost of raw materials increased *2¹/₂* times since 1972.

**Decimal Amounts.** Decimals are always expressed in figures. No comma is used in the decimal part of a number.

The annual rate of interest is exactly *12.14167* percent.

When no whole number precedes the decimal point, use a zero before the decimal unless the decimal itself begins with a zero. The zero calls attention to the decimal.

0.667 (clearer than .667)          .07

**Sums of Money.** In sentences, whole dollar amounts do not require a decimal point and two zeros (.00).

I paid a sales tax of *$16* on that *$200* camera.

In a column of numbers, however, if one number contains cents, add the decimal and two zeros to whole dollar amounts to make the column even.

Sums of money in round numbers of a million dollars or more may be expressed in several ways:

3¹/₂ billion dollars   OR   3.5 billion dollars   OR
$3¹/₂ billion   OR   $3.5 billion

Large amounts of money expressed in fractions (not mixed numbers) should be either completely spelled out or written all in figures.

one half of a million dollars   OR   $500,000
(NOT: ¹/₂ of a million dollars   OR   $¹/₂ million)

**Ages.** Generally, use figures for ages to show that the numbers are significant or technical. Spell out ages if the numbers are nontechnical or the writing is formal.

Elise Melior, *32*, has been named assistant manager.
Our business is exactly *2 years 3 months and 4 days* old.
BUT: This typewriter is less than *two years old*.

**Clock Time.** Always use figures with *a.m.* and *p.m.* Also use figures with *o'clock* (except in formal writing). Note that a colon (with no space before or after it) separates the hour from the minutes in clock time.

4:30 a.m.          6:20 p.m.          11 o'clock

Use figures with periods of time expressed in minutes, hours, days, weeks, and so on; however, a reference that is nontechnical should be spelled out if it does not require more than two words.

20 minutes          6 hours          4 weeks          9 years
BUT: Our logotype was designed more than *twenty years* ago.

Decades and centuries may be expressed as follows:

the 1940s  OR  the '40s  OR  the nineteen-forties  OR  the forties
the 1800s  OR  the eighteen hundreds
eighteenth-century fashions          the eighteenth century

**Percentages.** Use figures with percentages, and spell out the word *percent*. (Use the symbol % only in tables, forms, and technical copy.)

The sales tax is now *8 percent*.

**Plurals of Numbers.** To form the plural of a figure, add *s*. To form the plural of a spelled-out number, add *s* or *es*.

the 1970s          in the high 80s          all these W-4s
ones and twos          tens and twenties          fifties

**Hyphen With Numbers.** A hyphen is sometimes used instead of the word *to* in a continuous sequence of numbers.

pages 97-102          the years 1976-1979          the week of June 12-19

**Measurements.** Use figures with metric and customary measurements (unless the measurement has no technical significance).

4 kilometers     17 miles     16 kilograms     5 pounds
BUT: I must have gained *five pounds* in the last two days.

**Symbols and Abbreviations With Numbers.** Symbols and abbreviations may be used in typing forms, tables, and technical copy. Always use figures with symbols and abbreviations.

2%    32°F    17′ OR 17 ft    9″ OR 9 in    24¢    $14

In a range of numbers or a series of numbers, a symbol is repeated with each number, but a spelled-out word or abbreviation is given only with the last number.

20%-30%   OR  20 to 30 percent
10%, 20%, and 30%   OR  10, 20, and 30 percent
32°-44°F   OR  32 to 44 degrees F
3′ × 5′   OR  3 × 5 ft   OR  3 × 5 feet

# PUNCTUATION SIMPLIFIED

This section offers a concise listing of the punctuation principles that writers, secretaries, and editors most frequently question. For a more extensive treatment of the principles of punctuation, see *The Gregg Reference Manual*, Fifth Edition, by William A. Sabin (McGraw-Hill Book Company, 1977).

## Comma

**Comma With Nonessential Expression.** Writers sometimes insert a comment or an explanation that could be omitted from the sentence without changing its meaning. These added comments and explanations are called *nonessential* and are separated from the rest of the sentence.

I saw him yesterday, *however*, and he looked well.
Don't forget that we, *too*, want to go on the trip.
Frances, *or maybe it was Julia*, suggested this revised agenda.
If, *when you have reviewed the brochure*, you decide to order a sample copy, just use the enclosed form.
Carl Lovell, *not Carla Lowell*, should receive a carbon copy.

Because the italicized words and expressions are not essential to the meaning of the sentence, they are set off by commas. Some expressions, however, require judgment to determine whether they are essential or nonessential to the meaning of the sentence. Usually the expressions introduced by *that, which, who*, and *whom* cause difficulty.

The volume *that was published last year* was very successful.
The volume, *which was published last year*, was very successful.

The writer of the first sentence treats the dependent clause *that was published last year* as an essential part of that sentence. The writer of the second sentence treats the clause as nonessential to the meaning of the sentence and sets it off with two commas. Note the use of *that* to introduce the *essential* clause and *which* to introduce the *non*essential clause. Study the following examples:

The applicant *who submitted this letter* looks promising.
The applicant, *who submitted this letter*, looks promising.
This report is from Pat, *whom we are promoting*.
This report is from the secretary *whom we are promoting*.

A special type of parenthetical expression, called an *appositive*, is explained below.

**Comma With Appositive.** Sometimes a writer mentions a certain person or thing and then, in order to make the meaning perfectly clear to the reader, says the same thing in different words.

In many cases these constructions, known as appositives, resemble the constructions in which the commas are used to set off nonessential expressions.

You should talk to Mrs. Melendes, *our accountant*, about that.
Two important factors, *time and money*, must be studied carefully.

An appositive may occur at the end of a sentence, in which case only one comma is needed.

I'll see you on Monday, *the first day of school*.

**Comma in Series.** When three or more similar expressions (words, phrases, or clauses) occur in a series with a conjunction before the last expression, a comma should be placed before the conjunction and between the other items.

We need a microphone, a podium, and a screen.
I wrote, I telephoned, and I visited their office.
The broker found the house she wanted, arranged the mortgage, and made the sale.

**Comma After Introductory Expression.** A comma is used after an introductory expression such as *for instance* or *on the contrary*. A comma is also used after an *if* clause, a *when* clause, an *as* clause, or any similar dependent clause at the beginning of a sentence.

If you don't understand the estimate, please let me know.
When I see you after the meeting, I'll discuss it with you.
As you already know, we must have the form notarized by Friday.

When such a clause *follows* the main clause, however, a comma may or may not be needed to separate the two clauses. If the second clause is *essential* to the meaning of the sentence, then no comma is needed; if the second clause is *not essential*, then a comma should be used to separate this "extra" information.

Please let me know if you don't understand the estimate.
I'll discuss it with you when I see you after the meeting.

In the above examples, no comma is needed to separate the dependent clauses *if you don't understand the estimate* and *when I see you after the meeting* when they follow the main clause; they are essential to the meaning. But note:

We must have the form notarized by Friday, as you already know.

In this sentence, the comma is needed to separate the dependent clause *as you already know* because it is *not essential* to the meaning of the sentence.

Other kinds of introductory expressions that should be set off by commas are illustrated below.

In addition to the many telephone requests, we received about 750 letters and postcards. (Prepositional phrase.)

To be sure that your report is up to date, ask for a revised inventory schedule. (Infinitive phrase.)

Working at my desk, I heard the noisy machines all morning. (Participial phrase.)

**Comma to Indicate Omission of *And*.** Usually two adjectives preceding a noun are separated by a comma.

He is a charming, brilliant speaker.

The comma is not used if the first adjective modifies the second adjective and the noun as a unit.

She is a clever young attorney.

## Semicolon

**Comma or Semicolon Between Independent Clauses.** An independent clause (sometimes called a *main* or *principal* clause) is one that has a subject and predicate and could stand alone as a separate sentence. Each of the following sentences is an independent clause.

We will not raise the price.
We will discontinue free deliveries.
Ellen will order a copy for you.
If you prefer, she will lend you ours.

When two independent clauses are closely related, writers may combine them into one new sentence by using (1) a comma plus a conjunction such as *and, but, or*, or *nor* or (2) a semicolon.

> We will not raise the price, but we will discontinue free deliveries.
> We will not raise the price; we will discontinue free deliveries.
> Ellen will order a copy for you, or if you prefer, she will lend you ours.
> Ellen will order a copy for you; if you prefer, she will lend you ours.

Use a semicolon to separate two independent clauses that are joined by transitional expressions such as *moreover, however, for example*, and so on.

> We asked for a revised estimate; moreover, we requested an itemized list of all costs.
> Mr. DeRienzo has ordered the new equipment; however, the machines will not be delivered until January 15.
> Mrs. Rader made some excellent suggestions; for example, she recommended several ways to cut overhead costs.

**Semicolon Required Because of Comma in Independent Clause.** When two independent clauses are connected by *and* or some other coordinating conjunction and one of the clauses contains a comma, use a semicolon before the conjunction joining the clauses if the use of a comma before the conjunction might cause confusion or misinterpretation.

The use of a comma to separate the independent clauses in the following sentence is confusing:

> We ordered duplicating paper, onionskin paper, and carbon paper, and bond letterheads, plain bond paper, and cellophane tape were delivered to us instead.

Using a semicolon to separate the independent clauses makes the sentence easier to read and understand.

> We ordered duplicating paper, onionskin paper, and carbon paper; and bond letterheads, plain bond paper, and cellophane tape were delivered to us instead.

**Semicolon in a Series Containing Commas.** If one or more of the items in a series requires the use of a comma (as in a series of city and state names), use a semicolon to separate the items in the series.

The early American settlers brought with them many names from Europe such as *Boston*, Massachusetts; *New London*, Connecticut; *New Rochelle*, New York; and *New Orleans*, Louisiana.

## Colon

A colon is used after an expression that introduces a long quotation, an explanation of a general statement, a list, or an enumeration.

There are three secrets to learning shorthand: practice, practice, practice.

A credit card has this advantage: it can be used instead of money in all fifty states.

## Quotations

**For Direct Quotes.** Use quotation marks to set off someone's direct quotes—that is, someone's exact words.

Mr. Beluga said, "Vacation schedules must be submitted by May 1."

Do not use quotation marks for indirect quotes.

Mr. Beluga said that vacation schedules must be submitted by May 1.

Use single quotation marks for quotes within quotes.

"Please mark each envelope 'Confidential' before mailing them," said Mr. Fowler.

**For Emphasis.** Quotation marks may be used to emphasize words and phrases.

Tell the messenger this is another "special rush."

**For Titles.** Quotation marks are used to set off the titles of *parts* of complete published works and of article and song titles.

> She wrote Chapter 2, "Plan Ahead!"
> Have you read his article, "How to Save Half Your Paycheck"?

NOTE: Periods and commas always go *inside* the closing quotation mark; semicolons and colons, *outside*. Question marks and exclamation points go inside when they are part of the quoted material, outside when they are not. Study the examples above.

## Hyphenation

**Compound Nouns.** A compound noun may be spelled with a hyphen (*by-product*) or with a space (*back door*), or it may be spelled solid (*checkup*). Since no rules can simplify all the possible variations, always be sure to check *20,000 Words* for the spelling of each compound noun.

**Compound Verbs.** Many compound verbs are hyphenated: to *air-condition, dry-clean, tape-record,* and so on. Others, however, are spelled solid: to *handpick, highlight, proofread,* and so on. Moreover, some are spelled as two words: to *check in, make up, mark down,* and so on. Again, always check *20,000 Words* for the correct spelling.

**Compound Adjectives.** The hyphenation of compound adjectives is one of the most troublesome aspects of style. A compound adjective consists of two or more words that are used as one unit. Generally, these compounds are hyphenated when they occur *before* a noun, because in this position the compound words are out of order: our *up-to-date* statistics, a *well-known* actress, and so on. When such compound adjectives *follow* the noun, they are not hyphenated if the words fall in normal word order: statistics that are *up to date*, an actress who is *well known*, and so on. If the words are not in normal order, retain the hyphen: *government-funded* projects; projects that are *government-funded*. BUT: projects that are *funded by the government*.

There are exceptions to these general rules: (1) Do not hyphenate compounds like *high school* and *real estate* even when they are used before a noun, because such compounds are well known. (2) Do not hyphenate compounds that contain *ly* adverbs (a *carefully planned* report, a *privately funded* program). (3) Do not hyphenate proper nouns such as *Supreme Court, Park Avenue*, and so on, when they are used as compound adjectives: a *United States* citizen, the *New York* theaters, and so on.

# THE RIGHT PREPOSITION

Usage requires that certain words (usually prepositions) be used in certain combinations. For example, writers should say "identical *with*" and "retroactive *to*," not "identical *to*" and "retroactive *from*." In addition, writers should say "annoyed *by* some*thing*" but "annoyed *with* some*one*." The following list includes those combinations which are most frequently misused and gives a correct sample sentence for each combination. Use these sample sentences as patterns for correct usage.

**account for**   We asked him to account *for* his inaccurate estimate.
**account to**   He must account *to* Mrs. Peltz for his estimate.
**act for**   Our attorney will act *for* us in our absence.
**act on**   Let's act *on* this matter immediately.
**agree on** *or* **upon**   All of us agree *on* the discount that we will allow.
**agree to**   Mrs. Patulski agreed *to* the conditions in the contract.
**agree with**   Only Mr. Volpe agrees *with* Miss Harrow's suggestion.
**angry about**   Mrs. Henson was angry *about* the errors she found.
**angry at**   Mr. Aliano was angry *at* the needless delay.

**angry with**   We were angry *with* Roy for arriving so late.
**annoyed by**   She was understandably annoyed *by* Frank's remarks.
**annoyed with**   She was understandably annoyed *with* Frank.
**answer for**   We must be ready to answer *for* our actions.
**answer to**   Have you received an answer *to* your request?
**apply for**   Miss Schwartz applied *for* a sales position.
**apply to**   She applied *to* Mr. Zanna, the sales manager.
**argue about**   Mr. White and Mrs. DuBois argued *about* the new tax.
**argue with**   Mr. White argued *with* Mrs. DuBois.

**belong in**   All negotiable securities belong *in* the safe.
**belong to**   These folders belong *to* Mr. Charnow.
**belong with**   This book belongs *with* the others in the set.
**break in**   If you must break *in* during the meeting, please be brief.
**break into**   Suddenly they broke *into* laughter.
**break up**   Let's break *up* the meeting at 6 p.m.

**call for**   I will call *for* you at lunch time, Mr. Castro.
**call for**   Chess games call *for* great concentration.
**call on**   May I call *on* you next Thursday morning?
**capable of**   Neither one is capable *of* interviewing applicants.
**carry on**   She carried *on* the business that her father had founded.
**carry over**   Let's carry this discussion *over* to Monday morning.
**charge of**   Mr. Bogardis is in charge *of* both departments.
**charge to**   That invoice should be charged *to* our travel account.
**charge with**   Both partners were charged *with* obstruction of justice, according to published reports.
**compare to**   Compare this color *to* that one, then make your choice.
**compare with**   Please compare your estimate *with* mine. (*With* indicates a more-detailed comparison than *to*.)
**comply with**   We shall comply *with* the union's request.
**conform to**   The quality does not conform *to* our standards.
**consists in**   Success consists *in* getting along with others.
**consists of**   Her plan consists *of* three separate campaigns.
**convenient for (suitable for)**   Which day is more convenient *for* Homer?
**convenient to (near)**   This bank is convenient *to* all our stores.

**differ about**   Both of them differed *about* the plan that was presented.

**differ from**  This plan differs *from* any other he has offered.

**differ with**  I agree with you on the price, but I differ *with* you on the discount.

**different from**  This printing is different *from* that one.

**divide among**  The money was divided *among* the three of us.

**divide between**  The money was divided *between* two people.

**divide into**  The money was divided *into* equal shares.

**eager for**  Stella is eager *for* you to join us.

**eager to**  Stella is eager *to* see you again.

**familiar to**  That title is not familiar *to* me.

**familiar with**  No, I am not familiar *with* Mr. Loo or *with* Miss Vandermeer.

**foreign to**  The whole idea is foreign *to* us.

**get at**  What are you getting *at*?

**get off**  Please get this telegram *off* immediately.

**get over**  It seems as if we cannot get *over* this first hurdle.

**give in to**  Do not give *in to* her so easily.

**give up**  We gave *up* trying to change his bad habits.

**go about**  How do I go *about* obtaining permission?

**go against**  Do not go *against* the regulations.

**go by**  Be sure to go *by* the rules.

**go through**  Mr. Paoli went *through* all the *folders* quickly.

**grow up**  Sometimes I think he'll never grow *up*.

**hand down (announce)**  The court has not yet handed *down* its decision.

**hand down (bequeath)**  Traditions are handed *down* from generation to generation.

**hand in**  Hand *in* your papers before you leave.

**hand out**  Please hand *out* one form to each applicant.

**hear about**  Did you hear *about* the planned merger?

**hear from**  Did you hear *from* Mr. Kull yesterday?

**hear of (agree to)**  We tried to convince her to postpone her trip, but she wouldn't hear *of* it.

**hear of (know of)**  Did you ever hear *of* this company before?

**hold in**  He should learn how to hold *in* his anger.

**hold off**  Can we hold *off* reprinting until next July?

**hold out**   We need the loan now; we cannot hold *out* any longer.
**hold over**   That hit play is being held *over* another week.
**hold up (delay)**   This strike threat is holding *up* production.
**hold up (endure a test)**   Mrs. Robb holds *up* well under pressure.

**identical with**   Is this pattern identical *with* that one?
**impatient at**   Miss Schlein was impatient *at* the needless delay.
**impatient with**   Miss Schlein was impatient *with* me.
**independent of**   He has become independent *of* his family's wealth.
**interest in**   She has a sincere interest *in* helping others.
**interfere in**   Mr. Heinz never interferes *in* petty arguments.
**interfere with**   My supervisor seldom interferes *with* me.

**let down**   If you ask him for a favor, he will not let you *down*.
**let in**   Do not let any customers *in* after six o'clock.
**let off**   The judge let both of them *off* with small fines.
**let out**   This fits too tightly; please let *out* the waist.
**let up**   We hope that the storm lets *up* by noon.
**liable for**   You are liable *for* your actions.
**liable to**   You are liable *to* have an accident.
**live at**   Mrs. Partuk lives *at* 27 Elm Street in White Plains.
**live in**   Her sisters live *in* Scarsdale.
**live on**   Her brother lives *on* Elm Street too.
**live on**   All of them are retired and living *on* pensions.
**look after**   We will look *after* your store while you are away.
**look ahead**   Young people must look *ahead* to plan for their future.
**look around**   I will look *around* for a lower price.
**look at**   Did you look *at* the display case in the lobby?
**look for**   Our plant is now slow, so we are looking *for* more work.
**look into**   Please look *into* this further and report back to me.
**look on**   Mr. Mazda looks *on* his secretary as his greatest asset.
**look through**   Miss Ruiz looked *through* the catalog carefully.
**look to**   Look *to* your friends in time of need.
**look up**   For the correct meaning, look the word *up* in a dictionary.

**make out (understand)**   I can never make *out* his handwriting.
**make out (write)**   Make *out* a check for the entire amount.
**make up (create)**   He always makes *up* plausible excuses.
**make up (decide)**   Stop delaying; make *up* your own mind at once.
**make up (take a substitute for)**   Will you have to make *up* the exam?

**part from**   We parted *from* Joanne at the airport.
**part with**   I could not part *with* my favorite painting.
**pass for**   She could easily pass *for* her sister Doris.
**pass on**   I am not qualified to pass *on* your argument.
**pass out**   Please pass *out* these application forms.
**pass up**   Never pass *up* a chance to help a friend.
**pay back**   I plan to pay *back* the loan by November.
**pay for**   We suggest that you pay *for* everything in cash.
**pick out**   Please pick *out* the color that matches best.
**pick up (accelerate)**   Business will surely pick *up* in the fall.
**pick up (take into a vehicle)**   Please pick me *up* at 4:30 p.m.
**pick up (learn)**   She picked *up* our billing system in just a few days.
**plan for**   Are you already planning *for* the next convention?
**plan on**   How long do you plan *on* staying in San Francisco?
**plan to**   We plan *to* stay in San Francisco two weeks.
**present to**   The dean presented the award *to* Henry.
**present with**   The dean presented Henry *with* the award.
**prohibit by**   As you know, we are prohibited *by* law.
**prohibit from**   We are prohibited *from* advertising cigarettes on TV.
**pull into**   Pull the car *into* the garage.
**pull out**   The train pulled *out* as we arrived at the station.
**pull over**   Let's pull *over* to the curb and ask for directions.
**put away**   Try to put *away* a few dollars each payday.
**put off**   Do it now—don't put it *off* any longer.
**put out**   Put *out* the lights before you leave the house.
**put through**   Put *through* a conference call to our Detroit office.
**put up (build)**   Our new building will be put *up* next spring.
**put up (list)**   The Marshalls have put their house *up* for sale.
**put up with (tolerate)**   I can't put *up with* this system any longer.

**reason with**   He always tries to reason *with* his opponents.
**reconcile to**   We are reconciled *to* our economic condition.
**reconcile with**   Mrs. Abel has reconciled her differences *with* us.
**retire for**   Mr. York will retire *for* reasons of health.
**retire from**   General Moyers has retired *from* the army.
**retire on**   Will he retire on a pension?
**retire to**   Mrs. Columbo will retire *to* a warmer climate.
**retroactive to**   This pay increase is retroactive *to* July 1.
**reward by**   Miss Janus rewarded him *by* giving him a promotion.
**reward for**   We rewarded the young boy *for* helping us.

**reward with**   For their efforts, they were rewarded *with* a free trip.
**rule on**   Mayor Gibson will have to rule *on* that question.
**rule out**   We cannot rule *out* any possibility in this case.
**rule over**   Victoria ruled *over* England more than 60 years.
**run against**   Who will run *against* Governor Schwartz this year?
**run away**   Never run *away* from problems; they will follow you.
**run for**   Who will run *for* mayor this year?
**run off**   How many copies of this pamphlet should we run *off*?
**run out**   Once again we have run *out* of postage stamps.
**run up**   At our convention we ran *up* a tremendous bill.


**set back**   The strike has set us *back* about two months.
**set forth**   This pamphlet sets *forth* the committee's findings.
**set off**   His recent comments have set *off* a series of complaints.
**speak to (tell something to)**   Please speak *to* Joan about these errors.
**speak with (discuss)**   Let's speak *with* Maria when we go to Dallas.


**take for**   Both of us took you *for* James Bradley.
**take off**   I will take one week *off* next month.
**take on**   I cannot take *on* any more projects at this time.
**take out**   I suggest that you take *out* a life insurance policy.
**take up (assume)**   When did you first take *up* chess as a hobby?
**take up (occupies)**   He takes *up* all my time with foolish questions.
**turn down**   Did you turn *down* the volume?
**turn in**   Turn *in* your report during the coffee break.
**turn on**   Please turn those lights *on*.
**turn out**   Turn that lamp *out*.
**turn over**   While I am away, be sure to turn your work *over* to John.
**turn up**   Anne, please turn *up* the volume slightly.


**work for**   We work *for* a meticulous manager.
**work on**   She works *on* her thesis every evening.
**work off**   I work *off* my "extra" pounds in the company gym.
**work out**   I can't seem to work *out* this puzzle.

# ACRONYMS AND THEIR MEANING

| | |
|---|---|
| **A (Bomb)** | Atom Bomb |
| **A1** | First Class or First Quality |
| **AA** | American Airlines, Inc. |
| **AAA** | American Automobile Association |
| **AAAA** | American Association of Advertising Agencies |
| **AAD** | Association of American Dentists |
| **AALA** | Associate in Arts in Liberal Arts |
| **AAMC** | American Association of Marriage Counselors |
| **AAMCH** | American Association for Maternal and Child Health |
| **AAP** | Academy of American Poets |
| **AAP** | Association of American Publishers |
| **AAR** | Association of American Railroads |
| **AASR** | Ancient Accepted Scottish Rite (Masonic) |
| **AAUW** | American Association of University Women |
| **AAVS** | American Anti-Vivisection Society |
| **ABA** | American Bankers Association |
| **ABC** | Alcoholic Beverage Control (Board) |
| **ABC** | Audit Bureau of Circulations |
| **ABLA** | American Business Law Association |
| **ABM** | Associate in Business Management |
| **ABP** | Associated Business Publications |
| **ABS** | Absent |
| **ABS** | American Board of Surgery |
| **ABWA** | American Business Women's Association |
| **AC** | Air Corps |
| **AC** | Alternating Current |
| **ACLD** | Association for Children with Learning Disabilities |
| **ACLU** | American Civil Liberties Union |
| **ACR** | American College of Radiology |
| **ACS** | American Cancer Society |
| **AD** | Anno Domini (In the Year of Our Lord) |

| | |
|---|---|
| **ADA** | Americans for Democratic Action |
| **ADC** | Aid to Dependent Children |
| **ADCC** | Associated Day Care Centers |
| **ADL** | Anti-Defamation League of B'nai B'rith |
| **AEA** | Actors' Equity Association |
| **AEA** | Atomic Energy Act |
| **AEC** | Atomic Energy Commission |
| **AEP** | Adult Education Program |
| **AF** | Air France |
| **AFA** | Air Force Academy |
| **AFA** | Armed Forces Act |
| **AFDC** | Aid to Families with Dependent Children |
| **AFDCS** | American First Day Cover Society |
| **AFL** | American Federation of Labor |
| **AFL-CIO** | American Federation of Labor and Congress of Industrial Organizations |
| **AFT** | American Federation of Teachers |
| **AGMA** | American Guild of Musical Artists |
| **AHES** | American Humane Education Society |
| **AHF** | American Heritage Foundation |
| **AHQ** | Army Headquarters |
| **AHS** | American Humane Society |
| **AIA** | American Inventors Association |
| **AIDA** | Associated Independent Dairies of America |
| **AIGA** | American Institute of Graphic Arts |
| **AIM** | American Institute of Management |
| **AIR** | Action for Industrial Recycling (An organization) |
| **AIU** | Action for Interracial Understanding |
| **AJI** | American Jewish Institute |
| **AKA** | also known as |
| **ALA** | American Library Association |
| **ALA** | Authors League of America |
| **ALD** | American Library Directory |
| **ALGCU** | Association of Land Grant Colleges and Universities |
| **ALSS** | Association of Lutheran Secondary Schools |

| | |
|---|---|
| **ALTA** | Airline Traffic Association |
| **AMA** | American Management Association |
| **AMA** | American Medical Association |
| **AMCROSS** | American Red Cross |
| **AMEX** | American Stock Exchange |
| **AMIH** | Association for Middle-Income Housing |
| **AMS** | American Montessori Society |
| **AMVETS** | American Veterans of World War II |
| **ANG** | American Newspaper Guild |
| **ANS** | American Numismatic Society |
| **AOA** | American Optometric Association |
| **AOB** | Alcohol on Breath (Police term) |
| **AP** | Author's Proof |
| **APF** | American Psychological Foundation |
| **APH** | Association of Private Hospitals |
| **APhA** | American Pharmaceutical Association |
| **APHB** | American Printing House for the Blind |
| **APO** | Army Post Office |
| **APS** | American Peace Society |
| **APSA** | American Psychologists for Social Action |
| **APTA** | American Physical Therapy Association |
| **ARA** | American Railway Association |
| **ARAMCO** | Arabian-American Oil Company |
| **ARF** | Advertising Research Foundation |
| **ARF** | American Retail Federation |
| **ARIA** | Adult Reading Improvement Association |
| **ARS** | American Radium Society |
| **ART** | Advanced Research and Technology |
| **ASA** | Acoustical Society of America |
| **ASA** | Actuarial Society of America |
| **ASA** | American Society of Anesthesiologists |
| **ASC** | American Safety Council |
| **ASCA** | American School Counselor Association |
| **ASCAP** | American Society of Composers, Authors and Publishers |
| **ASCE** | American Society of Civil Engineers |

| | |
|---|---|
| **ASCU** | Association of State Colleges and Universities |
| **ASE** | American Society of Engineers |
| **ASIM** | American Society of Internal Medicine |
| **ASMA** | American Society of Music Arrangers |
| **ASME** | American Society of Magazine Editors |
| **ASO** | American Society of Orthodontists |
| **ASPA** | American Society for Public Administration |
| **ASQDE** | American Society of Questioned Document Examiners |
| **AST** | Association for Student Teaching |
| **ASTA** | American Society of Travel Agents |
| **ASTHMA** | A Society to Help the Morale of Asthmatics |
| **ASXT** | American Society of X-Ray Technicians |
| **ATCMU** | Associated Third Class Mail Users |
| **ATESL** | Assoc. of Teachers of English as a Second Language |
| **ATPI** | American Textbook Publishers Institute |
| **ATST** | Atlantic Standard Time |
| **AT&T** | American Telephone and Telegraph Company |
| **AV** | Audio-Visual |
| **AVS** | Anti-Vivisection Society |
| **AVTP** | Adult Vocational Training Program (HEW) |
| **AWOL** | Absent Without Official Leave (Military) |
| **AYD** | American Youth for Democracy |
| **AZC** | American Zionist Council |
| **AZF** | American Zionist Federation |

## B

| | |
|---|---|
| **BA** | Bachelor of Arts |
| **BAC** | Business Advisory Council |
| **BBA** | Big Brothers of America |
| **BBB** | Better Business Bureau |
| **BBC** | British Broadcasting Corporation |
| **BCA** | Boys' Clubs of America |
| **BCSE** | Board of US Civil Service Examiners |
| **BE** | Bill of Exchange |

| | |
|---|---|
| **B of E** | Board of Education |
| **BERA** | Business Education Research Associates |
| **BFI** | Business Forms Institute |
| **BHE** | Bureau of Higher Education (Office of Education) |
| **B/L** | Bill of Lading |
| **BMOC** | Big Man on Campus (Slang) |
| **BOMC** | Book-of-the-Month Club |
| **BP** | Blood Pressure |
| **BPOE** | Benevolent and Protective Order of Elks |
| **BPW** | Business and Professional Women's Foundation |
| **BROS** | Brothers |
| **BS** | Bureau of Standards |
| **BSA** | Boy Scouts of America |
| **BSMCP** | Blue Shield Medical Care Plans |
| **BSO** | Boston Symphony Orchestra |
| **BU** | Boston University |
| **BVM** | Beata Virgo Maria (Blessed Virgin Mary) |
| **BVS** | Bureau of Vital Statistics |
| **BYO** | Bring Your Own (Liquor) (Party invitation notation) |
| **BYPU** | Baptist Young People's Union |

## C

| | |
|---|---|
| **C** | Celsius (Centigrade) Temperature Scale |
| **C** | Circa (About) |
| **Ca** | Circa (About) |
| **CAA** | Civil Aeronautics Authority |
| **CAB** | Civil Aeronautics Board |
| **CALTECH** | California Institute of Technology |
| **CARA** | Chinese American Restaurant Association |
| **CARE** | Cooperative for American Relief Everywhere |
| **CASE** | Council for Advancement of Secondary Education |
| **CAT** | Clear Air Turbulence (Aviation) |
| **CAUSE** | College and University System Exchange |
| **CBB** | Catholic Big Brothers |

| | |
|---|---|
| **CBI** | Cumulative Book Index |
| **CBS** | Columbia Broadcasting System, Inc. (NYSE symbol) |
| **CC** | Cubic Centimeter(s) |
| **CCSB** | Credit Card Service Bureau (of America) |
| **CD** | Congressional District |
| **CDS** | Certificates of Deposit |
| **CEEB** | College Entrance Examination Board |
| **CEU** | Christian Endeavor Union |
| **CFG** | Camp Fire Girls |
| **CFM** | Cubic Feet per Minute |
| **CFS** | Cubic Feet per Second |
| **CG** | Coast Guard |
| **CGM** | Centigram(s) |
| **cgs** | Centimeter-Gram-Second |
| **CIA** | Central Intelligence Agency (of the US) |
| **CIF** | Cost, Insurance, and Freight (Business and trade) |
| **CKA** | Catholic Knights of America |
| **COB** | Close of Business (With date) |
| **COD** | Collect on Delivery |
| **COED** | Concise Oxford English Dictionary |
| **COL** | Column |
| **COPE** | Committee on Parenthood Education |
| **COPES** | Conceptually Oriented Program in Elementary Science |
| **CORE** | Congress of Racial Equality |
| **COT** | Checkout Time |
| **CPA** | Certified Public Accountant |
| **CPFF** | Cost Plus Fixed Fee (Business and trade) |
| **CPM** | Cost Per Thousand (Advertising) |
| **CPPC** | Cost Plus a Percentage of Cost |
| **CPS** | Certified Professional Secretary (National Secretaries Association) |
| **CRC** | Civil Rights Commission |
| **CRD** | Confidential Restricted Data |
| **CREF** | Cross Reference |
| **CRS** | Child Rearing Study |

| | |
|---|---|
| **CS** | Christian Science |
| **CSA** | Confederate States of America |
| **CSB** | Civil Service Board |
| **CSC** | Civil Service Commission |
| **CSF** | Civil Service Forum |
| **CSR** | Certified Shorthand Reporter |
| **CTC** | Cold Type Composition |
| **CTCLS** | Court of Claims |
| **CTS** | Contract Termination Settlement |
| **CW** | Clockwise |
| **CWPM** | Correct Words Per Minute (Typewriting, etc.) |
| **CWS** | Child Welfare Service |
| **CWT** | Hundred Weight |

## D

| | |
|---|---|
| **3-D** | Three-Dimensional (Pictures or films) |
| **DAR** | Daughters of the American Revolution |
| **DART** | Data Analysis Recording Tape |
| **DAT** | Differential Aptitude Test (Psychology) |
| **D & B** | Dun & Bradstreet, Inc. |
| **DBA** | Doing business as |
| **DC** | Direct Current |
| **DCA** | Digital Computers Association |
| **DD** | Doctor of Divinity |
| **D/D** | Demand Draft |
| **DDC** | Dewey Decimal Classification |
| **DDS** | Doctor of Dental Surgery |
| **DE** | Distributive Education |
| **DECAL** | Decalcomania |
| **DEP** | Depart(ure) |
| **DEPT** | Department |
| **DF** | Damage Free |
| **DID** | Data Input Display (Data processing) |
| **DIV** | Division(al) |

| | |
|---|---|
| **DJ** | Disc Jockey |
| **DJI** | Dow-Jones Index |
| **DK** | Don't Know |
| **DKL** | Dekaliter |
| **DL** | Deciliter |
| **DLO** | Dead Letter Office (US Postal Service) |
| **DNA** | Deoxyribonucleic Acid (Biochemistry, genetics) |
| **DNB** | Dictionary of National Biography |
| **DO** | Ditto |
| **DOA** | Dead On Arrival (Medicine) |
| **DOT** | Dictionary Of Occupational Titles |
| **DOZ** | Dozen |
| **DPC** | Data Processing Control |
| **DPI** | Disposable Personal Income |
| **DQC** | Data Quality Control |
| **DSO** | District Sales Office |
| **DT's** | Delirium Tremens |
| **DV** | Deo Volente (God Willing) |
| **DWD** | Driving While Drunk |

## E

| | |
|---|---|
| **EAL** | Eastern Air Lines, Inc. |
| **EBS** | Emergency Broadcast System |
| **EBSR** | Eye-Bank for Sight Restoration |
| **ECC** | Employee's Compensation Commission |
| **ECG** | Electrocardiogram (Medicine) (Also, EKG) |
| **ECM** | European Common Market |
| **ECS** | Educational Career Services (an organization) |
| **ECT** | Estimated Completion Time |
| **ED** | Edition |
| **Ed D** | Doctor of Education |
| **EDD** | Estimated Delivery Date |
| **EDPRESS** | Educational Press Association of America |
| **EEC** | European Economic Community (Common Market) |

| | |
|---|---|
| **EEOC** | Equal Employment Opportunity Commission |
| **EET** | Education Equivalency Test |
| **EFF** | English for Foreigners |
| **EFL** | English as a Foreign Language |
| **EHME** | Employee Health Maintenance Examination |
| **EKG** | Electrocardiogram (Medicine) |
| **ELS** | Extra-Long Staple (Cotton) |
| **EMA** | Employment Management Association |
| **EMCEE** | Master of Ceremonies (Slang) |
| **EMMA** | Eye-Movement Measuring Apparatus |
| **EMP** | End of Month Payment |
| **ENRT** | En Route |
| **EOA** | Effective On or About |
| **EOD** | Every Other Day (Advertising) |
| **EQ** | Educational Quotient (Psychology) |
| **E/R** | En Route |
| **ERB** | Educational Records Bureau |
| **ERCA** | Educational Research Council of America |
| **ERICR** | Eleanor Roosevelt Institute for Cancer Research |
| **ERT** | Educational Requirements Test |
| **ES** | Electrostatic |
| **ESCRU** | Episcopal Society for Cultural and Racial Unity |
| **ESL** | English as a Second Language |
| **ESOL** | English to Speakers of Other Languages (Program) |
| **ESQ** | Esquire |
| **ETA** | Estimated Time of Arrival |
| **ET AL** | Et Alii (And Others) |
| **ETD** | Estimated Time of Departure |
| **ETLT** | Equal To or Less Than |
| **ETR** | Estimated time of repair |
| **ETS** | Educational Testing Service |
| **EWC** | Electric Water Cooler |
| **EXAM** | Examination |
| **EXIM** | Export-Import Bank |

| F | Fahrenheit |
| FA | Free Alongside |
| FABB | Filene's (Boston) Automatic Bargain Basement |
| FABX | Fire Alarm Box |
| FAM | Foreign Air Mail |
| FAQ | Fair Average Quality |
| FAT | Fixed Asset Transfer |
| FATS | Fight to Advertise the Truth about Saturates |
| FAX | Facsimile |
| FBI | Federal Bureau of Investigation |
| FBL | Form Block Line |
| FC | File Copy |
| FCDN | Ferrocarril de Nacozari (AAR code) |
| FCE | Foundation for Character Education |
| FCPO | First Class Post Office |
| FDA | Food and Drug Administration (of HEW) |
| FDR | Franklin Delano Roosevelt |
| FEA | Foreign Economic Administration |
| FEAST | Food Education and Service Training |
| FEP | Fair Employment Practice |
| FET | Federal Excise Tax |
| F & F | Furniture and Fixtures |
| FHY | Fire Hydrant |
| FICB | Federal Intermediate Credit Bank |
| FIFO | First In, First Out (Inventory) |
| FIP | Fairly Important Person |
| FIT | Federal Income Tax |
| FITW | Federal Income Tax Withholding |
| FLB | Federal Land Bank |
| FLETC | Federal Law Enforcement Training Center |
| FLTST | Flight Steward |
| FMVSS | Federal Motor Vehicle Safety Standard |
| FO | Fuel Oil |

| | |
|---|---|
| **FOB** | Free On Board |
| **FORTRAN** | Formula Translation (Data Processing) |
| **FOT** | Free On Truck (Business and Trade) |
| **FPS** | Foot-Pound-Second (System) |
| **FRA** | Federal Reserve Act |
| **FRD** | Federal Reserve District |
| **FREC** | Federal Radio Education Committee |
| **FS** | Final Settlement |
| **FSEE** | Federal Service Entrance Examination (Civil Service) |
| **FSI** | Foreign Service Institute |
| **FSP** | Food Stamp Program |
| **FT** | Foot (or Feet) |
| **FTA** | Future Teachers of America |
| **FT-C** | Foot-Candle (Illumination) |
| **FTI** | Federal Tax Included |
| **FTLB** | Foot-Pound |
| **FTRF** | Freedom to Read Foundation |
| **FUNY** | Free University of New York |
| **FWL** | Foundation for World Literacy |
| **FYA** | For Your Attention |
| **FYI** | For Your Information |
| **FYIG** | For Your Information and Guidance |

## G

| | |
|---|---|
| **GAD** | Grants Administration Division (Environmental Protection Agency) |
| **GAI** | Guaranteed Annual Income |
| **GAL** | Gallon(s) |
| **GAO** | General Accounting Office (of the US government) |
| **GASP** | Greater (name of city) Alliance to Stop Pollution |
| **GATT** | General Agreement on Tariffs and Trade |
| **GBF** | Great Books Foundation |
| **GCA** | Girls Clubs of America |
| **GCD** | Greatest Common Denominator |
| **GCT** | Greenwich Conservatory Time |

| | |
|---|---|
| **GD** | General Delivery |
| **GDR** | German Democratic Republic (East Germany) |
| **GE** | Federal Republic of Germany (NATO) |
| **GESTAPO** | Geheime Staats Polizei (Secret State Police) |
| **GI** | Soldier (Wartime slang) |
| **GIA** | Goodwill Industries of America |
| **GIGO** | Garbage In, Garbage Out (Data processing) |
| **GM** | General Manager |
| **GMV** | Guaranteed Minimum Value |
| **GND** | Ground |
| **GOAT** | Goes Over All Terrain (Vehicle) |
| **GOP** | Grand Old Party (the Republican Party) |
| **GOSPLAN** | From the Russian for Central Planning Commission |
| **GPM** | Gallons Per Mile |
| **GPO** | Government Printing Office |
| **GQA** | Get (or Give) Quick Answer |
| **GR** | Government Regulation |
| **GSA** | Girl Scouts of America |
| **GST** | Greenwich Sidereal Time |
| **GTC** | Good Till Canceled (as in a brokerage order) |
| **GTM** | General Traffic Manager |
| **GU** | Gastric Ulcer |
| **GW** | Guerrilla Warfare |
| **GZTS** | Guilford-Zimmerman Temperament Survey |

## H

| | |
|---|---|
| **HAA** | Housing Assistance Administration (HUD) |
| **HBP** | High Blood Pressure (Medicine) |
| **HDBK** | Handbook |
| **HER** | Human Error Rate |
| **HEW** | Department of Health, Education, and Welfare |
| **H/F** | Held For |
| **HFR** | Hold For Release |
| **HH** | His Holiness |

| HIAS | Hebrew Immigrant Aid Society |
| HL | Height-Length |
| HLS | Holograph Letter Signed |
| HMV | His Master's Voice (Phonograph records) |
| HON | Honeywell, Inc. (NYSE symbol) (Formerly, M-H) |
| HOPE | Help Obese People Everywhere (an organization) |
| HP | Horse Power |
| HQ | Headquarters |
| HS | High School |
| HSCP | High-Speed Card Punch (Data processing) |
| HSCR | High-Speed Card Reader (Data processing) |
| HSPT | High School Placement Test |
| HT | Height |
| HUD | Department of Housing and Urban Development |
| HV | High Velocity |
| Hz | Hertz (Cycles per second) |

# I

| IA | Immediately Available |
| IAA | International Advertising Association |
| IABA | Inter-American Bar Association |
| IACHR | Inter-American Commission on Human Rights (OAS) |
| IAGLP | International Association of Great Lakes Ports |
| IATA | International Air Transport Association |
| IAVG | International Association for Vocational Guidance |
| IBC | International Business Corporation |
| IBI | Interpersonal Behavior Inventory (VA) |
| IBM | International Business Machines Corporation |
| IBP | Institute for Better Packaging |
| IBS | International Bach Society |
| IBT | Irrational Beliefs Test (Psychology) |
| ICAO | International Civil Aviation Organization |
| ICBM | Intercontinental Ballistic Missile |
| ICBMS | Intercontinental Ballistic Missile System |

| | |
|---|---|
| **ICBO** | Interracial Council for Business Opportunity |
| **ICC** | Interstate Commerce Commission |
| **ICFA** | Independent College Funds of America |
| **ICG** | Interviewer's Classification Guide |
| **ICI** | Imperial Chemical Industries |
| **ICPI** | Insurance Crime Prevention Institute |
| **ICS** | International Correspondence School |
| **ICU** | Intensive-Care Unit (of a hospital) |
| **ICZ** | Isthmian Canal Zone |
| **ID** | Identification |
| **IDA** | Intercollegiate Dramatic Association |
| **IE** | Id Est (That is) |
| **IEEE** | Institute of Electrical and Electronics Engineers |
| **IFO** | Identified Flying Object (Air Force) |
| **IFS** | Irish Free State |
| **IG** | Imperial Gallon |
| **IGCC** | Intergovernment Copyright Committee |
| **IGS** | Institute of General Semantics |
| **ILA** | International Longshoremen's Association |
| **IMBE** | Institute for Minority Business Education |
| **IMF** | International Monetary Fund |
| **INC** | Incorporated |
| **IOG** | Intercollegiate Opera Group |
| **IOU** | I Owe You (Business and trade slang) |
| **IPM** | Inches Per Minute |
| **IPS** | Inches Per Second |
| **IQ** | Intelligence Quotient |
| **IRA** | Irish Republican Army |
| **IRC** | Internal Revenue Code |
| **IRIS** | IBM Recruitment Information System |
| **IRS** | Internal Revenue Service (Treasury Department) |
| **ISBN** | International Standard Book Number |
| **ISC** | International Student Conference |
| **ISC** | Interstate Commerce |
| **ISME** | International Society for Musical Education |

| | |
|---|---|
| **ITA** | Initial Teaching Alphabet |
| **ITED** | Iowa Tests of Educational Development |
| **ITT** | International Telephone and Telegraph |
| **ITTF** | International Table Tennis Federation |
| **ITU** | International Typographical Union |
| **ITU** | Income Tax Unit |
| **ITV** | Instructional Television |
| **IWW** | Industrial Workers of the World ("Wobblies") |

## J

| | |
|---|---|
| **JA** | Job Analysis |
| **JAIM** | Job Analysis and Interest Measurement |
| **JAL** | Japan Air Lines |
| **JAP** | Joint Apprenticeship Program (Department of Labor) |
| **JB** | Juris Baccalaureus (Bachelor of Laws) |
| **JCET** | Joint Council on Educational Television |
| **JD** | Job Description (Department of Labor) |
| **JD** | Justice Department |
| **JDC** | Job Description Card |
| **JDL** | Jewish Defense League |
| **JE** | Job Estimate |
| **JET** | Jobs Evaluation and Training |
| **JETP** | Jet Propelled |
| **JFK** | John Fitzgerald Kennedy |
| **JI** | Job Instruction |
| **JIS** | Job Information Service (Department of Labor) |
| **JM** | Juris Magister (Master of Laws) |
| **JOBS** | Job Opportunities for Better Skills |
| **JOM** | Job Operation Manual |
| **JOR** | Job Order Request |
| **JOTS** | Job-Oriented Training Standards |
| **JOY** | Job Opportunity for Youth (NASA) |
| **JP** | Justice of the Peace |
| **JQ** | Job Questionnaire |

**JR** Junior
**JRC** Junior Red Cross

## K

**K9** Canine (K9 Corps - Army Dogs) (World War II)
**kc** Kilocalorie
**K of C** Knight(s) of Columbus
**KD** Knock(ed) Down (i.e., disassembled)
**KELP** Kindergarten Evaluation for Learning Potential
**kg** Kilogram(s)
**KKK** Ku Klux Klan
**KO** Knockout (Boxing)
**KP** Key Punch
**kph** Kilometers per Hour
**KPO** Keypunch Operator
**kw** Kilowatt(s)
**kwh** Kilowatt-Hour

## L

**LA** Latin America
**LAW** Left-Handers Against the World
**LB** Pound
**LC** Library of Congress
**LC** Lower Case (i.e., small letters)
**LCD** Liquid Crystal Display
**LCM** Least Common Multiple (Mathematics)
**LCM** Lowest Common Multiple
**LDC** Less-Developed Countries
**LDS** Latter-Day Saints
**LEA** Law Enforcement Assistance Program
**LED** Light-Emitting Diode
**LF** Lightface (Type)
**LH** Left Hand
**L/I** Letter of Intent

| | |
|---|---|
| LISA | Life Insurance Society of America |
| LLB | Bachelor of Law(s) |
| LLD | Doctor of Law(s) |
| LMRA | Labor-Management Relations Act |
| LOC | Library of Congress |
| LOCATE | Library of Congress Automation Techniques Exchange |
| LOG | Logarithm |
| LOX | Liquid Oxygen |
| LP | Long Play(ing) (Phonograph record) |
| LSAT | Law School Admission Test |
| LT | Lieutenant |
| 1LT | First Lieutenant (Army) |
| LTD | Limited |
| LWOP | Leave Without Pay (Civil Service) |

## M

| | |
|---|---|
| M | One Thousand (Roman numeral) |
| MA | Master of Arts |
| MAG | Magazine |
| MA in LS | Master of Arts in Library Science |
| MAP | Manpower Absorption Plan (Department of Labor) |
| MAS | Management Advisory Services |
| MASA | Mail Advertising Service Association International |
| MAT | Minimal Aversion Threshold (to noise) |
| MAUDE | Morse Automatic Decoder |
| MBF | Thousand Board Feet (Lumber) |
| MBM | Thousand Feet Board Measure |
| MC | Member of Congress |
| MCCR | Medical Committee for Civil Rights |
| MCHS | Maternal and Child Health Service |
| MCP | Male Chauvinist Pig (Feminist term) |
| MD | Doctor of Medicine |
| M/D | Man Day |
| MDAR | Minimum Daily Adult Requirement |
| MDD | Doctor of Dental Medicine |

| | |
|---|---|
| **MDP** | Malicious Destruction of Property |
| **MDR** | Minimum Daily Requirement (of a vitamin, etc.) |
| **MDS** | Master of Dental Surgery |
| **MDT** | Mean Down Time |
| **MDV** | Doctor of Veterinary Medicine |
| **MEMO** | Memorandum |
| **MERC** | Music Education Research Council |
| **MERCY** | Medical Emergency Relief Care for Youth |
| **MET** | Magic Eye Tube |
| **MF** | Microfiche (Sheet microfilm) |
| **MFA** | Malicious False Alarm (Firefighting) |
| **MFBM** | Thousand Feet Board Measure (Lumber) |
| **MFC** | Microfilm Frame Card |
| **MFD** | Minimum Fatal Dose |
| **MFN** | Most-Favored-Nation (Tariff) |
| **MF (p)** | Microfiche (Positive) |
| **M/G** | Miles per Gallon |
| **MGM** | Metro-Goldwyn-Mayer |
| **mgm** | Milligram |
| **MGR** | Monsignor |
| **MH** | Man-hours |
| **MHR** | Member of the House of Representatives |
| **MHT** | Mean High Tide |
| **MHW** | Mean High Water |
| **MIA** | Missing in Action (Military) |
| **MICR** | Magnetic Ink Character Recognition (or Reader) |
| **MIG** | Mikoyan-Gurevich, a Russian aircraft |
| **MIK** | More In the Kitchen (Family dinner-table expression) |
| **MIN** | Minimum |
| **MIP** | Methods Improvement Program (IBM) |
| **MIRACODE** | Microfilm Information Retrieval Access Code |
| **MISC** | Miscellaneous |
| **MITS** | Man in the Street (the average man) |
| **MLLE** | Mademoiselle |
| **MLT** | Mean Low Tide |

| | |
|---|---|
| **MLW** | Mean Low Water |
| **mm** | Millimeter (Metric) |
| **MME** | Madame |
| **MMES** | Mesdames |
| **MO** | Money Order |
| **MOG** | Metropolitan Opera Guild |
| **MOMA** | Museum of Modern Art (New York) |
| **MONY** | Mutual of New York (Insurance company) |
| **MP** | Member of Parliament (British) |
| **MP** | Military Police (Army) |
| **MPG** | Miles Per Gallon |
| **MPH** | Miles Per Hour |
| **MPM** | Miles Per Minute |
| **MRM** | Mail Readership Measurement |
| **MS** | Manuscript |
| **MSGR** | Monsignor |
| **MSS** | Manuscripts |
| **MTL** | Mean Tide Level |
| **MTU** | Metric Units |
| **MV** | Mean Variation |
| **MV** | Megavolt |
| **mV** | Millivolt |
| **MVD** | Doctor of Veterinary Medicine |
| **MWL** | Mean Water Level |

# N

| | |
|---|---|
| **n** | Nano (a prefix meaning divided by one billion) |
| **NA** | National Archives (of the United States) |
| **NAB** | National Association of Broadcasters |
| **NABISCO** | National Biscuit Company |
| **NABS** | National Association of Black Students |
| **NABTE** | National Association for Business Teacher Education |
| **NACA** | North American College of Acupuncture |
| **NAD** | National Academy of Design |

| | |
|---|---|
| **NAFMB** | National Association of FM Broadcasters |
| **NAGA** | Negro Actors Guild of America |
| **NALS** | National Association of Legal Secretaries |
| **NAME** | National Association for Minority Education |
| **NAPA** | National Association of Purchasing Agents |
| **NARA** | Narcotic Addict Rehabilitation Act |
| **NARAS** | National Academy of Recording Arts and Sciences |
| **NAS** | National Audubon Society |
| **NASA** | National Aeronautics and Space Administration |
| **NASC** | National Association of Student Councils |
| **NASCL** | North American Student Cooperative League |
| **NATO** | North Atlantic Treaty Organization |
| **NATTC** | Naval Air Technical Training Center or Command |
| **NAWA** | National Association of Women Artists |
| **NB** | Nota Bene (Note Well) |
| **NBA** | National Bankers Association |
| **NBA** | National Bankruptcy Act |
| **NBA** | National Bar Association |
| **NBCU** | National Bureau of Casualty Underwriters |
| **NBEDC** | National Black Economic Development Conference |
| **NBFU** | National Board of Fire Underwriters |
| **NBME** | National Board of Medical Examiners |
| **NBS** | National Bureau of Standards (Department of Commerce) |
| **NC** | No Charge |
| **NCADH** | National Committee Against Discrimination in Housing |
| **NCEC** | National Committee for an Effective Congress |
| **NCEY** | National Committee on Employment of Youth |
| **NCH** | National Committee on Housing |
| **NCI** | National Cancer Institute (of NIH, *q.v.*) |
| **NCIP** | National Council for Industrial Peace |
| **NCJSC** | National Criminal Justice Statistics Center |
| **NCOC** | National Council on Organized Crime |
| **NCSH** | National Clearinghouse for Smoking and Health |
| **NCSS** | National Center for Social Statistics (HEW) |
| **NCSW** | National Conference on Social Welfare |

| | |
|---|---|
| **NCTA** | National Cable Television Association |
| **NCTE** | National Council of Teachers of English |
| **ND** | No Date (of publication) |
| **N/E** | Not Exceeding (Business and trade) |
| **NEA** | National Education Association |
| **NEGRO** | National Economic and Growth Reconstruction Organization (Negro entrepreneurial organization) |
| **NET** | National Educational Television |
| **NFL** | National Football League |
| **NGSM** | National Gold Star Mothers |
| **NHA** | National Health Association |
| **NHEF** | National Health Education Foundation |
| **NHLA** | National Housewives' League of America |
| **NHTSA** | National Highway Traffic Safety Administration |
| **NIH** | National Institutes of Health |
| **NIRA** | National Inter-Racial Association |
| **NIT** | Negative Income Tax |
| **NLRA** | National Labor Relations Act |
| **NLRB** | National Labor Relations Board |
| **NMA** | National Management Association |
| **NMUC** | National Medical Utilization Committee (HEW) |
| **NNPA** | National Negro Press Association |
| **NNPA** | National Newspaper Publishers Association |
| **NO** | Number |
| **NOA** | National Opera Association |
| **NOIBN** | Not Otherwise Indexed by Name (Tariffs) |
| **NP** | Notary Public |
| **N/P** | Notes Payable |
| **NPC** | National Press Club |
| **NPPA** | National Probation and Parole Association |
| **NPS** | National Park Service |
| **NPU** | National Postal Union |
| **NPV** | No Par Value |
| **NQB** | No Qualified Bidders |
| **NRC** | National Reading Council |

| NRS | National Reemployment Service |
| **ns** | Nanosecond |
| NSAS | Non-Scheduled Air Services |
| NSBA | National School Boards Association |
| NSBA | National Small Business Association |
| NSF | Not Sufficient Funds (Banking) |
| NSMS | National Sheet Music Society |
| NSOB | New Senate Office Building |
| NSSR | New School for Social Research |
| NTL | National Temperance League |
| NTSA | National Traffic Safety Agency |
| NTUC | National Trade Union Council for Human Rights |
| NTX | National Teletypewriter Exchange |
| NUEA | National University Extension Association |
| **nW** | Nanowatt |
| NW | Net Weight |
| NWAA | National Wheelchair Athletic Association |
| NWBA | National Wheelchair Basketball Association |
| NWH | Normal Working Hours |
| NYC | New York City |
| NYME | New York Mercantile Exchange |
| NYSE | New York Stock Exchange |

## O

| OAA | Old-Age Assistance (HEW) |
| OAB | Old-Age Benefits |
| OAS | Old-Age Security |
| OATS | Office of Air Transportation Security (FAA) |
| OC | Office Copy |
| OCR | Optical Character Reader (or Recognition) |
| ODB | Office of Dependency Benefits |
| OE | Old English (language) (i.e., before 1150 or 1200) |
| OEEO | Office of Equal Educational Opportunities |
| OIO | Office of International Operations (of IRS) |

| | |
|---|---|
| **OIR** | Office of International Research (of NIH, *q.v.*) |
| **OJ** | Orange Juice |
| **OJT** | On-the-Job Training |
| **OK** | All Right (From *Old Kinderhook* or *Oll Korrect*) |
| **OKA** | Otherwise Known As |
| **OMB** | Office of Management and Budget |
| **OMBE** | Office of Minority Business Enterprise |
| **ONT** | Our New Thread (Clark thread designation) |
| **OPEC** | Organization of Petroleum Exporting Countries |
| **ORC** | Opinion Research Corporation |
| **ORR** | Owner's Risk Rates (Shipping) |
| **ORUS** | Official Register of the United States |
| **OS** | Old Style (Calendar, previous to 1752) |
| **OSC** | Order to Show Cause |
| **OSG** | Office of the Secretary General (UN) |
| **OSHA** | Occupational Safety and Health Act (1970) |
| **O/T** | Overtime (Business and trade) |
| **OTB** | Off-Track Betting |
| **OTC** | Over the Counter (Stock) |
| **OTJ** | On the Job |
| **OWI** | Operating While Intoxicated (Traffic offense) |
| **OWM** | Office of Weights and Measures (National Bureau of Standards) |

## P

| | |
|---|---|
| **PA** | Purchasing Agent |
| **PAA** | Pan American World Airways, Inc. |
| **PAC** | Put and Call (Stock market) |
| **PACE** | Projects to Advance Creativity in Education (HEW) |
| **PAL** | Police Athletic League (New York) |
| **PAN-AM** | Pan-American World Airways, Inc. |
| **PAR** | People Against Racism (Civil Rights organization) |
| **PATH** | Port Authority Trans-Hudson (New York) |
| **PAU** | Present Address Unknown |

| PB | Passbook (banking) |
| PBA | Patrolmen's Benevolent Association |
| PC | Peace Corps |
| PCC | Panama Canal Company |
| PCEEO | President's Committee on Equal Employment Opportunity |
| PCEH | President's Committee on Employment of the Handicapped |
| PCML | President's Committee on Migratory Labor |
| PCMR | President's Committee on Mental Retardation |
| PCTS | President's Committee for Traffic Safety |
| PCV | Petty Cash Voucher |
| PDF | Parkinson's Disease Foundation |
| PDQ | Pretty Damn Quick |
| PFC | Private, First Class (Army) |
| PG | Parental Guidance Suggested (movie rating) |
| Ph D | Doctor of Philosophy |
| PINS | Persons in Need of Supervision |
| PJ | Presiding Judge |
| PL | Price List |
| PLO | Palestine Liberation Organization |
| PLS | Professional Legal Secretary |
| PM | Post Meridiem (After noon) |
| PNYA | Port of New York Authority |
| PO | Post Office |
| POB | Post Office Box |
| POPE | Parents for Orthodoxy in Parochial Education |
| POPS | People Opposed to Pornography in Schools |
| POW | Prisoner(s) of War (Also, PW) |
| PP | Pages |
| PP | Planned Parenthood |
| PPFA | Planned Parenthood Federation of America |
| PR | Public Relations |
| PRC | People's Republic of China (Mainland China) |
| PROF | Professor |
| PROP | Proprietor |
| PRS | Performing Right Society |

| **PS** | Post Scriptum (Written afterwards; a postscript) |
| **PSF** | Pounds per Square Foot |
| **PSI** | Pounds per Square Inch |
| **PSL** | Pressure Sensitive Label |
| **PT** | Pacific Time |
| **PTA** | Parent-Teacher Association |
| **PTO** | Please Turn Over (the page) |
| **PW** | Packed Weight |
| **PWP** | Parents Without Partners (an organization) |

## Q

| **QAR** | Quality Assurance Representative |
| **QB** | Qualified Bidders |
| **QC** | Quality Control |
| **QE 2** | Queen Elizabeth 2 (Luxury Liner) |
| **QF** | Quick Freeze |
| **QI** | Quarterly Index |
| **QT** | Quiet (or Sub Rosa, as, "On the QT") |
| **QV** | Quod Vide or Quod Videte (Which see) |

## R

| **R** | Restricted (Movie rating) |
| **3R** | Readin', Ritin', and Rithmetic (Also, RRR) |
| **RADA** | Radioactive |
| **RADAR** | Radio Detection and Ranging |
| **RAPP** | Registered Air Parcel Post |
| **RC** | Roman Catholic |
| **R & CC** | Riot and Civil Commotion |
| **RCIA** | Retail Credit Institute of America |
| **RCT** | Rorschach Content Test (Psychology) |
| **RDD** | Research and Development Division |
| **RECD** | Received |
| **REIT** | Real Estate Investment Trust (Generic term) |
| **REM** | Rapid Eye Movement |

| | |
|---|---|
| **REO** | Real Estate Owned (Banking) |
| **REV** | Reverend |
| **RH** | Right Hand |
| **RHEO** | Rheostat |
| **RIE** | Retirement Income Endowment (Insurance) |
| **RIMPTF** | Recording Industries Music Performance Trust Funds |
| **RIMR** | Rockefeller Institute for Medical Research |
| **RIP** | Requiescat in Pace (May he, or she, rest in peace) |
| **RL** | Retarded Learner (Education) |
| **RM** | Room |
| **R/M** | Revolutions Per Minute |
| **RN** | Registered Nurse |
| **ROT** | Rule of Thumb |
| **RPH** | Registered Pharmacist |
| **RPM** | Revolutions Per Minute (phonograph records) |
| **RR** | Railroad |
| **RR** | Rural Route |
| **RS** | Reformed Spelling |
| **RSP** | Receiving Stolen Property |
| **RT** | Released Time |
| **RTE** | Route |
| **RTW** | Right to Work |
| **R/W** | Right-of-Way (Also, ROW) |
| **RY** | Railway |

## S

| | |
|---|---|
| **/S/** | Signed (Before signature on typed copy of a document, original of which was signed) |
| **SA** | Salvation Army |
| **SABE** | Society for Automation in Business Education |
| **SABW** | Society of American Business Writers |
| **SAE** | Self-Addressed Envelope |
| **SAE** | Society for the Advancement of Education |
| **SAGA** | Society of American Graphic Artists |
| **SAJ** | Society for the Advancement of Judaism |

| | |
|---|---|
| **SALT** | Sisters All Learning Together (Feminist group) |
| **SANKA** | Sans Caffeine (Acronym used as brand name) |
| **SAP** | Soon As Possible |
| **SAR** | Sons of the American Revolution |
| **SASE** | Self-Addressed Stamped Envelope |
| **SAT** | Scholastic Aptitude Test |
| **SATB** | Soprano, Alto, Tenor, Bass (Music) |
| **SBLI** | Savings Bank Life Insurance |
| **SCAN** | Stock Market Computer Answering Service |
| **SCAT** | School and College Ability Test (of ETS) |
| **SCL** | Senior Citizens League |
| **SCORE** | Service Corps of Retired Executives |
| **SCRAP** | Society for Completely Removing All Parking Meters |
| **SDS** | Students for a Democratic Society |
| **SEAM** | Society for the Emancipation of the American Male |
| **SEC** | Securities and Exchange Commission |
| **SEEK** | Search for Education, Elevation and Knowledge |
| **SEN** | Senator |
| **SGD** | Signed |
| **SH** | Semester Hour |
| **SHAME** | Save, Help Animals Man Exploits |
| **SHAPE** | Supreme Headquarters Allied Powers Europe (NATO) |
| **SITCOM** | Situation Comedy (Television) |
| **SLD** | Specific Language Disability (Education) |
| **SLR** | Single-Lens Reflex (Camera) |
| **SMOG** | Smoke and Fog |
| **SMR** | Standard Mortality Rate |
| **SMSG** | School Management Study Group |
| **SN** | Stock Number |
| **SNAFU** | Situation Normal, All Fouled Up (Military) |
| **SODA** | Stamp Out Drug Addiction |
| **SONS** | Society of Non-Smokers |
| **SOP** | Standard Operating Procedure |
| **SOS** | Save Our Ship (or Souls) |
| **SPCA** | Society for the Prevention of Cruelty to Animals |

| | |
|---|---|
| **SPCC** | Society for the Prevention of Cruelty to Children |
| **SPM** | Strokes Per Minute |
| **SPQR** | Small Profits, Quick Returns |
| **SPR** | Society for Psychical Research |
| **SQM** | Square Meter |
| **SR** | Senior |
| **SRCC** | Strikes, Riots, and Civil Commotions |
| **SRO** | Single-Room Occupancy (New York housing term) |
| **SRO** | Standing Room Only (Theater) |
| **SS** | Saints (as in "SS Peter and Paul") |
| **SS** | Social Security |
| **SSA** | Social Security Administration (of HEW) |
| **SSAT** | Secondary School Admission Test Board |
| **SSU** | Sunday School Union |
| **ST** | Saint |
| **ST** | Sensitivity Training |
| **ST** | Short Ton (2000 lbs.) |
| **STAR** | Safe Teen-Age Rocketry |
| **STB** | Soprano, Tenor, Bass |
| **STD** | Standard |
| **STE** | Sainte |
| **STEP** | School to Employment Program |
| **STP** | Standard Temperature and Pressure |
| **STS** | School Television Service |
| **SUBS** | Subscription |
| **SUNY** | State University of New York |
| **SUNYA** | State University of New York at Albany |
| **SUNYAB** | State University of New York at Buffalo |
| **SWAK** | Sealed With A Kiss (Correspondence) |
| **SWALK** | Sealed With A Loving Kiss (Correspondence) |
| **SWEAT** | Student Work Experience and Training |
| **SWORD** | Separated, Widowed, Or Divorced |
| **SWP** | Summer Work Program |
| **SY** | Square Yard |
| **SYD** | Scotland Yard |

| | |
|---|---|
| **T** | Tutti (Sing or play together) (Music) |
| **TA** | Teaching Assistant (In a university) |
| **TAG** | The Acronym Generator (An RCA computer program) |
| **TAP** | Teacher's Aide Program |
| **TARMAC** | Tar Macadam |
| **TARP** | Tarpaulin |
| **TARS** | Teen-Age Republicans |
| **TAS** | Telephone Answering Service (or System) |
| **TB** | Tuberculosis |
| **TBA** | To Be Announced |
| **TBSP** | Tablespoon |
| **TCPO** | Third-Class Post Office |
| **TEF** | Temperance Education Foundation |
| **TEFL** | Teaching English as a Foreign Language |
| **TEMP** | Temperature |
| **TENES** | Teaching English to the Non-English-Speaking |
| **TESL** | Teaching English as a Second Language |
| **TESOL** | Teachers of English to Speakers of Other Languages |
| **TEST** | Teen-Age Employment Skills Training, Inc. |
| **TF** | Till Forbidden (i.e., repeat until forbidden) |
| **TGIF** | Thank God It's Friday |
| **THAT** | Twenty-four-Hour Automatic Teller |
| **TIP** | To Insure Promptness |
| **TL** | Trade-Last |
| **TLC** | Tender Loving Care |
| **TM** | Transcendental Meditation |
| **TMH** | Tons per Man-Hour |
| **TML** | Three-Mile Limit |
| **TO** | Table of Organization |
| **T/O** | Table of Organization |
| **TOP** | Temporarily Out of Print |
| **TPQI** | Teacher-Pupil Question Inventory |
| **TPRI** | Teacher-Pupil Relationship Inventory |

| TR | Tape Recorder |
|---|---|
| **TSP** | Teaspoonful |
| **TT** | Teletype |
| **TTP** | Total Taxable Pay |
| **TTPE** | Total Taxable Pay Earned |
| **TTY** | Teletypewriter |
| **TV** | Television |
| **TWA** | Trans-World Airlines, Inc. |
| **TWK** | Typewriter Keyboard |
| **TWX** | Teletypewriter Exchange Service (Western Union) |

## U

| **UA** | United Air Lines, Inc. |
|---|---|
| **UC** | Upper Case (i.e., capital letters) (Typography) |
| **UFO** | Unidentified Flying Object ("Flying saucer") |
| **UHF** | Ultra-High Frequency |
| **UL** | Underwriters' Laboratories (Inc.) (Also, ULI) |
| **UN** | United Nations |
| **UNAUS** | United Nations Association of the United States |
| **UNESCO** | United Nations Educational, Scientific and Cultural Organization |
| **UNGA** | United Nations General Assembly |
| **UNSC** | United Nations Security Council |
| **UNSG** | United Nations Secretary General |
| **UPI** | United Press International |
| **UPS** | United Parcel Service |
| **US** | United States (of America) |
| **USA** | United States of America |
| **USBS** | United States Bureau of Standards |
| **USCC** | United States Chamber of Commerce |
| **USCG** | United States Coast Guard |
| **USDC** | United States District Court |
| **USES** | United States Employment Service |
| **USIA** | United States Information Agency |
| **USJCC** | United States Junior Chamber of Commerce (JAYCEES) |

# METRIC (SI) SYSTEM
## OF WEIGHTS AND MEASURES

etric (SI) system the base unit for length is the meter (m); and weight, the gram (g); and for capacity, the liter (l). prefixes are used to indicate multiples and submultiples base units.

| Quantity Prefix | Multiplication Factor |
|---|---|
| mega (M), as in *megagram* = | 1 000 000 |
| kilo (k), as in *kilometer* = | 1 000 |
| hecto (h), as in *hectogram* = | 100 |
| deka (da), as in *dekagram* = | 10 |
| deci (d), as in *decimeter* = | 0.1 |
| centi (c), as in *centigram* = | .01 |
| milli (m), as in *milliliter* = | .001 |

### ENGLISH–METRIC EQUIVALENTS

1 inch = 2.54 centimeters
1 foot = 0.3048 meter
1 yard = 0.9144 meter
1 mile = 1.6093 kilometers

1 ounce = 28.349 grams
1 pound = 0.453 kilograms
1 short ton = 0.907 metric ton

1 fluid ounce = 29.573 milliliters
1 pint = 0.473 liter
1 quart = 0.946 liter
1 gallon = 3.785 liters

### METRIC–ENGLISH EQUIVALENTS

1 centimeter = 0.3937 inch
1 meter = 3.281 feet
1 meter = 1.0936 yards
1 kilometer = 0.6214 mile

1 gram = .035 ounce
1 kilogram = 2.2046 pounds
1 metric ton = 1.1 short tons

1 milliliter = .06 cubic inch
1 liter = 61.02 cubic inches
1 liter = 0.908 dry quart
1 liter = 1.057 liquid quarts

| | |
|---|---|
| USLTA | United States Lawn Tennis Association |
| USMC | United States Marine Corps |
| USN | United States Navy |
| USNG | United States National Guard |
| USOC | United States Olympic Committee |
| USOE | United States Office of Education |
| USP | United States Pharmacopeia |

## V

| | |
|---|---|
| V | Versus (against) |
| VA | Veterans Administration |
| VC | Victoria Cross (British) |
| VEEP | Vice President |
| VET | Veteran |
| VET | Veterinary |
| VG | Very Good |
| VHF | Very High Frequency (Radio) |
| VIP | Very Important Person |
| VMD | Doctor of Veterinary Medicine |
| VOL | Volume |
| VP | Vice President |
| VS | Versus (Against) |
| VV | Vice Versa |
| VW | Volkswagen (German automobile) |

## W

| | |
|---|---|
| WAAC | Women's Army Auxiliary Corps |
| WAC | Women's Army Corps (Formerly WAAC) |
| WAM | Words a Minute |
| WAR | We Are Ridiculous (Antiwar slogan) |
| WASP | White, Anglo-Saxon Protestant |
| WAVES | Women Accepted for Volunteer Emergency Service |
| WCA | Workmen's Compensation Act |
| WCTU | Women's Christian Temperance Union |

| | |
|---|---|
| **WF** | Wrong Font (Typesetting) (Proofreader's mark) |
| **WHO** | World Health Organization (United Nations affiliate) |
| **WIN** | Workshop in Nonviolence |
| **WITCH** | Women Incensed over Traditional Coed Hoopla |
| **WPA** | Works Progress Administration |
| **WPM** | Words Per Minute |
| **WPS** | Words Per Second |
| **WSJ** | Wall Street Journal (A newspaper) |
| **W/TAX** | Withholding Tax |
| **WUMP** | White, Urban, Middle Class, Protestant |
| **WWI** | World War I |
| **WWII** | World War II |

## X

| | |
|---|---|
| **X** | Movie Rating for "Persons under 18 not admitted" |
| **XQ** | Cross-Question |
| **X-REF** | Cross Reference |
| **XXX** | International Urgency Signal |

## Y

| | |
|---|---|
| **Y** | Young Men's (or Women's) Christian Association |
| **YMCA** | Young Men's Christian Association |
| **YM–YWHA** | Young Men's and Young Women's Hebrew Association |
| **YW** | Young Women's (Christian Association) |
| **YWCA** | Young Women's Christian Association |
| **YWCTU** | Young Women's Christian Temperance Union |
| **YWHA** | YoungWomen's Hebrew Association |

## Z

| | |
|---|---|
| **Z** | Zero |
| **Z** | Zulu Time (Greenwich Mean Time) |
| **ZPG** | Zero Population Growth |

| USLTA | United States Lawn Tennis Association |
| USMC | United States Marine Corps |
| USN | United States Navy |
| USNG | United States National Guard |
| USOC | United States Olympic Committee |
| USOE | United States Office of Education |
| USP | United States Pharmacopeia |

## V

| V | Versus (against) |
| VA | Veterans Administration |
| VC | Victoria Cross (British) |
| VEEP | Vice President |
| VET | Veteran |
| VET | Veterinary |
| VG | Very Good |
| VHF | Very High Frequency (Radio) |
| VIP | Very Important Person |
| VMD | Doctor of Veterinary Medicine |
| VOL | Volume |
| VP | Vice President |
| VS | Versus (Against) |
| VV | Vice Versa |
| VW | Volkswagen (German automobile) |

## W

| WAAC | Women's Army Auxiliary Corps |
| WAC | Women's Army Corps (Formerly WAAC) |
| WAM | Words a Minute |
| WAR | We Are Ridiculous (Antiwar slogan) |
| WASP | White, Anglo-Saxon Protestant |
| WAVES | Women Accepted for Volunteer Emergency Service |
| WCA | Workmen's Compensation Act |
| WCTU | Women's Christian Temperance Union |

| | |
|---|---|
| **WF** | Wrong Font (Typesetting) (Proofreader's mark) |
| **WHO** | World Health Organization (United Nations affiliate) |
| **WIN** | Workshop in Nonviolence |
| **WITCH** | Women Incensed over Traditional Coed Hoopla |
| **WPA** | Works Progress Administration |
| **WPM** | Words Per Minute |
| **WPS** | Words Per Second |
| **WSJ** | Wall Street Journal (A newspaper) |
| **W/TAX** | Withholding Tax |
| **WUMP** | White, Urban, Middle Class, Protestant |
| **WWI** | World War I |
| **WWII** | World War II |

## X

| | |
|---|---|
| **X** | Movie Rating for "Persons under 18 not admitted" |
| **XQ** | Cross-Question |
| **X-REF** | Cross Reference |
| **XXX** | International Urgency Signal |

## Y

| | |
|---|---|
| **Y** | Young Men's (or Women's) Christian Association |
| **YMCA** | Young Men's Christian Association |
| **YM–YWHA** | Young Men's and Young Women's Hebrew Association |
| **YW** | Young Women's (Christian Association) |
| **YWCA** | Young Women's Christian Association |
| **YWCTU** | Young Women's Christian Temperance Union |
| **YWHA** | YoungWomen's Hebrew Association |

## Z

| | |
|---|---|
| **Z** | Zero |
| **Z** | Zulu Time (Greenwich Mean Time) |
| **ZPG** | Zero Population Growth |

# METRIC (SI) SYSTEM
## OF WEIGHTS AND MEASURES

In the metric (SI) system the base unit for length is the meter (m); for mass and weight, the gram (g); and for capacity, the liter (l). Quantity prefixes are used to indicate multiples and submultiples of these base units.

| Quantity Prefix | Multiplication Factor |
|---|---|
| mega (M), as in *megagram* = | 1 000 000 |
| kilo (k), as in *kilometer* = | 1 000 |
| hecto (h), as in *hectogram* = | 100 |
| deka (da), as in *dekagram* = | 10 |
| deci (d), as in *decimeter* = | 0.1 |
| centi (c), as in *centigram* = | .01 |
| milli (m), as in *milliliter* = | .001 |

## ENGLISH–METRIC EQUIVALENTS

1 inch = 2.54 centimeters
1 foot = 0.3048 meter
1 yard = 0.9144 meter
1 mile = 1.6093 kilometers

1 ounce = 28.349 grams
1 pound = 0.453 kilograms
1 short ton = 0.907 metric ton

1 fluid ounce = 29.573 milliliters
1 pint = 0.473 liter
1 quart = 0.946 liter
1 gallon = 3.785 liters

## METRIC–ENGLISH EQUIVALENTS

1 centimeter = 0.3937 inch
1 meter = 3.281 feet
1 meter = 1.0936 yards
1 kilometer = 0.6214 mile

1 gram = .035 ounce
1 kilogram = 2.2046 pounds
1 metric ton = 1.1 short tons

1 milliliter = .06 cubic inch
1 liter = 61.02 cubic inches
1 liter = 0.908 dry quart
1 liter = 1.057 liquid quarts